The Hunt of a Lifetime

The Practical Guide to Planning and Executing
Your Dream Hunt

By Colonel Michael A. Abell

This book is dedicated to my Mother, Barbara Jean, who was a badass and encouraged me to follow in her footsteps.

Contents

Chapter 1 - The Grind

Chapter 2 - Fundamentals

Chapter 3 - Navigation

Chapter 4 – First Aid and Medical

Chapter 5 – Communications

Chapter 6 – Weapons

Chapter 7 – Gear

Chapter 8 – Packing

Chapter 9 – Logistics

Chapter 10 – Planning

Chapter 11 – Cooking

Chapter 12 – Colorado Bear

Chapter 13 – Mountain Lion

Chapter 14 – Colorado Elk

Chapter 15 –Turkey and Hogs

Chapter 16 – Pronghorn

Chapter 17 - Friends Family Tribe Nation

Chapter 18 - Black Death on the Rocks

Chapter 19 – Great White Bear

Chapter 20 - Man Plans, God Laughs

Chapter 21 - Four Days Late

Introduction

If I've heard the following statement once, I've heard it one too many times – "Wow man, that is my dream hunt, wish I could do that!" The hunt of a lifetime is really just the hunt of a summertime when you learn how to make it happen. This book in unapologetically aimed at hunting, fishing and the outdoors, but the principles I am advocating apply to everyone.

I'm also trying to push my peers, middle-aged folks, to get out and do something before it's too late. I find it a little bit sad how many middle-aged adults are slaves to the grind of their urban lives. Competing with other adults in their community, for no apparent reason with the material goods they can buy or how much they can earn, usually at marginally meaningful or totally meaningless jobs. The truth is, when all is said and done, life is meant to be lived. Life is always too short. There is never enough time. So, do something with what you've got left.

A good family life is fundamentally important to anyone's happiness. My wife is my best friend. But a good relationship is not built on being around each other and being in contact 24/7/365. It's about the bonds of friendship, love, trust and passion. How in the name of the Good Lord can you have any passion in your life if you have nothing going on but servitude to the responsibilities of your life? How are your kids going to respect you, if you don't ever do anything for yourself? I am not suggesting you don't provide for your family. I am not suggesting that you don't serve others. What I am suggesting is – if that is ALL you do, you've got problems. By the time most adults are ready to retire, they don't have a memoire to write or a journal that will inspire their grandkids. They're done. They're spent. They're ready to move to somewhere warm and vegetate until the very end.

At best, they worked hard to "leave the kids something." At worst, they are regretful and angry. They're regretful and angry because they didn't live life to it's fullest and now it's gone or they're too old and feeble to do anything worthy of being written in a memoire.

If you're the kind of adult that steals a day for yourself, you might golf, get your hair done, go shopping or hang out and watch the game with friends. That's fine, but that's not enough. That is a timeout, nothing more. That's a break from the day to day doldrums of a life of servitude. Family is good. Service to others is good. Work is good. But that cannot be all you do with your life or you'll be sorry when it comes to an end.

So, what do I suggest? Do something big. Go on an adventure. It doesn't mean you have to liquidate your kid's college fund or risk your life in some unnecessary way. But what it does mean is that you must get out of the routine and spend time on yourself. Doing something you might have always wanted to do or have dreamed of doing. Because, if you cannot be true to yourself, how can you be the best spouse, parent, boss, employee, teammate or friend? And it doesn't mean you have to abandon your family. If they're game, take them with you.

I've taken many people on their first real adventure. They are all shocked how easy and inexpensive it was. In fact, through that first mentored adventure they learned they can do it themselves and have since done it repeatedly. The bottom line is easy: (1) figure out what you want to do (2) make a simple plan (3) train if necessary (4) execute the plan (5) be proud of yourself. Then you come home and get back to your normal life of service to others and your job, but you'll go back to your normal life with a story worth telling. I guarantee you, that story, an adventure story, will touch a part of your aboriginal soul. The pride you feel from adventures comes from a place 20,000 years ago, when your nomadic ancestors told stories around a campfire. It's something most people don't even know they need until it's too late.

In the end, is having a better car than your neighbor more important than memories of a Rocky Mountain backpacking trip or pictures you took at the Great Barrier Reef? What are you going to be prouder of when you're 70 years old: that you had the Honda Odyssey Touring Elite Minivan or that you took that photographic safari in Namibia? Yep, it is the adventure you'll be talking about, not the minivan. Ever seen anyone bust out their phone and say, "Dude check out how the seats fold up to allow me to haul cargo? I love the folding seats." That never happens. In real life it goes like this, "Yes, the Great Barrier Reef is loaded with sharks. Here look at the pictures of the great white I saw there."

Chapter 1 - The Grind

Once our nomadic hunter gatherer ancestors started cultivating wheat and tending the land, division of labor was invented. Fast forward tens of thousands of years and our labors are now subdivided into finite niches. So, we all must work in our niche, grand or small, that work pays our way in this world. But we must escape our niche as often as we can to remind ourselves that we are more than just our work. There is a time in all our lives when we are making our way, working, and raising a family and putting in the necessary work required to be responsible adults. The problem with those years, even those decades is that along the way too many of us lose sight of who we are, who we were and who we wanted to be. We get stuck on wash, rinse, repeat. It is sad, because by the time we figure it out we have run out of health before we have run out of time or money. Outdoor adventure rekindles the connection we all still have deep within us to our ancient ancestors who wandered this land with the seasons. Finding your place on the landscape, ocean, mountains, desert, or forest and living out that event, whatever the adventure is for you, will rekindle that aboriginal spark. It will also fuel the rest of your life and make you better when you go back to the grind.

Modern society makes it popular and easy to say, "Well I am a good family man and that's my identity." I think that is a copout. Our air conditioned, well-groomed soft lives make it easy for us to become fat and lazy. Eventually we find ourselves living lives without imagination. We blend in and buy the minivan. Then we buy a McMansion in a subdivision. We find a way through out consumerism to fit in.

Small rebels grow a long beard or color their hair pink or drive something totally impractical to work and back home. Small meek minded rebels try to stand out in meaningless and superficial ways. Maybe they even dream of doing something, something big. But they still go back to their little house and tend to their family the same way their practical neighbors with normal hair colors and minivans do. It is cool to have your own style. We should all be ourselves, but if you are coloring your hair as a form of mild rebellion, that's not what you need.

You need to follow your instincts and get out there and do something. Your kids are not going to show their friends pictures of your cool hair color or your Land Rover. They will show friends pictures of you taking them on a rafting trip down the Flathead River in Montana. In fact, they will keep showing those pictures to their kids and grandkids. They will tell your grandkids how you saved money every paycheck so that every two years you could take a month off and hike the Appalachian Trail. They will tell your grandkids that you drove a piece of junk for years, so that you could save the money it took to attend NASCAR driving school every summer and how you were the best race car driver that never raced. They will be proud of you. They will be proud of your determination and discipline and that you went and did it. They will certainly tell the story of what it felt like when they turned 16 and you invited them to come along for the first time.

Do you think they are going to tell the story of how you went to Disney World with all the McFamilies in their McMinivans every year? Nope. I have got a good friend that takes his daughter on a cow elk rifle hunt every year. They go with friends and stay in a nice lodge. They eat wonderful meals, have a great time and bring back a years' worth of the best free-range organic meat that God ever made. You think that young lady wants to go to Disney World? Nope, she wants to go to Colorado every year and hunt elk with her Dad. Wonder how many dads and daughters have a bond like that?

The weak and unimaginative people will default by saying, "We cannot afford it. We have to save for our kid's college." That is a load of manure. Once your car is paid off, keep it. Do not buy a new car. Keep that old thing running and put that money in the "annual adventure fund." Or wait tables half a day every weekend and put that money in the "annual adventure fund." Live within your means during your regular life so that you have the means to live an adventurous irregular life!

There will be some who read this book who are young, poor, and living paycheck to paycheck. I will tell you that those people can also find ways to save a little money. That money might not be enough to take an adventure, but it might be enough to take time off for an adventure. That time off could be spent on a church mission to an exotic place or doing a tour with the Job Corps or Peace Corps. Those experiences can also be used to build a resume. That resume will not only be full of experience, it will be full of adventure.

It will be illustrative of someone who turns a small amount of resources into wisdom. That wisdom can then be turned into a better job. That better job will bring more resources with which to go on adventures and experience the world. In a few decades, the person who had nothing has a memoire to write that most middle-class middle-aged urbanites would die for.

While there are certainly, dream trips for hunters and fishers out there, like Kodiak Brown Bear, Dagestan Tur, Brazilian Peacock Bass or Giant Trevally in the Seychelles, there are adventures within everyone's reach here in the good ol' United States of America. Going on a weeklong float down the best trout river in your region or a backpack elk hunt on public land in the Rockies is NOT a dream. It is totally doable, and it takes a few simple things (1) a little money (2) a little knowledge (3) a little skill (4) a little time and (5) a little motivation.

Once you do it, you'll never stop doing it. You say you cannot get any time off work? Well, I've worked a lot of places in my life, was a Soldier for well over two decades, and was even a small city mayor. There was always a way to get time off work.

While the recipes in this book are for hunting, fishing and outdoor adventure, the principles could be applied to someone that loves Asian culture. They could figure a way to save the money necessary to go to a different country every three years. By the time they die, maybe they speak Cantonese and have awesome pictures of the Great Wall of China.

Or maybe you're one of those dads who is a sports fanatic, who also coaches your kid's baseball team. You might put money away to attend a seriously high-level coaches' clinic, where you work with professional and college coaches every couple years. Then when your kid graduates college, quits playing ball and decides to start coaching themselves they can look up and admire their dad – the coach. The one who not only led their local high school team to the championship three times, but who got to know the legends of the game by first name.

These things take extra effort. They will not help you fit into your suburban matrix, but they will help you live a life without regret. The fact is that too many adults get to a certain age and do something stupid to ruin their lives. They make bad money decisions or bad libido decisions and it is over. I think they make such decisions because they are "slave to the grind." They do not know what to do, so they act out. They have lost touch with who they are and who they wanted to be. Live long enough and a so called "mid-life crisis," is coming. That is the sad day when you realize you are stuck. You have got nothing to do but serve your family and try to get your 27 years at the General Electric assembly plant.

Small people, with small minds think they need to change or they need another mate. They act out and everything they worked for was lost. How much better would it have been for them to plan events or adventures that allowed them a break from the grind. Time away doing something worthwhile, but also time away to remind you of what is at home. Time away to allow you to miss your spouse and look forward to the loving reunion, versus seeing them every single day for twenty-years, deciding they are boring and it is time to "trade up."

Some people are going to read this first chapter and say, "Helping my spouse and kids be successful is my job. I'm a provider." Okay, that is copout number two. It is easy to flip that one. Ask this question - whose job is it to make sure you are successful? Much less, whose job is it to make sure you do not feel taken for granted? Love is a plural word. Ask yourself, "Am I getting back what I give?" Most likely, you are not. Instead of finding some younger person to help you violate the sanctity of your marriage, take a short interlude, and go on an adventure. Take the time to be gone long enough to miss your spouse and luxuriate in the happy reunion. If you take an adventure and get home and the reunion is not luxurious, well you needed a new spouse to begin with.

I am not advocating against the family and harmony in a marriage. I am arguing that adventure makes it better. Here is another example. Think about the mom, who after months of sacrificing her weekends and struggling to budget for her kid's traveling volleyball team is at her wits end. Then she wakes one morning to see that her volleyball kid has packed her a great lunch, included a killer bottle of wine, gassed up the car and volunteered to watch her younger siblings so that Mom can have a picnic with Dad. That is a Hallmark movie. It will not happen. Dad if you are watching Mom suffer the grind every day, wake up and make something special happen. Get yourself in gear. Do not take her on a fancy night out and spend a bunch of money you do not have. Do some planning like I advocate in this book. Find a pretty campsite at a state park you can afford. Pack a decent meal and a bottle of wine. Call a babysitter. Gas up the car and go. Do not say much. Listen to her. When the wine is gone, go back to tent, and pretend you are ten years younger. Then wake up and go to Waffle

House and eat things you should not before you get back home.

It does not have to be a trip to see the Great Wall of China. But you have got to do something. Love is a plural word. Socrates, the ancient Greek philosopher, said at his trial, "The unexamined life is not worth living." You can get very deep into why he said this and how his love of wisdom and pursuit of it caused him to choose death over exile, but the statement is enough to make my point here. Planning and executing adventures, large and small, is the antidote to our mundane existence. If Socrates is too worldly and ethereal for you, how about the band, Rage Against the Machine, "You can't be king of the world if you're slave to the grind."

Chapter 2 - Fundamentals

Now, that I've got your attention, let's talk about the fundamentals necessary to make you an adventurer. Whatever your discipline, being proficient in the fundamentals is the prerequisite to adventure travel. These are not only the things you must be able to do routinely, but also the things you must be able to do in an emergency. You do not need to master the fundamentals, but you must be proficient enough in them to make your adventures enjoyable. When faced with adversity our inability to be minimally proficient in these areas will turn adversity into danger.

There are six universal fundamentals that must be done on every single trip: planning, navigation, first aid/medical, communications, logistics, and packing. These fundamentals apply to every type of travel. There are also specific supplementary skills that must be mastered if your adventure is in the outdoors. You will also need proficiency in shooting your weapon, game meat management, apex predator avoidance, behavioral patterns of your quarry, setting up a shelter, building a fire, field nutrition, knot tying, purifying water, and field hygiene. That is a few of the never-ending list of skills that will help you approach mastery of the outdoors, but certain things are foundational.

These foundational items are what I am going to call fundaments in the chapters to come. The six universal fundamentals will all be covered in their own chapter later, plus a few necessary to have outdoor adventures. We are not day tripping. We are escaping the grind. We are going on adventures long enough and immersive enough to get us out of our routine. If done right, these adventures are something we will be proud of. If you do not have proficiency in these fundamentals, that's okay. Building proficiency in these fundamentals will require smaller local trips, where you will gain skills and the confidence to take the bigger trips. Through these experiences you will find your way and figure out how to do it and what you want to do before you die.

Again, do you think your kids will be telling their kids that you drove a BMW? No, they will be showing them pictures of the time you climbed Mount Rainer. I am not throwing stones at being a parent or grandparent. I just think it is sad that the top three first questions asked when two middle-aged adults meet are: (1) are you married? (2) what do you do? and (3) do you have kids? Really? Is that all we have got? The hidden nuanced truth of adventure travel is that you also become a bigger, better person. You will see new places, meet new people, and experience other cultures. The experienced gained will make you a wiser and more well-rounded person. You will no longer be forming your opinions based on the talking heads on your favorite news show or sports news show. You will have actually gone someplace, seen things for yourself and formed your own opinions based on first-hand knowledge.

Back to fundamentals, let's say you're skeptical and are thinking of skipping the following chapters. Okay, maybe you have got the fundamental skills already or think you do. Well good for you. Here is a scenario for you before you skip the fundamental chapters. The scenario is: it's rained for eight straight days on your drop camp moose hunt west of Denali National Park in Alaska, your campsite is flooding, your devices are out of power because there has been no sun (solar power) to repower them and you're out of batteries. Your hunting partner cannot get warm and you think hypothermia might be setting in.

(1) Could you move to a dry location, shoot a resection, taking back azimuths, converting from magnetic north to grid north, transferring it to your map using two known peaks in the Alaska range, insuring you accounted for the declination to confirm your location?

(2)   What are your primary, secondary and tertiary forms of communication with the outside world now that you're out of power?

(3)   What is the single most important mode of treatment for hypothermia?

These are not complicated things, really. They are fundamental. Simple answers to the above questions are:

(1)   Moving to a dry location is easy, climb. However, resection involves shooting a magnetic azimuth with your compass at known points, then taking a back azimuth, then converting from magnetic to grid in order to plot the azimuths on your map. You draw two intersecting lines on your map and that is roughly where you are.

(2)   In a wet environment, with no power, and a hypothermic partner we are in emergency mode. My primary means of communication is the plan I left with the bush pilot listing my contingency locations, so they know where to search for me. Then I would need a signal. My primary signal would be a fire because I also need to warm my partner. However, it is raining and most folks, even experts struggle to build and maintain a fire in the rain. The fire will likely fail until the rain stops. I would mark my location using my blaze orange pack cover set out on a high point to be visible from a distance. If the rain broke and the Alaska State Police came searching with their helicopter, I would signal them with a chemlight tied to the end of a 4ft

length of paracord swung very rapidly in a large circle.

(3) No fire until the rain stops, and your partner is showing signs of hypothermia. First, you have got to warm them up. Then you have got to motivate them to hike to high ground with you and get out of the flooding valley. Their body will burn what little energy they have got left to get there, but in doing so will elevate their core temperature. Once you have gotten out of the flooding, get their wet clothes off them, and get them into a sleeping bag. If symptoms do not start to abate, get in the sleeping bag with them, you may have to zip two bags together. When symptoms abate, make hot beverages or warm food.

Taking the time to learn the fundamentals is actually fun. You will also gain a level of confidence that allows you to relax and enjoy your adventure. Fundamentals make the routine things routine and emergency tasks possible.

Chapter 3 - Navigation

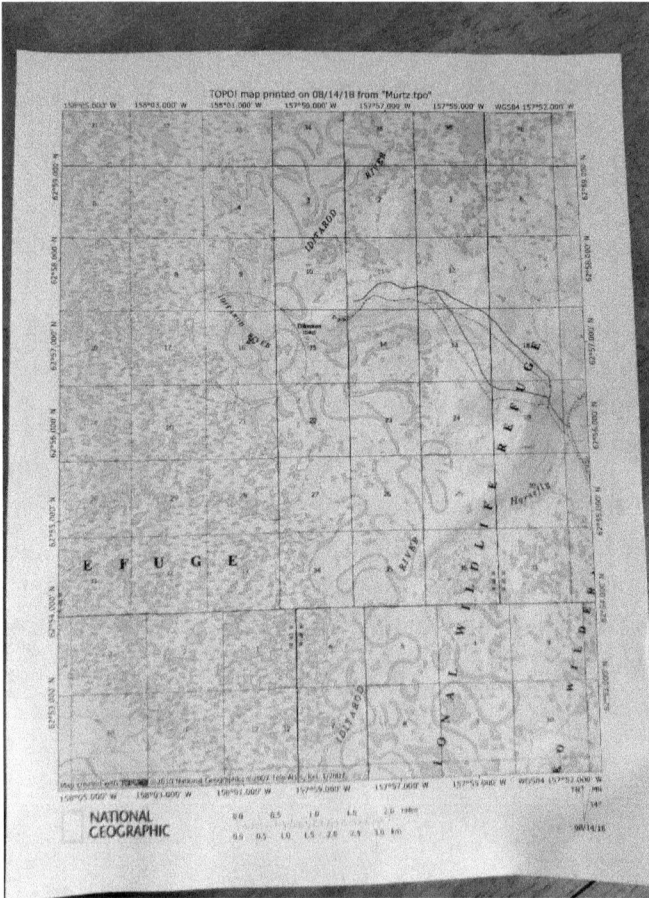

Navigation is not something you can learn simply by mastering Google Maps or onX. Far from it. Navigation is something you must learn through study, hone through trial and error, and burnish into your soul through experience. It starts with learning how to read a map, but many have bypassed this lesson and rely on technology. That is a failure.

Adventurers and especially outdoor adventurers must learn more. At the apex level, navigators read their maps, then visualize the map and compare it to what they are seeing in front of them. They synthesize what they see in their "mind's eye" with what they see with their own eyes. This skill is impossible without first learning the analog fundamentals.

When I was but a wee cadet in the Army ROTC program, my greatest pleasure and pride came from the fact that I could navigate. Where so many of my fellow cadets struggled with the land navigation tests, I would often plot my points and almost run to them, punching my score card and returning well in advance of the time limit. My Sergeants taught me to "see the terrain" and use the visualization of my route to my advantage. This skill helped throughout my career as an infantry officer.

The fact of the matter is that you cannot count on connectivity. Downloaded maps on systems like onX will absolutely help you, but all electronic systems fail. Thick forest or jungle canopies reduce satellite connectivity and render GPS units almost worthless. Battery power is not guaranteed either. The amount of rain in Alaska or the lack of sun light during fall and winter in northern latitudes may make even solar power a liability. So, you must not only be able to read a map and use a compass. You must also be able to navigate without any tools.

I have taken about a dozen new hunters with me to the Rockies to bow hunt for elk on public land with over-the-counter tags. Prior to going on the hunt, I have helped them in many ways and talked to them at length about altitude and terrain. It never ceases to amaze me how confused most of them are when we leave camp the first morning and hike up to the best water holes and wallows to hunt elk. They ask so many questions about where we are going and how to get back to camp. I guess it is my confidence in having been an infantry officer for over two decades, but I giggle at their questions. I can remember saying many times, "Calm down. Which direction have we been walking all morning?" To which they usually get confused and say something like, "Northwest…maybe north? Not sure." After I laugh out loud, I say in response, "Uphill, is the answer I was looking for. Not only uphill, but up a valley with high ground on three sides and you are going to hunt in this valley. If we get separated and you need to get back to camp, simply walk downhill and only downhill. Then you will see the lights of camp and you're home." It is a navigation aid ignored by most, but simply knowing the terrain and using elevation can get you home sometimes. In this case, by walking almost exclusively downhill, they would reach the valley floor and then camp.

I know sheep hunters who hunt a single mountain per day with spike camp on their back. They mark not only the location of their spike camp, but the elevation of it. So, that if they get stuck in a storm or if they are caught out at night, they simply must find the right elevation and walk until they bump into their camp. For them it is simple, just check the altimeter and it does not matter if you cannot see ten feet in front of your face due to weather conditions, you'll bump into your spike camp eventually. This kind of technique and the confidence to use it, comes with proficiency in the fundamentals.

Map reading is something most outdoorspeople believe they can do, but I've taught enough classes to know that folks don't really know what map symbols, grid reference systems, terrain features, contour intervals, marginal data and scale/distance really are. When I give them the test at the end of my course, most fail miserably.

Unfortunately, map symbols change from map to map. In fact, maps themselves change based on who developed them and based on their intended use. Game Management Unit (GMU) maps in Colorado differ greatly from USGS maps and even more so from military maps. Thus, the marginal data, method of depicting terrain features, the contour intervals, color key, scale and grid reference system also differ.

You need to figure out which type map or maps you will be using and learn how to use them. One of the biggest modern navigation failures is that folks use GPS data that does not match their map data. Then they wonder why they are confused. Here is the good news, terrain features are standard things and the vocabulary should not change from map to map or person to person. However, you need to be careful when speaking to the locals, because they may use a completely different word than cartographers or navigators. For instance, a draw might also be a coulee, wadi, or holler – just depends on which part of the country you are in.

The standard major terrain features are hill, valley, ridge, saddle, and depression. The standard minor terrain features are draw, spur and cliff. The supplementary terrain features are cut and fill. I bet you thought you knew all the terrain features, didn't you? There are yet others that are not covered in most navigation manuals like river, lake, stream, creek, bench, plateau, bay, marsh, and false hilltop. I did not develop the land navigation manuals, so I am not sure why certain features of terrain are not included. But like anything else, you need to learn the vocabulary.

Now, if you have figured out the items above, you might be ready to plan a route. Most folks do not understand how crucial this is to the success of their adventure, especially their hunt. It is important to consider different aspects of terrain regarding the type of terrain you are hunting in temperate forest, swamp, mountain, desert, jungle or arctic conditions all have different considerations when planning your route.

For instance, if you are hunting in mountainous terrain and you know the elk are sitting on cool north slopes during the heat of the day, you want to avoid those slopes on your hike into your hunting area. Then you want to consider the evening thermals so as not to give your position away with your scent as you move into your spot. This is a logical process, but it can get complicated and you have got to approach it with some serious thought and logical informed reasoning.

I have run into people that have said, "Wow, where did you kill that bull?" I might respond, "Well I got him about a mile east of here." Then I would hear, "I hunted that valley for a week last year and didn't see an elk." I try to seem surprised, but I am not always surprised. The fact is that they did not understand the relationship between the terrain, the prevailing wind, and the thermals. They simply blew the elk out on their way because they had a poorly planned route.

Once you have all that figured out, now you are ready to try navigating. The practical application of good map reading, and route planning is often foiled by a simple task called, "orienting your map". Most folks cannot grasp the fact that to read the terrain, visualize it and then interpret it on the map they must orient the map in the direction they are going. Most of these poor fellows, get befuddled right off the bat when we leave the classroom and walk out into the woods. They usually have their map straight up and down, north on top all the time. They cannot fathom the concept that if they are walking west, the top of the map should be the western edge of the map.

It does require a small amount of imagination to "see" the terrain in front of you and watch it magically appear on the map, but it is not hard once you get it. If you can orient your map and find your start point, you are better than most. Once you find your start point, then you have got to start using a method of navigation.

The simplest, most mechanical, and logical is called, "dead reckoning." This is where you figure out where you are on the map. Then you take a direction reading (azimuth) and a distance. Once you have that figured out, you simply keep going on that imaginary line (azimuth) until you get there. The trouble with this technique is that there are always obstacles you must navigate over or around.

The fact is that your imaginary line on the ground is quite often not going to get you to your destination. In fact, when you "dead reckon" through the woods, you will most likely end up far from your intended destination simply based on your dominant hand. Right-handed persons navigate around small obstacles to the right. They do it repeatedly along their route. If they are not aware of this fault, they end up far to the right of their intended destination.

One way to fix this is to account for it and simply use it to your advantage. If you know you have made the right distance and have not found your point, simply turn away from your dominant hand and start looking. For a right-handed navigator going north, who has not found their point, it is most likely west.

The best form of navigation is called terrain association or orienteering. The great thing about terrain association or orienteering is that terrain features do not move. A hill that God made is going to be there, the same as a valley or a river. The trouble with terrain association and orienteering is that they require an immense amount of practice and confidence to do well. So, for beginners dead reckoning is the best choice, despite its draw backs.

In dead reckoning you must be able to determine direction and distance on a map. Your direction is called an azimuth in navigation. Once you determine your azimuth on the map (grid) you must convert it into a magnetic azimuth. To do that, you must take declination into account. Declination is basically a measured plus/minus from your grid (map) azimuth to your magnetic azimuth you read on your compass.

You may ask why is there a difference? Good question, the gigantic iron deposit in the northern hemisphere of our planet causes compasses to point north, but it is not centered in the northern tip of the planet under the north pole. So, compasses are slightly off true north depending on where you are on the planet. So, there is a slight math problem, called declination, that you must do to determine the azimuth on your compass versus the azimuth on your map. Then you will need to determine the scale of your map very accurately, apply that scale to the map in the direction you intend to travel on your route.

When dead reckoning most routes will have multiple legs. It is best to plan each leg to begin and end at a verifiable terrain feature. If you have good GPS signal, you can also stop, turn it on, and verify you are at the end of leg 1 and starting leg 2.

This is where most folks ask why they cannot simply use their GPS, well throwing out power and connectivity, you should never navigate using a GPS. In a safe or relatively safe environment, you can put your head down and look at your GPS to find your way. In the wild outdoors, national forests, or wilderness areas you would be foolish to downright unsafe to navigate with your head down looking at a three-inch screen. A true navigator visualizes each leg of their journey and then moves with their head up, taking in everything around them. A fool navigates with their head down looking at a GPS or their phone. With your head down you miss game you are hunting, important terrain and rattlesnakes and grizzly bears.

Handling a compass would seem elementary, but it is anything but elementary. Gun barrels and any other heavy iron laden metals will skew your compass readings terribly. Holding your compass incorrectly or setting the bezel improperly will also get you lost. Like anything else, it is not just your equipment, but your technique with your equipment that matters.

Congratulations, you have got your azimuths converted properly from grid to magnetic and your route planned. How do you measure the distance you have traveled? The best way is a "pace count". There are other methods surely, like a pedometer or tracking on your GPS, but all mechanical devices are subject to failure and they cannot interpret slope or altitude gained. Even minor changes in elevation will skew your ability to interpret distance traveled relative to what you plotted on your map. The truth is that determining distance is an acquired skill. If you are using a pace count, then a set of Ranger beads might help keep your total distance traveled.

As a hunter, you might have a Laser Range Finder (LRF) on your person. That is a great solution to determining distance. If you are using your LRF you might need a pad of paper (use a pencil to write on it, ink runs in the rain) to keep track of each increment of each leg of your movement. If you can accurately determine distance traveled and keep track of it, assuming you determined your azimuth properly, then you can dead reckon.

There are advanced techniques to help you figure out where you are if you are lost, like intersection and resection. There are advanced techniques like catching features, running features, handrailing, and deliberate offset to learn someday too. But just like anything in life, without learning the fundamentals, you are screwed.

When you get good at this, you will be able to memorize your route. You will probably only take your map and compass out at the beginning and end of each leg. You might draw yourself a sketch or cartoon graphic of the entire route for reference. But when you become proficient, you will be navigating with your head up and looking at your environment.

Sure, nowadays there are phone apps like onX Maps and HuntStand. There are computer programs like Google Maps, Google Earth, and phone/computer interfaces for mapping software.

This technology makes planning your movement easier. But the fact is that if your head is down and looking at some form of technology, you are not navigating. You are missing the world around you and that could, in the very least ruin your hunt, and in the very worst get you killed.

Those electronic devices should only be used to confirm your location. A good navigator memorizes the next leg of their route and moves with their head up. When they stop for a rest break, they can drop their pack, hydrate, and turn on their device to confirm what they already know. Keeping your devices off and navigating also saves battery power in addition to allowing you to move with your head up, taking in your surroundings.

I am not going to cover alternative methods of determining direction like an analog watch/sun shadow, position of the sun, constellations/stars, or plant life. I am also not going to mention animal behavior, water flow direction or prevailing wind direction. Those nuanced environmental cues and direction determining techniques are next level. The readers of this book need to focus on fundamentals first.

This chapter was not meant to teach you how to navigate, not in any way, shape, or form. It was an introduction into the basics required for the task, to illustrate in most cases what you do not know but need to know. The ability to navigate does not come easy, but with some practice, you can be proficient and with proficiency comes confidence and confidence is so important when navigating. If you master the above-mentioned items and practice them in practical application, you can do a big trip and enjoy it, realizing that if you get lost, you can always be found. Even the great Daniel Boone said, "I was never lost, but I was bewildered once for three days."

Chapter 4 – First Aid and Medical

Medical is something you do not need, until you do. It is hard to say what's more important on an adventure trip than a fundamental proficiency in emergency medicine. The world we live in is fraught with danger, but when simple medical emergencies become tragedies because the "first responder" was ignorant it is doubly worse. There are far too many adventurers going into the backcountry with little to no medical training. A simple Red Cross First Aid or Life Saving class would go a long way to helping most wannabe backcountry adventurers. Here are a few examples to help you grasp the magnitude of the issue.

Three elk seasons ago, I killed a good 5x6 bull on public land with my bow. The friends that were along for the hunt were so happy they hung out and passed a flask of bourbon, talking and telling stories, while I caped the skull. Anyone who has caped a trophy animal knows it is a serious endeavor with small sharp knives or scalpels. Well, after one too many pulls on the bourbon flask and far too many jokes told while I was working, I lanced two fingers. It was pretty stupid, but not a problem – quick trip to the creek to scrub the wound clean, pressure to stop the bleeding, alcohol swap to clean the area, antiseptic ointment and a bandage until all the bleeding and oozing was complete, clean it again with alcohol wipes, then super glue it all back together, that's right – super glue.

I have some funny scars, but it required zero stitches and could have used about 9 maybe 14 stitches. As I write this, I am in Iowa hunting whitetails and today while camouflaging my blind, I ripped off the end of my left pinkie finger and cut the left ring finger severely. Not a problem – apply pressure until the bleeding stopped, clean up with alcohol swabs, apply a clean pressure dressing that could be worn around while I finished camouflaging the blind and until the bleeding was all done; then clean again and apply…you guessed it…super glue.

This past summer while hunting Colorado for elk and mule deer I ran into a bald-faced hornet (Dolichovespula maculate) nest in a bush, not 2ft off the ground. Thank God I saw it before I simply walked into it. I do not just carry things for cuts. I also carry pain killers, antihistamines, and an epi-pin. So, had I run into the hornet's nest (they are really wasps that are misnamed), I would have been upset and in pain, but not dead on the mountain.

You have to be prepared for the medical things you know you need, like your allergy medicine and for the things you don't know you need – emergency supplies. So, what are the major injuries or illnesses you will have to deal with? First, start with yourself. What are you prone to doing to yourself? What health issues do you have? Answering those questions will help you get your personal medical kit together. Then have a frank discussion with your hunting partner. What accidents are they prone to doing? What health issues do they have? What are they bringing into the field with them? I am personally prone to cutting myself, that is about it. I do not have a chronic or routine health issue, thank the Lord. But if you do or your partner does, you better carry the right stuff. If they are diabetic, you have got to plan for that. If they are allergic to bees, you have got to plan for that. If your hunting partner has had a previous heat injury, then they are susceptible to heat and will have the next heat injury quicker and more easily than the first. You must ask these questions and use the answers to build your kit and your skills.

Yes, you can purchase one of the commercial first aid kits with "everything you'll need" already in it. I think that is a bad plan. Those kits are loaded with things that people in the medical field use. If you are not familiar with them, then when you need to use them it will be a liability. Also, your kit must serve you when you are on your own, flying solo. While medical gauze is useful, it is not very absorbent, and it is expensive. I am more familiar with and like using high quality paper towels. While medical tape is useful, it is meant to be cut with scissors and is very hard to rip. I am more familiar with and like using athletic tape. If you get a bad cut on your hand, you can grab three or four paper towels out of the Ziplock bag in your first aid kit, apply pressure and wait for the bleeding to halt or slow. Then carefully fold a single towel into the size you need to cover the wound and tape it tightly with athletic tape. Paper towels are highly absorbent. Athletic tape rips easily with one hand and your teeth. That is a simple example, but it works for me.

Then there is the general first aid/trauma skills that everyone should know prior to taking on any kind of adventure. The list looks something like this:

(1) Evaluate a casualty

(2) Open an airway (conscious or unconscious) and restore breathing

(3) Stop bleeding (pressure dressing to tourniquet)

(4) Treat for shock

(5) Treat head, neck and spinal injuries

(6) Treat burns

(7) Treat fractures

(8) Treat climatic injuries (heat and cold)

(9) Treat bites and stings

(10) How to transport a casualty or if you should transport a casualty

I highly recommend you carry a "cheat sheet" in your medical kit to help you remember the steps in treating any one of the above listed conditions. There is a good chance you will not have Google, YouTube or WebMD where you're going. The cheat sheet with help you, but it is not enough. In an emergency you must know what you are doing. It cannot be discovery learning. When you pull out your first aid kit time is rarely on your side. There are many places you can learn basic first aid, but probably the best is your local American Red Cross. The class is less than $100 and you will learn invaluable skills that could save your life or someone else's life.

Once you have that skill set, you will need to build your personal kit. I make changes to my kit after each adventure. I learn and adapt from each trip.

Also, my health is changing as I age, so I will most likely never stop adapting my first aid kit. Going back to the example above, after experiencing some serious lacerations to my left hand, I realized I need less fancy medical supplies and more old-fashioned band-aids, paper towels, athletic tape, and alcohol swabs. I do not need fancy tapes, cremes, pain killing ointments and gauzes that seem like a good idea but are quite useless in the field. I got rid of the fancy things and added a higher quantity of the more useful items.

The weight in my pack is the same, but now I am safer and more functional. So many backcountry hunters, anglers and adventures cut their toothbrush in half to save weight and only go into the field with an absolute minimum first aid kit. That is just crazy if you ask me. My kit is comprehensive and weighs in at 1lb 5oz. I highly recommend you know how to use everything in the kit, and you would be amazed that it is cheaper if you build it yourself. A fundamental proficiency in first aid is something you must have, but the second order effect of gaining that proficiency is the confidence you will build. In the end, having confidence will help you enjoy the adventure.

Chapter 5 – Communications

Communication is something we have too much of in society today. The challenge is meaningful communication, that is appropriate and reaches the right audience. Well the same is true when you are in the field. Meaningful communication can be the difference between life and death. Even if you are okay, if someone believes you are not and calls search and rescue, it could cost you some serious money. The bottom line is that you owe it to yourself and your family to be able to call the cavalry if you're surrounded by hostiles, got your arm stuck under a boulder and are considering cutting it off with a dull knife or simply broke your ankle and cannot get back to the truck.

In the next part of this chapter I am going to cover means of communication. What I am not going to cover are companies that offer medical and emergency extraction from bad places all over the world. Companies like Global Rescue are necessary if you decide your adventures will take you to places outside North America that have no set protocols for rescuing folks or if you might find yourself unfortunately delayed (kidnapped) by a hostile organization who is short on cash and needs your family to help them get through their current budget crisis. These issues are a whole other discussion on communication and in those circumstances a satellite phone is without a doubt a must. We are talking mostly about practical things in this book and will save the Delta Force options for another time.

If you are hunting close to home and have a great deal of friends and family you might be able to simply leave them a note (written communication) about where you are hunting and when you expect to return. The note should have a few things in it and the good old "5Ws" is a great place to start. Here is an example: "Honey, I'm hunting alone (who) today. I will be "running and gunning" for turkey (what) all day. If I do not get one and get home sooner, I will be home an hour after dark (when). I will be hunting the Great Bear Wildlife Management Area in central Gallatin County (where). I love you (why) have a great day.

Michael." Now, you can write that on a piece of paper, in an email or in a text. It does not matter. That is enough information for your spouse to call your buddies when you are late getting home to discuss what to do.

It also helps if you text your spouse a couple times a day, so they do not worry. There are times where a text is very appropriate, like, "Safe up in my stand." This kind of simple note alleviates any worry or stress from your spouse and helps them to support your passions. If you're going to be hunting in an area, especially close to home, that has cell phone signal and you're more technically adept, you might want to consider a few hunting apps that help communicate with friends and loved ones. Those same hunting apps can enhance your hunt. My two favorites are HuntStand and onX Hunt. They allow you share your location but doing so could give away your spots. So, you would be balancing safety versus secrecy. A better plan is to add your favorite hunting app to your spouse's phone and share your exact location with them. It will alleviate worries of all kinds on their part. It will also provide them an accurate location in case you are lost or worse.

Then there are the adventures that require you to leave your state, region, time zone or even the Continental United States. Those adventures require more thoughtful planning of your communications. In those cases, I recommend a few things: (1) the Garmin inReach Explorer+ Satellite Communicator with GPS and (2) a SPOT Gen3 Satellite GPS Messenger for back-up. The Garmin inReach

Explorer is my favorite piece of electronic gear to come out in a long time. Before Garmin bought it, Delorme owned it and it was still a good emergency piece of communications equipment, but the GPS functionality was antiquated. Garmin added a fully functional map to the of the original Delorme, coupling very functional satellite text with very functional GPS. This eliminates one piece of equipment, either your satellite phone or your GPS. You will be carrying less, and it gives you confidence to go it alone even in places close to home that have no cell phone signal.

The Garmin inReach Explorer Plus is simple to operate. You set up an online account and add your family and friends cell phone numbers. Then you chose a plan that allows you to text as much as you need. If you are not using it, you can suspend the plan until you need it. It is easy to use. Not only does it have satellite texting capability anywhere in the world, it also has an SOS button that brings the search and rescue. That button has a security cover on it, so you do not accidently press it. All the while, it also functions as your GPS. It is not a compromise. Garmin made it a real serious satellite communicator and GPS all in one.

The only drawback is that the battery is internal, and you cannot simply put AAA batteries in when the old batteries run out. Thus, you need a power management plan and a recharging plan. My recharging plan is the Dark Energy Poseidon. It is a waterproof nearly indestructible battery back-up with a built in LED flashlight. It can recharge my phone or the Garmin about 3 times fully. I used the Garmin inReach for multiple seasons. There is nothing like being able to update your spouse, every time you move to a different valley in the Rio Grande National Forest. There is something special about reassuring your spouse a couple times a day with a simple text. They feel better about your hunt, knowing that you are okay. Everyone feels better knowing that if you are in real trouble and press the SOS key, it will send a message with your location to their 24/7/365 monitoring center. This service is included in the very reasonable connection plans they offer. If you must press the SOS button, they will work out the necessary search and rescue and help update your loved ones. It is also capable of device to device communication. So, no longer do you have to bitch and complain about how the two-way radios do not work that well, especially in mountainous terrain. You can text from one Garmin inReach Explorer to another. Finally, you can link it to your smart phone through an app and it amplifies your texting and communication abilities.

I could go on for another thousand words about this device. The point is that there are digital solutions that are cheap, relative to the risk you are taking in not using them. Mitigating the risk of being stuck and cutting off your arm, breaking a leg, falling from a tree stand or any other accident is a primary skill necessary to enjoy adventure travel. This device is inexpensive when you consider the alternative of not being able to get help or simply being late and your spouse calls search and rescue and you must pay for it.

The SPOT company has a couple great tools for communications as well. Their latest device is the X2 two-way satellite communicator. It is really a text messenger, which allows you to stay connected to the outside world when you are in the backcountry. It provides something all other devices do not, your own satellite phone number. So, you would have a different satellite number from which to contact everyone and vice versa. It also provides a compass, SOS functionality, tracking, and you can link it to social media. This is a great idea for someone who does not need a GPS like the Garmin inReach discussed above.

It is also significantly cheaper than the Garmin inReach discussed above unless you also need a GPS. Then you have got an additional expense and two devices to maintain to include two power/battery systems that go with the two devices. This device has a USB rechargeable lithium battery, so like the Garmin inReach you would need a backup power source to recharge it or a portable solar charger.

There are multiple service plans to choose from as well. The SPOT company also has a Gen3 Satellite GPS Messenger. This is another great tool, capable of digital communication, but it is a one-way device. It has four buttons that tell someone about your trip and a tracking feature, which allows people you have pre-programmed into your account to literally watch your trip on the map as you move. This is not a two-way device. It is a one-way device. It does have one advantage in my opinion, it runs on AAA batteries. So, if you are the kind of adventurer that has AAA batteries in all their other devices this is a good idea. On my long-range hunts, two weeks plus, where I am really in the middle of nowhere, think Alaska drop camp moose, I carry this device as a back up to the Garmin inReach Explorer.

Your SPOT account has multiple options that let you suspend service or upgrade to a package that lets your friends and family track your every move in almost real time. The device has four one-way communication buttons. They are:

(1) SOS – Send the Coast Guard and/or Search and Rescue

(2) Trouble – I am out of gas or have a flat tire

(3) Okay – I'm okay and here are my current coordinates and finally

(4) A button you program yourself into your online account prior to departing, that says whatever you want. A good example is, "Big bull down!"

The bottom line is that if you cannot afford the Garmin inReach Explorer then the SPOT device should be your primary device when you will be out of cell phone range.

Garmin also recently came out with the inReach Mini. This little powerhouse does everything its big brother, the Garmin inReach does, except a full functional GPS. It allows limited GPS functionality, like waypoint to waypoint navigation, but there is no map on the device. Now, if you pair it with your smartphone and add the Earthmate app from Garmin, it adds mapping, weather, and some other useful things. It is also lighter and smaller than the Garmin inReach at only 3.5 ounces.

Probably by the time this book hits the streets there will be even smaller and more capable emergency communication devices available. The fact is that you need one if you are going to be out of cell phone range for any reason. These devices are cheap, readily available and they work. It would be foolish to go afield without one anymore.

Emergency signaling is something most folks just do not understand and never think will be useful, so they don't plan for it. Without these skills you could find yourself in the very tragic position of being almost rescued. These are things like a signaling mirror, a chemlight with a length of cord attached, a whistle, a traffic safety flare, or a marine grade flare/flare gun. Yes, there may come a time when you are lost or worse. You might even be able to hear the helicopter, but it cannot see you. Worse yet, it cannot see you. This is when you must have "close in recognition" signals that make sense and are truly useful.

One of the best at night or in low light is simply a chemlight with a string tied to the end, swung very fast in a circle. This simple lightweight signal is extremely effective. From the air it appears to be a circle of light. Chemlights are "one shot one kill," so you've got to be sure you can see the rescuers before you do it, because if you can see them, they can see you. Another good choice is a simple road flare, yep the kind you use when your rig breaks down on the side of the highway. If you are in bear country and are considering taking a non-lethal means of bear defense a marine flare is a great dual-purpose option. In the event you are in bear trouble they have been reported to work. It also lasts much longer than a can of bear spray. The downsides to flares are (1) they are a pyrotechnic and can start a fire, so if you're going somewhere dry, that has any risk of forest fire do not take them and (2) they are single use devices.

During the day, nothing says, "Come and save me", like the reflection from a signal mirror, but alas you must have sunlight for that. Even without sunlight a signal mirror has a dual purpose of letting you fix your face, should you cut it or get something in your eye. The final good visual signal is your warming fire. The challenge with a warming fire is that it is more easily hidden than you think. The plan to signal with a fire, is not the fire. It is the smoke. The more smoke you can make the better. So, if you are going to keep a warming fire going, consider having some smaller branches of a tree with leaves or needles attached in a pile next to the fire. Should you hear a helicopter or believe you do, start adding the green boughs to the fire. What you want is a steady thick plume of smoke, without smothering and putting out your fire. Yes, fire is a great signaling device, but it is the smoke that billows and rises that will be seen from any angle. That black thick plume of smoke works night and day, especially if there's good moonlight. So, do not be afraid to add those green boughs even after sunset.

Audible signals come in many forms, but your voice is the last resort. Yelling is not energy efficient, nor is it loud enough to carry very far. Also, at a distance, it sounds like other natural sounds in the forest. The key is something that makes a loud sound, foreign to everything else. Banging your cookpot on a rock works. Shooting your gun if you have plenty of ammo works. But if you can breathe, you can blow a whistle, and nothing produces a louder sound that carries with minimal effort like a whistle. The best whistles do not have a ball in them like your high school gym teacher had. In very cold weather a metal whistle can stick to your lips and be very painful to remove. Also, if it gets wet from snow, rain or even just your breathing on it, the ball inside a metal coach's whistle can freeze up and render it almost useless. The best whistles are specifically designed for the outdoors. They are made of plastic and have no ball in them. A whistle costs nothing and weighs nothing, put one on your pack today.

So, what do I carry? Well it depends on the adventure certainly, but let's just say I'm hunting alone in the Rocky Mountains. In that case I carry: the Garmin inReach Explorer Plus Satellite Communicator with GPS, a SPOT Gen3 Satellite GPS Messenger for back-up, and a Dark Energy Poseidon for backup power for the Garmin. I do not keep the Garmin on. I turn it on only when I want to check my location against what my map and compass are telling me, or I want to text my wife. I have never run the Garmin out of power. Usually, I turn it on about once every hour when I stop to rest. I check my location, text my wife, and then I turn it off. I have the SPOT Gen3 just in case and I do not even put batteries in it. I have a headlamp that works on AAAs and carry a back-up set of AAAs in my pack for the headlamp. If I need the SPOT device, something has gone wrong and I am operating on a contingency plan. My daytime signaling device is the mirror inside my compass or smoke from a fire. My nighttime signaling device is a chemlight tied to a string and swung around in a circle. If I am out of chemlights I can tie my headlamp to the same string and do the same thing. And again, there's always fire. If I have got my pants on, I have got a whistle and a knife.

Taking this discussion one step further, I carry the following stuff on guided and unguided hunts: first aid kit, communications gear, map, compass, GPS, thirty feet of 10mm rope. Even if my guide were the great Jim Shockey himself that gear would be in my pack or on my person. Because, while my guide might know the territory and the game better than me, I'm not sure they have the survival skills and the training I've got from being an Airborne Ranger Infantry Officer. Probably not, so why in the world would you completely and totally trust your future and coming home safely to your guide? I am not saying to distrust them, not at all. What I am saying is that if you "fail to plan – it is a plan to fail".

Chapter 6 – Weapons

What is the appropriate weapon for your hunt? This is a question often not asked. If it is asked, it is asked out of context. If you ask someone, "What weapon are you taking on that mountain goat hunt?" You are likely to hear this, "Well I'm a bowhunter."

While there are millions of bowhunters in the United States, when you hear that statement, it really means, "I'm exclusively a bowhunter." I think you should ask yourself, "What is the appropriate weapon for this hunt," in the context of a second question, "Can you afford to do this hunt again?" If you chose to do a "once in a lifetime" hunt with a bow, you must be okay with going home empty handed. It is a mathematical issue. The probability that you will get an ethical shot within your effective range with a bow is low. With a rifle, especially if you are smart about caliber, bullet choice and ballistics, you increase your probability of successfully harvesting your quarry exponentially. If a hunt is truly going to be once in a lifetime, you need to consider very carefully your choice of weapon.

Your choice of weapon also requires you to have an ethical conversation with yourself. When the probability of an ethical shot opportunity is low, the probability of an unethical shot opportunity is high. If you decide to take your bow on that "once in a lifetime" hunt, you must be prepared to pass on marginal shots. I suggest you meditate long and hard, even go so far as using visualization techniques to help yourself pass marginal shots. As a "once in a lifetime" bow hunt comes to a close, the pressure to "get it done" will grow exponentially. That pressure will feel very heavy and real. If you are not prepared to deal with it, because you failed to discipline your mind and set goals that include coming home empty handed, you are putting yourself into a terrible position.

I define a "once in a lifetime" hunt using a few factors. The biggest factor is, "will I be able to afford a hunt like this again?" If the answer is, "no" or "yes but it will smother all my other adventures," I take a rifle. There are only so many hunting seasons in a lifetime. If you want to have a broad deep experience all over the world, like I do, there will not be enough seasons, nor enough money to do it all. This awareness helps me to set aside my favorite hunting method, bow hunting, and pick up my rifle without a second thought. The increased probability of successfully harvesting my quarry tilts the scales for me.

The second factor is what type of tag can I draw in my lifetime. The chances that I will draw a bighorn sheep tag anywhere is low. I can buy over-the-counter elk tags in multiple western states. This simple example means that I am only applying for rifle tags for bighorn sheep and I almost always hunt elk with my bow. Now, there are caveats and some nuance here regarding archery tags being easier to draw. There are many caveats weather, your age, your health, time off, but we are concerned here with weapon selection only. In the end, the probability of success is math problem. Math is finite and cannot be disputed. I use probability to help curb my desire and to help meet my goal. Harvesting my quarry is always my goal. Personally, I can live with not achieving my goals if and only if, I gave myself the best probability of succeeding.

I hunt with a short list of popular rifle calibers: .243 Winchester, .308 Winchester, .300 Winchester Magnum and .375 Holland & Holland Magnum. The first reason I hunt with popular calibers is that ammunition is easier to get. I travel the world to hunt and because airlines require you to ship your firearm and ammunition in separate cases, there is always a chance my ammunition will not arrive. If I am hunting with a popular caliber, then the chances are better that I will find ammunition if I need it. If my rifle does not arrive, then there is a good chance I can borrow one and at least I have ammunition. The second reason I hunt with popular calibers is that things break and if I need work done on short notice, the local gunsmith might have what I need on hand.

When I travel to hunt, I also use larger calibers than necessary for the game I am hunting. For instance, a good match for deer is a .25 caliber rifle with 115-grain well-made bullet. I am likely to use my .300 Win Mag with a 180-grain well-made bullet. That same .300 Win Mag with a 180-grain well-made bullet is an excellent choice for elk, but I am likely going to use my .375 H&H with a 260-grain well-made bullet for elk. Some folks are going to find my choices strange, but for me it goes back to probabilities. If I am traveling to hunt, my time and my access to good terrain are going to be limited. If my hunt is further limited by weather, hunting pressure of other hunters, or some other factor outside of my control, I might have only one chance. If that chance is quartering toward me, then I am much more likely to make an ethical decisive shot with a larger more powerful caliber and bullet. Sure, the smaller, perfectly matched caliber and bullet will do the job if I am offered a perfect or nearly perfect shot opportunity. However, late in a hunt that perfectly matched caliber becomes a liability when a perfect or nearly perfect shot, does not materialize. The larger caliber and heavier bullet simply increase my chances or once again, the probability I will be successful.

Finally, let's talk about how you load your rifle. Most folks load the exact same bullet all the time. I believe that is a mistake. If I am hunting a big game animal that is thin skinned, weary and lives in difficult terrain I might have a long shot. I will still use a larger caliber than necessary, most likely a .300 Win Mag. I will choose a well-made long-range bullet, such as a Nosler Ballistic Tip or a Berger VLD in 165 or 168 grains. I would zero my rifle using whichever bullet performed best at 200 yards. I would have all the data or "dope" for that load painted on the right side of my rifle stock. I would practice out to 500 yards with that load and make sure I knew exactly where the bullet was hitting between 200 yards and 500 yards. But when it came time to load my rifle, I would load a 180 grain Nosler Partition in the chamber and load the 165 grain bullets in the magazine. I do this for the contingency that my quarry shows up unexpectedly, right in front of me. In that contingency, I would want a well-made heavier bullet that I could drive right through their shoulder without thinking about the shot. On the contrary, if I have time to get myself set up and prepare for the shot, then I also have time to cycle the bolt and put that lighter weight, higher velocity bullet I planned to shoot into the chamber. If I am hunting elk and using my .375 H&H, I will load a 300-grain solid bullet in the chamber. If an elk pops up unexpectedly in close range, I have only to imagine where the heart is and then I can shoot clean through the entire body from any angle to get the job done with that bullet.

There are two valid points of criticism with my method. One, is that I am giving myself one less bullet in my rifle by cycling the bolt and removing the round in the chamber. Most rifles only hold 3 or 4 rounds in their magazine and cycling the bolt removes "one chance," to make the shot. My response is, "If you need three shots to kill an animal you weren't prepared in the first place." I have also been told I am over thinking it. Well I have seen lighter, higher velocity bullets hit bone and wound animals at close range. They are simply not made to break bone and drive through an animal. The worst-case scenario is that you shoot your high velocity bullet at close range, where its performance is marginal, wound the animal, and never recover it. If that happens, then you suffer as the animal suffers.

Archery tackle is an accuracy game. There are times when a very heavy arrow, with a forged single bevel broadhead, is appropriate, but you cannot "drive" an arrow through bone to hit the vitals like you can with a bullet. In archery, you must hit the vitals as your arrow fully penetrates and passes through your quarry. This is a must to insure an ethical kill and a good blood trail. This means that your most important archery skill is accuracy. In order to be accurate, you must be able to easily draw and hold your bow on target. Because of this, I believe your most important consideration is draw weight.

Your second consideration then must be, your arrow and broadhead combination because that is what does the killing. There are many kinetic energy (KE) charts that will require you to enter the speed of your arrow and the weight of your arrow. This will help you calculate the KE you're shooting and decide if it is enough to penetrate the game you seek. I would advise you to be careful with these charts because they give more importance to velocity. The kinetic energy equation is $KE = Mass \times Velocity2$, so velocity is squared, while mass is not. This factor has pushed many archers to favor velocity over mass, which I believe is a mistake. There is an old question that people use to demonstrate the difference, "Would you rather be hit by a scooter driver going 40mph or a dump truck going 30mph?" Most folks are going to say, "The scooter." I prefer to judge my projectiles terminal performance by using momentum, which is very simply $P = MV$. In that equation, mass is equal to velocity.

Once you know the necessary energy or momentum required to ethically kill your animal, you must decide how to put everything together, the general factors are: draw weight, arrow shaft composition, arrow spine, broadhead weight, broadhead style (fixed or mechanical), and total arrow weight. This can become extremely technical in nature and I recommend you enlist the assistance of a trained archery technician at your local pro shop to help you.

If you are an experienced archer, you do not need my advice, but I would still give you some, based on my experience. Always shoot fixed blade broadheads at elk and larger game. Finally, remember that only hits to the vitals count. You can ruin a hunt by taking a marginal shot on any animal with archery tackle. Wait for your shot and then execute an excellent one.

"Beware of the man who only has one gun. He probably knows how to use it!" Clint Smith is credited with that, but it has probably been quoted so many times, who knows. The fact is that most world class shooters have had their go to gun repaired repeatedly. Many even refuse to upgrade, even though they are sponsored and could have a new gun every season. The same is true with some tournament archers. Once they are dialed in, they simply refuse to change. Maybe it is just confidence in that weapon, maybe it is something else. Maybe it is an uncanny familiarization with how that gun hits targets, even more important, maybe it is an uncanny familiarization with how that gun misses targets. Whether it is confidence, familiarization, or a combination of both, it matters not. The more time you spend shooting your weapon, prior to your hunt, the better your odds will be of making a successful ethical shot when the time comes.

I will not recommend any drills or exercises. What I will recommend is joining a league and competing with your hunting weapon. Yes, with your hunting weapon. Your goal is not to win the league championship with some highly technical competition style weapon. Your goal is to learn to shoot your "hunting rig" under pressure. The kind of pressure it takes when you are about to take an animal's life can only be replicated by the pressure of competition. Even then, it is not quite the same, competition has made me a better shooter and archer, it can make you better too.

Chapter 7 – Gear

Gear is everything else. It is not your weapon, your communications equipment, nor your first aid kit. It is your clothes, your tent, your stove, your water filtration system, your tent pegs and all the other paraphernalia required to live outdoors for the duration of your hunt.

Gear is the least of my worries and the greatest of new adventurer's worries. In the first few years of my mentoring life, when I was helping others achieve their goals, I was shocked to find out just how much gear meant to people. I remember the first person I took on a remote DIY Alaska hunt and their regular tension related to the trip. I could not figure out why they were so tense. Then about sixty days prior to the trip, I insisted that we do a "lay out" of all our gear and figure out who had what and what we needed. By the end of the day, my partner was calm and collected. As I drove home, I remember thinking, "Of all the things that would reassure someone, it was the gear, wow, never would have thought it." In my mind, it is the terrain, the weather, the behavior or habits of our quarry, not the gear, that matters. To a new hunter or someone new to adventure, the gear matters immensely.

The most popular adventure hunt is DIY archery elk hunting in the Rocky Mountains. I have helped numerous people go on their first archery elk hunt. I am always amazed about their concerns related to gear. My advice is this, "Your archery deer hunting gear will work just fine." The fact is that archery elk hunts normally occur in warmer months before the rut. And, if it's your first one, you're probably not going to hike in seven miles for a backcountry remote adventure. Chances are that you will hunt with an outfitter or you will have help or friends.

After your first trip, you will know what you did right and what you did wrong, what you want to change, and works for you. Those are invaluable lessons for a new adventure hunter. You should have that experience and that adventure before you spend thousands on the "latest and greatest" gear. You can easily spend more money on gear than what it costs to do the hunt. I think it's much more important that you get out there, have an adventure and try things for yourself with the gear you have or the gear you can borrow. Then you will know what to sink your money into that's right for you. If you look at some of our modern hunting superstars, you will see that they started off hunting the backcountry for deer using regular gear. In some of the pictures you will see them wearing tennis shoes and blue jeans.

The fact is that the most important thing you can do is get your mind ready to hunt. Then practice and get in shape. The last thing to worry about is gear. Having said that, let me give you a big caveat. If you are planning to hunt the Rocky Mountain High Country, British Columbia or Alaska, for your first adventure hunt, don't. Simply put, you are not ready. The Rocky Mountain high country, British Columbia or Alaska will kill you if you are not ready. The weather and the rapidity with which the weather changes require serious planning and expedition quality gear. Unless you are hiring a full-service outfitter and guide, stay away from the Rocky Mountain High Country, British Columbia and Alaska for your first real adventure.

Once you have a few adventures under your belt, you are going to develop a system or at least you should want to develop a system for your gear. I break my gear down into sets, kits, and outfits. A set is something I might use for a specific day. Kits are the standard subgroups of gear that I will need on any hunt. Outfits are everything I will need for a particular hunt. A set could be my archery deer tree stand hunting set. A kit might be my kill kit, first aid kit or electronics kit. An outfit might be everything I need to archery pronghorn hunt, from spot and stalk to blind hunting.

Let's look at it more in depth. Sets are simple things that apply to your daily hunting or fishing tactics. If you're going to spot and stalk animals on the prairie, your set might include: a Montana decoy, an ultralight tarp for shade during the midday heat when you're glassing, a spotting scope and potentially a ghillie suit top. If you are going to be fishing for flathead catfish your set might include a heavy-duty rod and reel, bait hooks, swivels, heavy leader material, sinkers, and bait. If you're going to bow hunt deer during the pre-rut on public land your set might include: a climbing stand, a grunt call, rattling antlers, an orange vest or panel to wear or have by your stand, a pack frame and game bags. The key to success is to have your sets planned and to pack them the night before, then the next morning check the set, recheck the set, lace up your boots and go.

Kits by comparison are the type of thing that goes with you no matter what the set is. Based on the examples above, it does not matter if you are going after antelope, flathead catfish or public land deer – you should have your first aid and electronics kits with you. There are other kits you might need to develop and tailor to your own style of hunting or fishing. I have tailored my own kits and they include what works very well for me. It is in the tailoring of your kits that you can save weight and be efficient. Initially you will carry too much stuff. Do not worry, that is normal. There are other kits that people forget about. A survival kit, weapons maintenance kit, bivy or spike camp kit, mess kit, and hygiene kits just to name a few.

Some folks believe that separating such compulsory kits into bags increases the space required to carry them. I agree, it does. But it also makes me very efficient. If I must leave my camp because we have seen a record book ram at last light on public land, I will grab my bivy kit and move to the last place we saw the ram. I will sleep cold and more uncomfortable than in my camp, but I will be in range of that ram at sunrise. If you must dump your pack and build a bivy kit, it is usually too late. By having your kits ready, you are ready for any contingency.

Separating your gear into kits also allows you to pack better. You should have a packing list by item in each kit. Those kits should go on every hunt. Those items should be useful and if possible dual purpose to save weight. A good example, is the athletic tape in my medical kit. It does great as medical tape, but it is cotton and burns well too.

Another example is petroleum jelly. It makes good lip balm, can help with torn up feet, helps with burns if you get one and oh by the way it is a great fuel to get a fire started.

Outfits are macro level things. Literally, they are overall hunting or fishing gear lists. Imagine your gear list to fish for steelhead in Michigan. Imagine your gear list to hunt pigs in Georgia. Imagine your gear list to hunt pronghorns in southeast Colorado. You get the point. While you will need waders to fish steelhead in Michigan, you probably will not use them to hunt pronghorns in southeast Colorado. Having said that, some gear translates and is present in almost all outfits.

There are strange pieces of gear, you would never think of until you need it. I learned a long time ago from the British Paratroopers that women's knee-high panty hose absolutely prevents blisters. I wore them on my mountain goat hunt. We climbed and descended over 12,000 feet and I did not get a single blister. I translated that idea to horseback hunts. If you are doing a horseback hunt that requires a long ride, you will need a couple pairs of waist high women's pantyhose. You might think that is a weird recommendation. But trust me, if you do not normally ride horses, an all-day ride might wear the insides of your thighs and your ass cheeks so raw you cannot hunt. Women's nylon hose or panty hose is the ultimate ultrathin slippery layer that prevents any kind of chaffing, boot blisters or saddle sores. Man-up and put on your pantyhose big boy.

Gear recommendations from experts and regular people are both important. One of the best sources of information is the references on an outfitter's website. Many outfitters will list references by name and give a phone number for them. These people have already done the hunt you are planning to do and have agreed to be a reference for the outfitter. Here is a little trick, they do not know if you are booking with that outfitter or not. If you call them and discuss their trip, 9 times out of 10, they will want to tell you their hunting story. You will learn something if you listen. One of my Alaskan outfitters recommended rubberized hip boots for their float plane hunts. One of their previous clients told me,

"Those damn hip boots are worthless. First, they're heavy as hell. Second, you only use them to get off the plane. Half the time the water was so deep they're worthless. The smartest guy in camp hunted in lightweight chest waders and wading boots. He never got wet feet. He did not have to carry wet weather pants, just a jacket. The only drawback to his plan was he had to roll his waders down to pee. By the end of the hunt we wished we were all wearing ultralight chest waders."

I took that advice and hunted in light weight chest waders and wading boots for Alaskan Moose for seventeen days. The guys in my camp thought I was a genius and recommended the outfitter change their packing list.

When it comes to gear, take a smaller lower dose trip for your first trip. Take notes and use that adventure as a test or a dry run for your current equipment. Do not buy anything new until after that "dry run" trip. Then you have a point of reference for what works for you. If you're booking with an outfitter, make some calls, talk to some people, and get their advice. They've, "been there, done that" and your ability to listen and make it count, could be the difference between surviving your adventure and enjoying your adventure.

Chapter 8 – Packing

Most people think they know how to pack. Most people are wrong. Packing is a talent that comes from years of adventure travel. There are many things to consider, but the first is, "How are you getting there?" Are you going to drive? Are you going to fly? Is it an international flight? Will you have to remain overnight enroute? What if a flight is delayed and you must remain overnight unexpectedly? Will you have to get to an interim destination and then catch a float plane or a bush plane? All these questions must be answered first, then you can figure out how to pack.

One of the best examples is remote Alaskan adventures. They will require you to pack for a commercial carrier from your home to Anchorage. Then a regional carrier from Anchorage to say McGrath. Then a bush plane to your destination. Each plane will be different. Each plane will have different rules. Each plane will have different weight limits. Each plane requires planning and specific packing.

If you are going to hunt big game in North America, I suggest you drive. Further, I suggest you drive a pick-up truck or large SUV. In my experience this gives you the best way to get your meat, horns, and hide home. You can use coolers. If they are in the bed of your truck you can use dry ice. If they're inside your SUV you'll have to use traditional ice. One of the best ways to get your meat home is to freeze it before you leave. Put it in the coolers and then drive home. If you do not open the coolers until you get home your meat will be fine. This requires significant prior planning. You will have to take your meat to a meat locker, some other facility, or travel with a freezer.

Modern chest freezers are lightweight, energy efficient and cost less than a high-end Yeti or Pelican cooler. I have a chest freezer and power in the back of my pick-up specifically to bring home my meat and hide. Before I had fulltime power capable of running a freezer in the back of my truck, we pulled a small enclosed trailer with a freezer in it and used shore power from a local rancher. Back then we paid to stay on his property and from there accessed public land to bow hunt elk and black bear. The rancher would help us with many things and was our greatest Rocky Mountain hunting mentor. As soon as we had an elk or bear packed back to the ranch, we would plug our freezer in and use his tack shed to debone the meat and put it in the freezer. We would leave the freezer plugged in and go hunting until we had another animal down or the trip ended. If we left the freezer lid closed and got home in two days, the meat stayed frozen.

There are famous people that travel in a group that includes a film crew and producers. Their trip is usually made when the celebrity has harvested the quarry. They freeze the meat, divvy it up, put it in well-made carry on coolers and fly home. They can then just send their euro mount skull and/or hide home salted and have little worry it will get there. If you fly, the only way to send the meat home is to use a service that butchers it, freezes it, and sends it next day express to your home. This is how I've had to do it on all my Alaskan trips and it's time consuming and expensive. It usually involves staying an extra day in Anchorage, which is expensive. Then you will have to go to a butcher shop that provides the service and shipping, this is expensive. Then you will have to go to a taxidermist that will flesh and salt your trophy and send it to your taxidermist, which is expensive. The cost to buy an extra chest freezer for your big game hunting trips and figure out a power solution is much less expensive.

When driving, your challenge is not what to pack or even how much. The challenge is planning the trip and packing appropriately for the stops. You should also pack differently for the return trip than you do for the trip out. A few examples are obviously necessary here. Let us say you're going on an elk hunt to New Mexico from Pennsylvania. That is at least a two-day drive. On the way to New Mexico, you will want to plan two overnight stays at a comfortable campground. Two nights because you do not want to arrive exhausted at the beginning of your hunt. I recommend you stay at a campground. If you stay at a hotel, you are accepting risk. It is risky to leave your expensive items in the vehicle, so you will have to unpack and take them all into the hotel with you and then repack in the morning. At a campground you can sleep right next to your rig or in your rig. You will also be able to get a hot shower when you get there before sleeping, when you get up in the morning or both. Campgrounds, especially established ones like KOA and Good Sam RV Parks, are very safe places. Most have small basic cabins for rent, and you can park your rig literally, right outside the door and sleep with the window open. There have been times when someone I traveled with insisted on a hotel and wore me down. When we got to the hotel, they were tired and did not want to unpack the truck. When I volunteered to sleep in the truck to make sure our gear did not disappear, they apologized profusely.

Do not put yourself through that, get a campsite or a cabin at a reputable campground.

There's also pressure to get home right after the hunt, especially if you have meat in the vehicle. A reputable campground will have sites or cabins with electric. If you took the earlier advice to use a chest freezer, you will be in good shape because you will be able to plug in the freezer. Driving out and back gives you the flexibility to bring everything you could possibly need. But you must be thoughtful when filling the truck bed or cargo trailer. Be mindful to keep the things you might need during the trip close to the tailgate. You will want to pack your emergency roadside equipment and tools last. You will also want to pack an overnight bag with enough socks, underwear, and a toothbrush for each night you will stop on the trip. On the return trip you will want to do the same thing, but if you are using coolers, you will have the added complexity of adding ice and draining the warm bloody water. Even high-tech coolers like Yeti will need ice depending on how you load them and how much meat vs. ice are in them. It does not matter whether you use coolers or a chest freezer, if you have a bear in there you must watch the meat. If you left any fat on the bear it will turn rancid quickly, even in a freezer. If that happens it will ruin all the meat in the freezer that is in there with it. Be extremely diligent in getting the fat off your bear meat for this reason.

There are certain adventures that require you to fly. If the trip requires that you bring firearms on the plane, that is a specific process. Traveling with weapons can be intimidating. When you travel with firearms you have to be aware of the laws in the locality you're traveling to or through. If you are going overseas, you will need to do specific paperwork for the country your traveling to, certainly. But most important, prior to your travel date, you'll have to take your firearm to a U.S. Customs Office and complete a CBP form 4457, also known as the Department of Homeland Security, U.S. Customs and Border Protection Certificate of Registration for Personal Effects Taken Abroad. This form is used to verify that the firearm you took overseas is the same one you are bringing back into the United States. It is important, and some foreign countries require it as proof you own the firearm as well.

Your next step is to check your airline's website and make sure that you comply with their requirements to bring a firearm on a plane. Normally, it is quite simple. Generally, you put the firearm in a locked hard-side case with a TSA approved lock. The ammunition must be in another separate bag. Some airlines do not require that the ammunition is in a hard-sided locked case with a TSA approved lock, but I recommend it. I use a small pelican case and put that into my other checked bag. The tense part is when you get to the ticket or check-in counter. The airline ticket agent must verify your weapon is unloaded. This can be nerve racking, because you will have to open your gun case in front of people. Be cool, calm, collected, smile, do what you are told, and be helpful. You should be just fine if you've prepared and follow the agent's instructions.

When packing the actual rifle case, I always remove the factory padding. I put my rifle in a quality lightweight soft rifle case and then pack clothes and other items around it until the hard-lockable case is full. If you are traveling alone, you'll have to pay for an additional checked bag to put your ammunition and your other gear into. If you are traveling with a friend or spouse, one of you can put both rifles in a double gun case and the other can put all the ammunition in their checked luggage. Thus, you do not have to pay for two additional checked bags. This tactic has worked for me in the past, but please check with your airline and make sure you are doing what is legal according to their policies.

Your personal and carry-on bag should be your backpack that you will use on the hunt and then a small bag with items you will need during the trip. I recommend your carry-on include your valuable optics, batteries, communications gear, headlamps and the normal change of clothes and personal items. Finally, if you are going to Alaska for a remote hunt, you will likely have three flights and the planes will get smaller each time. I recommend that you pack specifically to get from your home to Anchorage on a commercial flight according to commercial flight rules. When you get to Anchorage go shopping for your food, fuel, and other items you will need that are hard or impossible to bring on the commercial flight – like

MSR IsoPro or Jet Boil fuel canisters. After you secure those items, you will have to repack to fly out on your regional flight or to leave Anchorage on the bush or float plane. Repacking might include a change of bag type, most bush plane pilots would rather you have soft sided cases and smaller soft bags they can easily fill the fuselage with. Large hard-sided rifle cases and luggage will be very difficult to get on a bush or float plane and the pilot might simply tell you "no." So, it is important to know what bags are required before you leave. Do not take anything for granted. Review the rules online. If that's not possible, call and speak with someone who knows at each airline.

If your adventure involves fishing, then flying is a good idea, even in the continental United States. You can usually get away with one checked bag, a carry-on bag and a personal bag. If you intend to bring fish home, then I recommend a very high-quality soft sided cooler as your carry-on bag. In your personal bag, put your camera, Garmin inReach, and other electronics you cannot live without. Use the soft-sided cooler as a regular carry-on and put whatever you normally put in a carry-on in there. Simply freeze the fish you intend to bring home before you leave and fill the soft sided cooler with the meat. I have done this many times and never had TSA or any authority at an airport even check it.

Depending on your type of trip you might need a bunch of different sets, kits, and outfits. When I use my truck as a base camp, I make sure I have a robust mechanic's tool kit, coupled with pioneer tools (shovel, ax, saw, etc.). It is a very complete outfit. When I travel with my bow to an austere environment, I not only take my normal bow maintenance kit, I add a second "back-up" bow and a more robust set of archery tools. The normal sets, kits and outfits revolve around the fundamental chapters of this book: medical, navigation, weapons, communication, cooking, but could also include items you use or routinely use. It is up to you to write the sets, kits, and outfits down. You should have a standard checklist for each one and then you should test them and improve them. If your sets, kits, and outfits are packed according to the list you develop, then you're ready for anything. This will help you relax and focus on your adventure. By way of example, you won't have to worry when your water system won't work, because the temperature dropped below freezing overnight and your filter froze. In your water filtration kit or part of your cooking kit, you should have a back-up system. Either the tablets or drops that chemically purify the water or spare fuel enough to boil what you need. That is what sets, kits and outfits are about. It does not matter what the contingency, whether things go to plan or not, you have what you need to continue the adventure.

Chapter 9 – Logistics

Logistics is something no one can overlook if they intend to accomplish the mission. In fact, the "American way of war," is based almost entirely on logistics. It is not about how fearsome and proficient our infantry, armor, artillery, and special operations forces are, it is about the blue-collar hardworking logisticians that make sure those warriors have everything they need. The numbers vary over the decades, but generally one in ten Soldiers, Sailors, Airmen or Marines does the fighting, the other nine work to make sure they have everything they need. Keeping the warfighters fully supplied, informed, maintained, and "in the fight" is actually what wins wars.

I believe the greatest adventure in the history of North America was the journey of Lewis and Clark. President Thomas Jefferson gave Army Officers, Captain Meriwether Lewis and Second Lieutenant William Clark, the mission to lead the Corps of Discovery to study the plant life, animal life and geography of the newly acquired Louisiana Purchase. President Jefferson wanted to know how the new territory could economically benefit the young United States, but ultimately, he wanted them to reach the Pacific Coast before foreign powers did claiming our sovereignty along the way.

If you read their journals, you will discover that logistics was always on their mind. So much so, that on their way from St. Louis to the Pacific Ocean they established caches of supplies for their return trip. They were beset with all manners of trouble: navigational, lingual, hostile native peoples, unending rain, terrible cold, hunger, swarms of mosquitoes, grizzly bear after grizzly bear, frozen mountain passes, horses that quit, and boats that sank. Nevertheless, they persevered and accomplished the mission. They were gone so long that they were given up for dead. When they paddled back into St. Louis two years, four months and nine days later the local people were in disbelief. The whole country soon heard about their adventure and they were heroes of such renown we still talk about them today. Their success is attributed to many things, but the most agreed upon were their ability to maintain discipline amongst the Corps and their ability to resupply.

A good logistical plan fundamentally underpins your adventure goals. Supplying your trip start to finish takes planning and practice. The practice is the same as shooting your bow or rifle. During my first season of extended backcountry hunting I learned many things. I spent thirty-three days traveling and bowhunting the State of Colorado for pronghorn, elk, mule deer, and black bear. I brought home a black bear and an antelope, but the real trophy were the lessons I learned along the way.

The most surprising thing I learned was that I needed far less food than I would have ever considered. The other lessons helped refine the way I power or repower my essential electronics, the way I sleep to wake refreshed and ready to go, the style of pack I carry and what's in it, the way I refuel my truck, the recovery tools I carry in my truck, the way I maintain my bow and accuracy with it, all of these lessons are logistical in nature.

In 2017, I ran into a fellow hunter who had been hunting for three weeks alone in a national forest. I was scouting not far from my truck when I heard what sounded like pots and pans banging. He was driving down a rocky road on a very flat tire and his rim. By the time I'd walked out to the road a large 4x4 maintenance truck from one of the gas or oil companies had stopped to help him. I wandered up and stood quietly. When the gas well workers shook their heads and said they could not help, the hunter with the flat tire was beset with anger and grief. I started to walk away, thinking that if the guys with all the tools and knowhow could not fix it, well than

I could not fix it. I am an infantry guy, not a mechanic.

The guy with the flat tire's name was Paul. Paul chased me from the road back into the forest and asked for my help. I looked skyward and thought, "Lord, you'd send someone to help me if I were in this situation, so I guess you sent me to help Paul." I went back to look at his problem and asked him to calm down. I said, "Don't worry we will fix it." He did not believe me, but about an hour later I'd improvised a way to get his locking lug nut off the wheel – seems he left home without the key socket. Paul's smile as he mounted his spare tire was something I will probably never forget.

Three days later I came out of the mountains without an elk, but undeterred. When I got to my truck there was a letter on my windshield. "Mike, I left you and immediately drove to town to replace the locking lug nuts and get a new tire. On the way a bull elk crossed the dirt road as I crested the mountain. I marked it on my GPS and went into town. The mechanics were done quick, so I went back to the waypoint and quietly walked into the woods. I saw movement and took a knee. It was a cow elk, she stood up and I made a great shot. I had her packed up and back at my truck by midnight. I never would have killed my first elk if it were not for you. Thanks, Paul."

Logistics is not just supply; it also includes maintenance. Paul's failure was simply traveling without his locking lug nut key. Truthfully, his tool set was woefully sparse. So, as you plan to drive to your next big game hunt consider where you will be driving, the type of roads you'll be on, and the weather. Then you should consider what kind of tools you will need. It is not just sockets, and wrenches, but a serious air compressor, some tire puncture repair kits, a tow chain/strap, a shovel, ax, saw, and a big hammer is always a nice touch

Carefully thinking out how you are prepared for emergencies, minor or major, is a logistical concern. Remembering that once you have these things planned for and are proficient, then you can relax and enjoy your adventure, because you are prepared. There are two types of logistics to discuss, macro and micro are the terms I will use. Micro logistics is what you carry on your back. Macro logistics is what you have in your truck or at your drop camp.

Here are a few easy examples to help explain. I carry a small multi-tool, folding saw, and hand spade in my pack. I have a full mechanic's tool kit, air compressor, cans of fix-a-flat, tire puncture kits, shovel, saw, ax, and much more in the truck. If I am going to be out for more than 2 days, I carry dehydrated meals and an MSR Reactor stove to cook with. Back at the truck I have plenty of food and an infrared cook top that plugs into my Goal Zero Yeti 1400 solar generator to cook. You get the point.

Many eastern hunters who travel out west to hunt for the first time fail to realize there is not a gas station every fifty miles. There will be places you travel out west where fuel stops may be further than the capacity of your vehicles on-board tank. Planning how you will refuel to get to distant locations and back is serious business. This is not just a point to point calculation. This also includes if you are going to have a "truck base camp" and then drive from there to mountain tops or trailheads daily. You will need to figure out the range of your vehicle carefully. Then calculate your daily usage and I recommend you add 25%. If you simply cannot make the fuel calculations work to get to your destination, you will have to give up that destination or devise a better logistical plan to get it done.

I like to use my truck as a base camp and spike out during the week. Because most folks work during the week and hunt on the weekends, I "give them the road" on the weekends. I hike in Monday morning and hunt through Friday morning. I'm back at the truck by Friday night, where I rest and refit Saturday and Sunday. I reward myself with a campfire, beers, and real cooked meals. I also conduct maintenance on my gear and weapon. If I am archery hunting, I will even practice. This work week hunting plan helps me prepare logistically. I pack for four nights in the woods and try to keep my camp on my back the whole time. I rarely cook more than once a day. My food consists of cold bars and energy powders for breakfast, snacks throughout the day, and a dehydrated meal with peanut M&Ms for dinner. Now some folks would flip, get diarrhea, constipation or just get bored. Not me, because I plan to hunt Monday through Friday and I know there are awesome meals waiting at the "truck base camp" to reward myself with, so I stay motivated. And if worse comes to worse, I can always pack back to the truck early.

A comprehensive description of logistical planning is not possible here. It is an entire book of its own. There are too many types of adventures and too many variables to consider. What I hope you take away from this chapter is that you must take charge of your logistical planning. This is even true on a guided hunt. If you have questions about logistics, ask your outfitter well in advance. If they are not bringing something you need, then bring it yourself, it is your hunt, not theirs. When you first start out, this might mean you bring too much and that is okay. It might hurt if you bring too much and must carry it. It might end your adventure if you bring too little. Thoughtful planning, short practice trips, trial and error, and well-kept notes will go a long way to helping you become a logistician.

Chapter 10 – Planning

Planning comes in many forms, but for the sake of this book we are going to use (1) long range (2) short range and (3) near term planning. Long range is next year to three years out. Short range is within the year. Near term is planning within ninety days. This may sound like entirely too much trouble. You may think that planning at this level of detail will take the fun out of it. Well I am going to tell you it's necessary. The old adage applies well here, "failing to plan is a plan to fail."

I understand that not everyone is a planner. I realize that most folks live in a warm home with a grocery store or a McDonald's close by. Those people can go through life not really worrying about what is coming around the corner, because in a contingency they simply get in their car and go get what they need. There is no problem living like this in the suburban or urban United States. However, if you want to succeed in your goal of adventure, you must be more thoughtful. You must have a plan.

All plans start at the same place. You must decide where you want to go. Then you must assess, "where you are at" in the context of where you want to go. Do not worry about what the obstacles are, just list them. They may include funding, time off, your fitness, finding a friend to go with you, your vehicle, and your spouse's comfort level just to name a few. If you are honest with yourself, they may also include developing a fundamental proficiency in navigation, survival, medical, logistics, planning, shooting or communications. Once you have your list completed, consider the context of how long it will take you to get ready, one year, two years, three years? It will all depend on your skill level. How much time you have off. If you have a mentor who can take you and show you and if you have the money to go now.

A simple example from one of my favorite hunts will help here. A DIY solo public land archery elk hunt with an over-the-counter tag is available in multiple states, but my favorite is Colorado. In order to execute a hunt like this you'll need to do many things well. If you do not have the ability to navigate, cut up a big game animal and pack it out, or you simply don't have the money, then you should consider a multi-year approach to this hunt. Plan the hunt based on the most limiting factor. The most limiting factor is almost always time, but it can also be money.

For this example, your most limiting factor is time. If you get ten days vacation a year and you always take a weeks vacation with family, then you have got three days you can save a year. Set your goal for saving five days over two years. This will allow you to dedicate a weekend, five days vacation and another weekend to your elk hunt. That is nine days total including travel, which is a fair amount of time to accomplish your goal. A good budget for a DIY hunt like this is $2,000. So, you will have to save about $1,000 per year to make it happen. Now you know what your long-range plan is, you must assess your personal readiness to accomplish your goal.

If you decide that you need some fundamental proficiency in multiple skills, in addition to saving time and money I suggest you enjoy some local hunts that mimic your elk hunt. If this year's short-range plan is thoughtfully executed, it will be part of your long-range plan to hunt elk. This year hunt public land with your bow for whitetail deer in your home state, with the goal of harvesting a deer, not a buck, just a deer. Hunt some place new to you that requires you to develop the skills you will need out west. Scout electronically using Goggle Earth, onX Maps, and other tools. Find three to five spots to begin your, "boots on the ground" scouting. Then go scout on the ground. Once you have done the on-the-ground scouting, narrow it down to three spots.

Never have less than three spots when hunting public ground because there is a good chance someone else has figured out where the same good spots are. So, you will always need a plan A, B and C. When you are fortunate enough to kill a deer, quarter them up or bone them out and pack them out. This is why your goal needs to be to kill a deer, not a big buck. You need to learn how to cut up a big game animal in the field and what it feels like to carry it out. If you can carry the entire deer and your gear out in one trip, that is what one trip will feel like on an elk. Remembering you will have to make at least five trips to carry out an elk. When you get to your truck you should have a beer and celebrate, because you have done a good rehearsal for your elk hunt. After you get home and put your meat in the fridge or freezer, grab a second beer and write down everything you could do better. Do not make it too formal, just write it all down. This will be your reference for your next "rehearsal hunt." If you do not write it all down while it is fresh in your mind, you will not remember it all. If you think you need to learn to navigate better because you got a little lost or maybe a first aid class would be good because you cut yourself deboning the meat, then add those classes to your new short-range plan.

With one fall gone, you are still inside your long-range plan to do your first elk hunt. As you progress, keep notes, and take your time getting resources together. Part of your long-range plan should be planning your more expensive equipment purchases over the two-year period, rather than all at once. Smart people might even ask for a pair of very high-quality boots that first Christmas and spend eighteen months breaking them in. That same smart person may ask for a better pack frame the second Christmas leading up to their hunt. People that fail to plan, end up buying boots and equipment in the near-term, the last 90 days before the hunt. Those people get blisters because their boots are not broken in and they get indebted to credit card companies too.

Once you begin to see the local public land hunts as rehearsals or warm-ups for the same thing on bigger game in the west you can really look forward to those hunts too. It is fun to learn and build fundamental proficiency. Most folks believe that bowhunting whitetail deer out of a tree stand and dragging it out with an ATV will somehow prepare them, it will not.

Near-term planning is conducted within your short-range plan and includes things like: buying your tags, having your bow tuned, getting the 100,000mi check up on your truck, and going to the dentist. Yes, a toothache will end a hunt faster than you can sing the national anthem. You will want to go over your packing lists in the near-term and make sure you have a separate list for things that expire easily. Food, batteries, snaplight sticks, fuel cells, and anything else you use that has an expiration date should be bought in the last thirty days.

Do not have a big race or physical fitness challenge in the near-term. Thinking you will do a marathon in the last few weeks before you leave to help you get through the hunt is only a way to injure yourself. Do simple slow things to maintain your fitness as the hunt draws closer. Make sure you are practicing with your bow wearing the clothes and gear you will be wearing when you are hunting. Check the parks and wildlife or department of fish and game website for the state you are hunting regularly over the last month. Closures due to weather and wildfires happen more than you think.

Be cool and realize that you are about to accomplish your goal, but most of all remember to set expectations in the near-term that allow you to enjoy the hunt. Maybe the first year if you get there safe, see elk, and get home safe you call that a victory. The ability to under promise and over deliver is always a valuable skill.

Finally, it is time to go. What is your driving plan? You must plan your drive with the idea that you will be ready to hunt when you arrive. Too many people drive somewhere like they are going to the hospital in an emergency. After two years of planning, rehearsing, training, and building toward your goal, do not ruin it with a poor driving plan. Planning for the hunt also includes a plan to get there in one piece. Take your time, be safe and most of all arrive ready to hunt. You have earned it.

Chapter 11 – Cooking

Why is this book a quasi-cookbook? Good question. Almost every cookbook starts with a philosophy or style of cooking. It is French, Southern, Latin, Caribbean, American or maybe it is a style like barbeque, frying, baking, or grilling that the book focuses on. This book is a "cookbook" because I offer recipes in the chapters that follow on how to "cook up adventures" yourself. Those recipes include a list of things you will need for the adventure (ingredients) and how I did it as an example (directions).

I believe folks, especially grown men, do not take on bigger things they dream of because they do not know how and as a grown man we are supposed to know how. So, there is some embarrassment or some strange shame in asking for help. Well this book should get you pointed in the right direction as a "how to" in the familiar form of a cookbook. If you substitute the word "cooking" for "hunting" in the next paragraph, you will get the point.

Most chefs have a style of cooking. My style is simple. If I can do it myself, I do. If it is best done with a guide, then I do that. There will be folks who try to hunt everything themselves and that is admirable. But to me, the quest for a mountain goat or cape buffalo is best done with help. If I can accomplish that goal on the first try with the help of a competent outfitter and guide, then that gives me more years to try to harvest a bighorn ram in "the unlimiteds" of Montana. There are only so many years that I will have the legs, back and willingness to hunt bighorn sheep in "the unlimiteds." It is steep dangerous rocky country that is also home to a thriving population of grizzly bears.

So, I've got recipes lined up in my long range plans you could say. In fact, I've specifically decided to save adventure fishing trips for after I'm no longer able to physically pack out a moose quarter or hunt bighorns in the mountains alone. I also choose to hunt with a rifle when I am hunting dangerous game. In that category I also include Alaskan moose and elk anywhere there is brown bears. The fact of the matter is that there are so many adventures I want to do before I die, that I simply am not going to limit myself to a style of hunting.

I admire hunters that decide to use a longbow for every animal. It is admirable to use methods that are more difficult. I question the guys who are using handguns and crossbows just to fill up the SCI record books, but that is another essay for another time.

The fact is that you must decide for yourself how you will "cook" up your adventures. No one else can do it for you. But just like cooking, you must have a plan, prepare things in advance, manage the process, and live with the outcome. My recommendation on how to decide where to start is simple - do what makes you happy.

All too often people, especially grown men, feel the need to succeed at everything they do, often forgetting the failures of their youth that got them where they are today. Those failures were the lessons required to get them where they are today. If you are starting something new, even if you are an uber successful professional, you are going to fail. So, make sure your failures are fun. Following are my stories and recipes. There is no right or wrong way listed, just the way I did it.

Chapter 12 – Colorado Bear

I am not sure who first said, "Bring enough gun," but they were right. They were talking about hunting dangerous game in Africa. When you are a hunter, the truth is that kinetic energy (KE) and momentum (P) are your friends. The more you hit the animal with, usually the better the result. This is especially true when your shot is not where you wanted it to be. There are always factors about the shooter and how much the shooter can handle. While all those factors are true, I am an advocate of shooting as much KE or P as you can accurately. That advocacy comes from experience and this hunt is part of that experience.

My hunting buddy, First Sergeant Marshall "Mark" Ware, and I both killed a bull elk on public land during the first week of elk season in 2009. Neither bull was a trophy by Pope and Young standards, but to us they were giants. We were elated with our success, but there was something else – during the hunt we saw a lot of black bears. During the long drive home, we decided that we should also hunt black bears during our 2010 elk hunt.

The challenge with hunting bears back then was getting the tag. The elk tags were unlimited and Over-the-Counter (OTC). The bear tags were capped, which meant "first come, first served". That year there were 40 tags available for black bear in the elk unit we hunt. To get a bear tag, we had to fill out an application online in July and sit there and wait for 11 a.m. Kentucky time, 9 a.m. Colorado time and immediately press "send". Then hope and pray we got one of the 40 tags, because they sold out instantly.

The big problem for us that year, was that Mark would be on vacation with his family on the day of the draw. So, there I was sitting at my computer, with two applications loaded on a split screen. I was waiting for the minute hand on my watch to click over to vertical, 11 a.m. It did and I hit send on Mark's application, then mine. Praise the Lord! We both got the bear tags. I probably should have bought a Powerball ticket.

Labor Day weekend rolled around, and Mark showed up to get me in his "Cowboy Cadillac" Dodge Pickup. He literally got every option Dodge had on that thing and the cockpit looked like Darth Vader's bathroom. We hooked up the trailer with the chest freezer in it, loaded the gear in it and headed west. We drove straight from Kentucky to Denver and stopped at one of the Super Walmarts. The bear tags were already in our pockets, but we had to buy the OTC elk tags. They did not go on sale until 12:01 that "morning." None of the regular employees on duty that late could help us, so we smiled and flirted with the night manager to help us. Finally, she logged on and sold us our elk tags. The elation of having the tags wore off quick and we made a poor decision to sleep in their parking lot.

Mark pulled up next to an island in the parking lot, gets into the landscaping, crawls into his sleeping bag, pistol in hand and goes right to sleep. I think, "Well he is a bit off center and always has been." I shrug my shoulders, got into the truck and fell into a deep sleep.

HOLY MARY MOTHER OF GOD!!!

What is that sound!

I bounced off the windows, seats, radio, and center console like a cat shoved into a microwave on high power. Mark's iPhone alarm was going off to the tune of, "BATTLE STATIONS! BATTLE STATIONS!"

I scrambled and cussed up a storm trying to find his devil phone. Unsuccessful, I bailed out of the truck screaming.

HOLY MARY MOTHER OF GOD!!!

It got worse.

When I opened the door the truck alarm went off, "BWANG! BWANG!"

At this point, I was high stepping across the parking lot and in the background, I could still hear his devil phone, "BATTLE STATIONS, BATTLE STATIONS!"

I am rolling across the parking lot half-dressed, shoeless and in a full-on Post Traumatic Stress Disorder moment. I turned back toward the truck, still cussing a blue streak, when I see Mark hopping around in his sleeping bag yelling, "Sir what the hell!"

He could not get the zipper down and has his Kimber 1911 pointing out the hole in the top of the sleeping bag. As he hopped toward me, he looked like one seriously mean, pissed-off, well-armed caterpillar. Then over his shoulder I saw the Walmart Rent-a-Cop coming our way full speed. The poor rent-a-cop turned toward the commotion, not knowing what he was getting into. When he saw us, the shock and fear were apparent on his face. He quickly turned around as fast as his little rent-a-cop car would carry him. I half expected to see the Denver Police Department next, but that never happened.

It took a while to calm down and start walking back toward the truck. Mark had turned off the "BWANG, BWANG" of the truck alarm, but the devil phone was still blaring, "BATTLE STATIONS, BATTLE STATIONS". When all was settled down, I said, "Well that 1 minute of sleep was awesome." We laughed our asses off and decide to find a Waffle House. Mark said, "We will get enough sleep when we are dead anyway."

Over waffles and egg sandwiches we realized that Mark meant to take his phone with him but failed to do that. He also failed to account for the time change when he set the alarm, so that is why it went off the instant we went to sleep. Even better, Mark locked me in the truck with his key fob. So, when I ran from the devil phone, it set the truck alarm off. The truly funny part was those two alarms nearly cost the Walmart Rent-a-Cop a bullet hole or two in his car.

We rolled into camp before lunch and were greeted by two of our favorite people in the world, Jim and Linda Hockenberry. We caught up about life since last year and decide it was time to hunt. The scenario was the same as last year – we walk about a half mile on Jim's ranch in any direction and reach the fence. When we cross the fence, we are on public land. We have hunted the public land around Jim's long enough to become acquainted with the names for all the good spots. Mark and I planned to hunt the same spots as last year. Mark hunted a place called "Teepee". I hunted "Emery's Pond".

Before we leave, Jim gave us the same advice as last year, "Look-it, listen-here, the elk in this basin have been chased into it by other hunters all around us. The elk stay because we've got good cover, good water, and good food. Don't chase them out and they will be here for the entire season. Sit real still until mid-morning when even the birds stop singing, then come in for lunch, a nap and shoot your bow. Then get back out and stay until you cannot see your sight pins anymore. Then come in for dinner. Do that all five days and I guarantee you'll see elk, probably kill one." Last year, we had six hunters in camp, and we took six elk following Jim's advice. That first evening, Mark saw three young bulls in range for the last hour before dark and decided not to shoot. I did not see a thing, but man was I happy to be back in the Rockies hunting again.

The next morning, as the other hunters head to the main house for breakfast, Mark and I choked down Cliff Bars, drank coffee, and hiked out to our stands. My walk was almost a mile uphill to 8,400 feet. It was my first morning at altitude and I took it slow. I was at my spot an hour before dawn. The grey morning light came long before the sun's warming rays peered over the mountain top.

I was shivering uncontrollably but tried to be quiet about it. It was in the low 90s when we left Kentucky two days earlier. It was 38 degrees that morning in Colorado. It took two hours for the sun's warm lusty rays to finally crest the ridge in front of me and hit my face. That morning had been graveyard still. Before long, the shivering stopped, the sun's rays warmed me up and I fell asleep. Then all hell broke loose and it went something like this…

"Aww heck, I'm stiff."

"What's that sound?"

"Leave me alone - I'm sleeping."

"Oh no! I've been sleeping!"

"What's that sound?

There it is again.

"Shit!"

There was an enormous black bear right in front of me.

They say that talking to yourself is the first sign of mental illness. Well a bunch of folks will tell you that it is too late for me. Which is why, the first thing I did was talk to myself, again.

"Okay Self, breath deep and quiet. He doesn't know you're here, be cool."

"He's about to drink. Get a range."

"Damn 24 yards, that's an easy shot."

"He raised his head. He's looking around and checking the air for scent of danger."

"Wait until he drinks again. Okay he's drinking, draw your bow, level the bubble, center the peep, pin on target, squeeze…"

WHAP!

The arrow hit's its mark.

The bear whirled about and crashed up hill. I was elated and checked my watch, 10 a.m. I regained my composure. I pulled out my pistol and went to check for blood. There was no immediate blood trail. I was shocked, certain my arrow went right through the bruin. Then I looked for the arrow. It sliced right through him and was stuck deep into the mud. A clean pass through is always a good thing. The arrow was covered in bright red blood, lung blood, which was another good thing. Now, I was sure that I brought enough bow and I hit my mark. Prudence dictated to leave him to die, go have lunch and come back with help.

Everyone in camp was buzzing with the news that I shot a bear on the first morning. All the normal questions were floated…

"How big is he?"

"Did he make the death moan?"

"How far was the shot?"

"Did you hear him go down?"

I tried to answer as best I could, but I was fired up and nervous.

After lunch we went to track the bear. Jim told me I didn't find blood right away because of their thick heavy coat, "Takes about 100 yards to really start dripping. Their coat soaks up the blood for a while, don't worry." We went about 70 yards and found good blood. Shortly after that, we found my bear lying flat on his back as if he were trying to get a suntan. All the sudden I realized what I had done. It was a big bear. Jim's son, BJ, killed the sixth largest black bear in Colorado history and was ranting about the size of my bear. He was convinced it was the second biggest bear they had ever taken in their camp, second only to his. I could only agree. What the hell did I know? It was my first bear.

What I could tell you is that even after we field dressed the bear, it took four grown men to roll it down the mountain. After getting the bear back to camp, I showered up and went back on stand to find the bull elk of my dreams. Wouldn't you know it, about 5 p.m. another big bear showed up on the exact same line as my bear, this one was light brown versus the jet black of my bear. He stopped a yard closer, 23 yards. All I could do was hope Mark was having the same luck at Teepee.

Later we took measurements of my bear's skull. It was more than enough to make the Pope and Young record book. Everyone in camp in was excited. After skinning the bear, we hung him overnight to cool. Later that night, one of the men in camp, Buddy Boone, direct descendant of Daniel Boone, came in and handed Jim an arrow covered in blood. Then he said, "I've got a present for you!" He had a gorgeous big 5x5 bull down. After seeing Buddy's bull, we all went to bed excited about the next day, until the next day came.

The weather turned foul on us and never stopped. It was a mixture of brief good conditions, then thunderstorms, freezing cold, gale force winds and weird rainbows in between downpours. The third night we had one of those discussions around camp, boastful discussions, about who was going to fill their tags in the morning. We had spent too much time indoors and started getting silly. I was quiet until the end. Then I got up and said, "Jim get the meat wagon ready about 9 a.m. I'll have an elk down by then." That boastful comment was met with, "Yeah right!" and "Sure you will" and uproarious laughter. I simply smiled and went to bed, because I thought it was going to happen.

The fourth morning was cold and quiet, but right as the sun was coming up it turned nasty. I hunkered down in my climbing stand, high up in an aspen tree and rode it out. Before too long, the storm blew over and the sun's rays warmed up my sorry soaking cold body. Then at exactly 8 a.m., a mature cow, a yearling cow, and a calf elk came thundering down the meadow to my left. They milled about and never set still. I had my bow ready to draw and was trying to stop shivering from the cold.

They never stopped nervously moving. The wind was right. I had an aspen tree to my left, whose branches totally concealed me. It wasn't me making them nervous. Something chased them over the mountain and into my meadow. About the time they were going to leave, the yearling cow started to walk calmly toward me. I drew my bow just as she was about to walk into the clear, but she stopped. I realized I could see a vertical crease in her golden hide through the tree limbs. I thought, "That's the crease behind the shoulder, I can hit her lungs from here." I relaxed, held dead aim and I let the arrow fly. It went just exactly where I intended. She spun and almost fell.

Then I realized, it was not her shoulder crease. It was her hindquarter crease. I had shot her through the hindquarter. I was instantly sick to my stomach. The energy from the arrow almost knocked her down. She was wobbly but managed to limp off. Then I heard a crash. I shook convulsively, thinking, "What just happened? Is she down? I heard a crash?"

I gathered myself and headed back to camp for lunch. It was 8:15am and I needed the meat wagon. I guessed I was right. We talked about the shot and decided to give her some time. We waited a full five hours before heading out to track her. The track was easy in some places, hard in others, but we found her. The truth is that Jim and BJ are amazing trackers. The best I've seen in the U.S. I was so happy to be tagged out in such terrible conditions. We were also lucky and blessed that the rain did not wash away the blood trail, because about the time she was hanging in the skinning shed, a hard rain poured down.

Later that afternoon I butchered my elk. To my surprise, when I cut the meat around the femur joint the entire leg fell to the ground. I was surprised I did not have to separate the femur from the hip socket in the pelvis. Upon further inspection I found that my arrow cut the femur bone in half. We have all heard the saying, "Bring enough gun." Well friends I am here to tell you that you should always, "Bring enough bow." Kinetic energy and momentum simply make up for bad shots. After the surprise wore off, I made short work of the wonderful meat and got it all into the freezer with the bear meat for the trip home to Kentucky.

As I waited for the sun to set on the last day of the hunt, I marveled at how tough Mark was. He hunted every single minute of daylight regardless of conditions. He had rutting moose all around him every day. Bears challenged him on the way to the stand in total darkness. He could also hear elk running the ridge three hundred yards up the hill behind him, but he never got a shot.

You cannot say, no one can say, he did not give it his all. He is also one of the best hunting partners God ever invented. So, I called his effort a success that week and still do today. Nevertheless, the long drive back to Kentucky was made better because we had an elk and a bear in the freezer. The only thing that could have made this trip better is having two elk and two bears in the freezer.

Recipe –

Here is what you need, "soup to nuts" to serve up your own similar elk hunt –

Ingredients:

_____ A willing soul, a semi-stout heart, good legs, feet, and hips – priceless

_____ Time Off – (# of days) x (what you get paid daily) until you get it done = ?

_____ Colorado Non-Resident Over the Counter Hunting Fishing Combo, Elk Tag and Habitat Stamp $661

_____ Colorado Non-Resident, Bear Tag OTC with caps and Habitat Stamp $351

_____ Fee to hunt with someone like Jim $2,250; he recovers your animals, provides meals and warm sheds to sleep in

_____ Gas & Travel $800 (KY to CO and back)

_____ Archery equipment – you should already own it your deer rig is perfect (fixed blade broadheads)

_____ Clothes and boots – you should already own it

_____ Blind or climbing stand – neither is necessary, but you should already own it

_____ Pack, binoculars, rangefinder, etc. – you should already own it – once again deer gear is fine

_____ Food & Water – Included when you hunt with someone like Jim

_____ Meat hauling – freezer and drop cord $250

Total Cost: $4,312

Directions:

Well this is my way to cook up and elk/bear combo. There are certainly other ways. You could pay an outfitter about $6,500 and get everything done for you and potentially hunt private land too. Or you could pay an outfitter $3,500 for a drop camp. Or you could go DIY on public land and reduce costs from what we paid, but you are going to need a lot more gear, food, and time. Realize that no matter how you decide to hunt, the cost of the licenses/tags are still there and they are expensive. You could just do elk or just do bear to reduce the cost.

Fall free range bear meat is good, if processed and cooked properly. You must get the fat off the meat quickly after the kill, but other than that, you can treat the meat like any other game meat – UNTIL you cook it. Then you must cook it well done due to the possibility of trichinosis. We have eaten many bears since this first bear and enjoy the meat. At the time I'm writing this article, I have another fall free range Colorado bear in the freezer awaiting processing.

Paying to stay with someone like Jim is a bargain when you consider you get the following: hot meals and snacks, hardstand cabins with beds to sleep in, very easy walk-in access to public land, and daily showers. Now, add in the fact that Jim will track and recover your elk, it is a great deal.

I highly recommend you drive to Colorado for the hunt. Elk and bear are big animals. Getting your meat processed by a commercial processor and then shipping it home is expensive. If you do that you still have to figure out how to get your horns, skulls, and capes home.

The way we traveled to this hunt was to pull a small cargo trailer with all our gear in it. We also put a medium sized chest freezer in the trailer. We froze our game solid before we left. Then we did not open the freezer until we got home. It stayed frozen until we got home.

Earlier in our elk hunting careers we tried coolers with dry ice and regular ice. Either way it's a mess and you'll spend $100 in ice or dry ice. A small chest freezer will not cost you $300 and you can use it for many seasons.

Please use only fixed blade broadheads on elk. I do not care what you see on TV. I have personally witnessed the loss of multiple elk due to mechanical broadheads being used and failing to penetrate. Most folks simply do not shoot enough KE or P. Now, if you are shooting an 80lb bow with 550 grain arrows – you could do it, but I would still go with cut on contact broadheads. All your deer gear is perfectly fine. My wife has killed 3 elk with a 53lb compound bow, shooting 370gr arrows.

You could save up the money for a hunt like this by putting away $125 in savings monthly and then you could do a hunt like this every three years. Cut costs and you get there sooner. Remember, the hunt of a lifetime is really the hunt of a summertime. Life is short.

Chapter 13 – Mountain Lion

Hunting in grizzly country takes on a whole new feel. The knowledge that you are in the territory of an apex predator, that could kill you in seconds, adds a sense of adventure and adrenaline that cannot be easily described. Every strange scent that wafts through the air, causes you to pause and investigate. Every bear track stops you in your tracks. Any stick that snaps behind you, causes a rise in adrenaline and your senses become fine-tuned, razor sharp and you feel especially alive. When you are certain there is a grizzly in the area you can almost taste the iron in your own blood as your heart races. If you actually see one, you'll never forget it as you sort out the situation and evaluate the threat. I've hunted in grizzly country. I have also hunted grizzlies. I have a very healthy respect for North America's largest predator, but I don't worry about them. I prepare for them and have a plan that allows me to hunt in grizzly country and enjoy it, without being paranoid or bear-a-noid.

The apex predator that gives me pause and worries me is the *Puma Concolor* – the mountain lion. While attacks on humans are rarer than bear attacks, the mountain lion's skill set and hunting technique is far more frightful in my opinion. They are expert ambush predators. Many folks throw the term "expert" around too loosely. Lions are absolute experts and there is nothing loose about that adjective in regard to their skills.

They kill and eat one deer per week. Think about that, it takes roughly 52 deer or deer sized animals per year to feed a mature lion. They are poor runners but are powerful short distance sprinters. So, they must get within a few yards of their prey undetected. Deer have amazingly acute senses of smell and hearing, yet a lion gets within successful sprinting distance of one deer per week.

Mature male lions can be as tall as 36" at the shoulder, can reach 9' in length, and can weigh 220lbs. Mountain Lions also have the largest range of any large predator in North America. Thus, many more people have hunted in mountain lion country than in grizzly country. I often wonder how many times a lion has stalked within mere feet of a human, just to see how close they could get. I also wonder how many times a lion has been close to me on a backcountry hunt and I didn't even know it. The thought causes me to look over my shoulder and I'm sitting in my office right now.

So, it was with a healthy respect that I started looking for an opportunity to hunt them. I spent a lot of time researching different lion hunts and learned quickly that most outfitters hire a houndsman and subcontract the hunt out to them. The outfitters I spoke with were knowledgeable and talking to them was insightful, but after I spoke with my first houndsman directly, I knew I wanted to find a houndsman who ran his own business. I was fortunate to find Chris Gressman. He spent a great deal of time on the phone with me and after we talked, I stopped looking and booked the hunt.

Chris picked us up at the airport in Salt Lake City in late December. We would be hunting over the New Year's holiday. I was still an active duty Army Officer at the time and that is all the time I could get off work. We left the airport and started driving toward the Wasatch Mountains. Along the way we got acquainted of course, but I stopped talking and started listening when Chris began discussing his hunting strategy. He reminded me that hunting lions is easier if there's snow on the ground and that there was not much snow right now. He also reminded me that the hunt would have been easier if I would have drawn a tag in a limited entry unit with private land access. But nevertheless, he was absolutely committed to getting me a public land lion on an over-the-counter harvest objective tag. Tomorrow morning, we would drive to a trailhead in sub-zero temperatures, drop the truck off and start trying to "cut a track" on snowmobiles. Aline and I were so excited we could barely sleep.

Upon arriving at the trailhead, it was impressive to see the system Chris used. He pulled a big custom trailer with snowmobiles and dog boxes with a heavy-duty diesel truck. He very quickly unloaded the truck, loaded the snowmobiles and we were off. As we departed the trailhead, Chris was up front, pulling a dog box on skis behind his machine. I trailed with Aline holding on behind me on my machine. The excitement I felt leaving the trailhead smoldered in my chest like a coal burning stove and the bitter cold grey morning rolled off my back like so much water off a duck.

As we climbed into the mountains, the sun cut through the somber grey sky and burnt off the clouds, revealing a bluebird gorgeous day. It was not long before we found a dead moose carcass and stopped to inspect it. Chris was surprised to find it and I was shocked. After scouting around, we found only bobcat tracks and moved on. The day came and went without cutting a track, but what an amazing day it was. Even if we were not lion hunting, a day snowmobiling through the Wasatch Mountains was more than enough.

Painful is the only way to describe how cold it was the second morning. I will never forget driving past the local bank and seeing -14F on the sign. At that kind of temperature hypothermia and frostbite are serious concerns. Aline and I had spent some time before leaving Kentucky double checking all our gear and rehearsing our survival skills. So, on the outside chance a tragedy occurred we were ready. Plus, we were hunting with an extremely competent and skilled outdoorsman. Still, -14F is painful – thank the good Lord we had the excitement of the hunt to help keep us warm and our skills to give us confidence. The second day came and went. We never stopped, from sunup to sundown, we drove our machines through the mountains, always on trails, some snowy and some barren and rocky. Alas, we cut no track.

As we drove to the next hotel, we talked about public versus private land lion hunting. Chris was positive and upbeat, but made it clear that the lack of snow across the Wasatch Mountains and the pressure put on the lions by the myriad of public land users, not just hunters, upped the degree of difficulty for the hunt. I took it all in and tried to learn anything I could from this experienced houndsman. I also realized that if we got it done, the fact that it was on public land with an over-the-counter tag, would make me that much happier. Chris would have preferred we came out after a snowstorm and hunted fresh powder. I could not come out any other time. I was a Lieutenant-Colonel commanding an Infantry Battalion and the holiday around New Year's was all the time I had to do it. Chris gently reminded me that if I were more flexible and waited until they had a good snow, that we would have cut a track by now for certain. Well, hell – if we did not get it done – so be it. I was certainly having fun snowmobiling with my lovely wife and trying to find a lion.

The quiet in the truck was heavy, as we set out on the third morning. We were going to a different area, with the same game plan and playbook. Driving through the mountains I drifted off and was in my own world, thinking about some far-off land or future adventure, when Chris abruptly stopped the truck. He jumped out and checked the snowbank on the side of the road, we just cut our first lion track. Aline and I were ecstatic as we watched Chris inspect the track. The lion had crossed the road not long before we drove on it. He was not far away. How Chris spotted the track from the cab of his big pickup as we drove through the predawn grey light is beyond me, but I was impressed. We had to get to another area and off the road before we could let the dogs go.

We got the truck to a safe spot. Then Chris walked them into the forest away from the road, up the cold snow-covered north face of a ridge and let them go where the lion tracks crossed into public land. As the dogs climbed the mountain, we were able to watch them with our binoculars. The snow on the north face of the ridge provided a stark contrast to the dogs and it was a memory I will never forget. Chris tracked them using their GPS collars. He drove us around in the truck and kept us in range of the dogs, which was exciting and warm.

About 10 a.m., the dogs lost the track of the lion on the south face of another ridge that was barren of snow. It was apparent they were going to be there a while figuring out which way the lion exited that snowless area. Chris asked, "Are you up for a hike?" We both responded, "Yep". Just like that, he found an appropriate place to park the rig, we checked our gear and away we went.

Aline was a trooper. She never slowed and kept up for the first two hours as we hiked from 6,000 to 9,000 feet on broken trails and spotty deep snow. Finally, we got to where we thought the dogs had the cat treed, but we could not see it. We dropped our heavy packs and Aline volunteered to "guard" them as Chris and I made the final push to see the lion. Well it was not the final push. The dogs continued and so did we. By the end of the day and nearly 14 miles covered on foot, up and down some of the steepest terrain Aline and I have ever hiked, the lion made it home. His den was the hayloft of a barn on a working a farm. Chris said, "It happens. Lions are more plentiful than people think, and they sometimes live right under their noses." Chris went to recover his dogs and Aline and I hiked back to the truck. On our way back to the truck, we realized it was New Year's Day – what a day, one we would never forget.

When the clock went off at 3:30 a.m. on the fourth day, I woke Aline and then tried to get myself moving. I was sore and stiff. By the time I was tying my boots, the promise of a new day had washed away fatigue or failure from the last three days. Once we were in the truck Chris went over the game plan. We would simply run the playbook again (1) leave in subzero temperatures (2) offload the snowmobiles at a trailhead and (3) ride the trails until we cut track, or the sun went down. As I mounted the snowmobile, I remember how good it felt to pull my ski goggles down over my eyes and give Chris the thumbs up. He was optimistic about the new day and that gave us a spark too. As he sped away in front of me, I felt Aline's grasp as she wrapped her arms around me on the back of my machine when I opened the throttle. Lion or no lion, this was one hell of a trip.

We were not alone on the trails today and passed a few folks doing some off-roading. It drove home the public nature of our hunt and we pushed deeper into the mountains. Chris seemed to slow down and look at things on the side of the trail more often today. Was I imagining it or was there more sign today? Mid-morning, he stopped and said he'd seen a track earlier he wanted to go back and give it a second look, that it was maybe last night's track or yesterdays, but it was certainly a lion. We doubled back and upon further inspection as the sun was starting to crest the southern sky, Chris decided to put the dogs out on the track. It was off the trail to the north and went straight down into a deep snow filled canyon. He said if it were fresh enough for the dogs to follow, we would know shortly.

Well it was fresh, and the dogs took off with tongues wagging and what looked like smiles on their faces. We sat and talked, sitting on the snowmobiles and watched the progress of the dogs. We were able to see them for a long time as they climbed the mountain across the canyon, then after they disappeared, we followed them on the GPS. The sun was strong and after an hour of waiting, we were all warming up. We were happily soaking up the sun when Chris stopped talking and walked back to his machine. He brought me back a radio and said, "The dogs have crested the mountain above tree line and are on the other side of the ridge. I cannot hear them, but the GPS says they've got a cat treed, which could really mean they are stuck on a dry spot and there's no cat at all. I will climb down into the canyon and up the other side until I can hear them. If they've really got a cat treed, I will know when I hear them. Take off all your extra layers, get your rifle ready, and listen for my call on the radio." I was so excited all I could say was, "Right, got it." Then Chris pitched off the trail, down the steep bank, into the canyon and was gone.

Twenty minutes later, we saw him climbing out of the other side of the canyon up the north face of the mountain. Then I heard it, "Mike they've got a cat treed – go." I kissed Aline and took off down the hill. The snow in the bottom of the canyon was old, crunchy, and deep. I post holed through it as best I could. Out of the canyon bottom and climbing the north face, I had to paw my way through dense layers of scrub trees and bushes. That is when Chris's second call came in, "I'm sure it's a lion they've treed... haven't seen it yet... come on buddy." I responded, "I'm rolling." I was still moving pretty good, when I cleared the brush into the timber and then into a line of dog hair thick blowdowns. My heartrate was in the yellow on the tachometer, as the snow got shallow, but the north face got steeper. I was climbing on all fours like a mountain gorilla as fast as I could go, when the third call came over the radio. My heart leapt and my legs began to feel like concrete when Chris said, "Mike they've got a big tom in the tree. Not sure how long he will be here. You still with me buddy?" As my heartrate began to run into the red on the tachometer all I could get out over the radio was, "Yep."

Oxygen was at a premium as I finally broke through the trees onto the barren ground above the tree line. Even though I stripped down to the thinnest layer I thought was safe, I was sweating profusely. The shallower snow and the fact that I could hear the dogs pumped life into my burning legs. I was doing the best I could to climb, when Chris's fourth call came in, "Mike you still with me?" I did not answer, all available oxygen was being used to move as fast as I could.

In a few moments, I was over the ridge and down into the timber on the other side. The sound of the dogs grew louder, and it sounded like the sweetest symphony I had ever heard. Chris was crouching and looking up when he saw me. He stood grabbed me by the arm and pointed up into the thick canopy of the trees, "There Mike, there's your Tom. He is a big boy. Let me tie up the dogs. You catch your breath and get ready to shoot." Exhausted and exhilarated I breathed deeply and forcibly tried to slow my heart rate. Then I realized the lion was in the very top of the tree and the shot angle would be severely vertical. I contemplated laying down to shoot straight up. I decided instead to lengthen the shot horizontally by walking uphill until I was nearly level with the lion's vitals. I found a good rest on the limb of a spruce and leveled my rifle on the lion's chest.

Chris was right, he was a big Tom. I took a couple deep breaths and watched the lion. The powdery white snow, the green and smoky blue of the spruce, the thinness of the air, the dark grey brown of the tree trunks, the smell of evergreen, the baying and barking of the dogs, the feel of the rifle in my hands, the cold air on my naked head, the sweat rolling down my spine, the magnificent gold of the lion's hide and the piercing menacing stare with which he regarded me are forever burned into my memory.

Chris finally got the dogs tied up, climbed quickly up to me, and said, "Whenever you're ready, take your time." I took one final deep breath, cocked the hammer, relaxed, put the bead of the front sight in the bed of the buckhorn rear sight, centered it on the lion's heart and began to squeeze the trigger. In my memory, the rifle's report happened in slow motion and I saw the slow moving 225 grain .44 Remington Magnum bullet impact just above the lion's heart. At impact, the lion fell out of the tree and Chris leapt down the mountain after it. I stood still and asked myself in a whisper only I could hear, "What happened?" Chris was gone. I said, again to myself in a whisper, "Did I miss?" No, I could not have missed. I saw the bullet hit the lion.

I do not know how much time passed, but like being jerked out of a dream I heard Chris say, "Mike, let the dogs go, I cannot find the cat!" I sat my rifle down and started downhill to the dogs. I stumbled and began to feel ill. I said out loud to myself, "I missed? How could I have missed." Then I dry heaved and forced some vomit back down my throat on the second heave. I reached the dogs and began to undo their tangled leather leads from their mooring, when I heard the most glorious calm voice coming up the mountainside, "Oh wait. No worries. The cat fell dead into a snowbank. I walked right passed him. We got him." Then I collapsed, stared at the sky, smiled, and thanked God. I am not sure how long I laid there, so happy and almost in tears. The emotions of having successfully taken a lion and the sweet sadness of triumph only hunters know washed over me, as my body started to shake. The adrenaline that had kept me warm was gone and I was a shivering mess.

Chris climbed back up to me in no time and we celebrated a bit as he guided me down the hill to my lion. We dug the lion out of the snowbank, and I marveled at him. A nearly perfect predatory animal now laid on the ground in front of me. I inspected his retractable claws, his teeth, his jaws, his ears, his coat – what a beautiful beast. I stood back up and smiled widely at Chris. We had done it. Chris asked, "We can take pictures, before I skin and debone him right here or do you want to drag him out to let Aline see him whole?" There was no thinking involved in those options. Aline was as big a part of this hunt as Chris, the dogs, the lion, and I were. We had to drag the lion out.

We decided that dragging it uphill and back down the way we came was not an option. So, we went straight down the mountain, through the blowdowns, deep snow, and brush to the frozen creek bottom. Then we went around the mountain that we went up and over earlier. It took a few hours and poor Aline was alone on the snowmobiles waiting and hoping the whole time with no idea what happened.

Poor me too, I learned I was allergic to mountain lions along the way. The longer we dragged, the redder and more swollen my face became. I also left a trail of snot on that frozen creek bottom, that rivaled any of the giant snails of Africa. As we worked, Chris explained that it happens regularly and a few of his clients have had severe reactions. There is no way to know beforehand if a client will be allergic, so now he carries an epi pen just in case. I was just annoyed. It was not a medical emergency. I am not allergic to anything or at least I was not – until I learned I was allergic to mountain lions. Now, on my annual physical when the doctor asks, "Allergies?" I get to respond, "Mountain Lion, no kidding, want to hear the story?"

The look on Aline's face was worth the hours it took to drag the lion back to the snowmobiles. We celebrated, took pictures, and enjoyed the late afternoon sun. Chris and I discussed taking the time to skin and debone the lion but decided it would be safer to use the remaining daylight to drive out of the mountains. We would worry about the skinning and deboning later, it was cold, and the meat would certainly not spoil. The lion was too big to strap to the seat behind Chris on his machine. He strapped it across the top of his dog box on skis that he pulled behind his machine. The lion was so big his head and his shoulders hung off one end, his hips hung off the other end and there were three full grown hounds in that box. By the time we got back to the trailhead it was dark and bitterly cold. We were too tired to skin and butcher the lion. I decided to spend the money and let a taxidermist do it in the morning after we checked it in with the Utah Division of Wildlife Resources (UDWR).

After a great dinner celebration, we went to a hotel close to the Salt Lake City Airport and crashed. We spent the next morning slowly regenerating some energy and power in our tired bodies. At breakfast Aline said proudly, "You know you climbed the mountain just as fast as Chris yesterday. I timed it from when he left us, until he broke tree line. You made it to the tree line in about the same time." I responded, "Wow, thanks baby, but Chris was navigating and talking on the radio like he was out for a Sunday stroll. All I had to do was follow his footprints in the snow and go as fast as I could. My heartrate was red lining and I couldn't even answer his radio calls by the time I climbed above tree line."

Chris picked us up and we checked in the lion at the UDWR. Then went to the taxidermist, paid him to skin and debone it. Then we did the paperwork to have the lion delivered from Salt Lake City to Kentucky. Just like that, the hunt was over.

There was an overwhelming sense of pride and accomplishment as we said goodbye to Chris. Nothing worth doing is ever easy and this hunt was anything but.

Recipe –

Here's what you need, "soup to nuts" to serve up your own lion adventure –

Ingredients:

_____ A willing soul, a semi-stout heart, good legs, feet and hips – priceless

_____ Time Off – one week – 7 x what you get paid daily

_____ Tag – Utah Non-Resident Harvest Objective Permit and license $358

_____ Houndsman – approximately $4,000

_____ Firearm – you should already own it _____ Round Trip Plane ticket - $350

_____ Ammunition - $100 (5 boxes of 20; 4 for practice and 1 for hunting)

_____ Clothes – you should already own it

_____ Ski goggles - $40

_____ Boots – you should already own it

_____ Pack – you should already own it

_____ First Aid Kit – you should already own it

_____ Survival Kit – you should already own it

_____ Food & Water – Breakfast $8; Lunch $8; Dinner $25: $41 per day x 6 days = $246

_____ Hiking Stick(s) – you should already own it or can make them yourself

_____ Taxidermy – in Utah to skin and flesh $155; price varies upon amount after that your choice

_____ Shipping – FedEx overnight frozen from Utah to Kentucky - $306

Total Cost: $6,055

Directions:

Start by finding a houndsman who books hunts themselves, not necessarily an outfitter. All the outfitters I spoke with took a cut of the price and subcontracted to a houndsman. Trips booked directly with houndsmen are cheaper than those booked through an outfitter. Remember that the entire price is not due at once, usually a deposit of 30% to 50% is due the year you book the hunt and the remainder is due the following year when you take the hunt. So, the cost is not "all at once" in that regard.

I recommended a lever action rifle with iron sights chambered in a large pistol caliber .357 or better. I used a Marlin Model 1894 chambered in .44 Remington Magnum. I also recommend you use the factory open sights and do not put a scope or optic on it. The firearm will have to be with you on every chase and along for the ride on snowmobiles, ATVs or horses - lightweight and durable is key. Many weapons will dispatch a lion, so if you decide on another weapon, consult your houndsman before you make the final decision.

Obviously, the less gear you must buy, the cheaper the hunt will be. You can do this hunt in your best cold weather whitetail deer hunting gear and do not need any specialty gear other than ski goggles. Ski goggles are really a must if you are going to be driving snowmobiles, nothing else will do really.

Food and drinks are your choice of course. The way we did it you ate quick in the morning and got on the road. Then we snacked all day, really whenever you stopped. Finally, we had a good healthy dinner and crashed into our beds.

You can find ways to get cheaper or more expensive plane tickets, that is your call. You could also drive, but that would require more days off work, so that is a tradeoff. Now that I am retired, I drive if it is at all practicable. That way I can get there on my own time and do some sightseeing along the way.

Chapter 14 – Colorado Elk

We knew we wanted to bow hunt elk. We knew how to hunt whitetails and turkeys. We had our Army training and we had the spirit to try. That sums up where we started our elk hunting journey. While planning that very first hunt, I was fortunate to meet Jim Hockenberry. Jim is a Vietnam Vet and he was an outfitter in Canada and Colorado. Jim knows elk and if you listen you will learn something. Jim still rents small cabins on his ranch and included in the rent is his help in recovering your elk. The priceless part of renting from Jim is his expert advice. It was a perfect fit for us, and we decided to stay with Jim that very first year.

Over a number of years, I have learned more from Jim about elk behavior, tracking, meat preparation, and how to hunt the Rocky Mountains than I could have ever learned in a book or in a seminar. His mentorship has been a real blessing and now I bring new hunters with me as often as I can. I help them, sure, but what I really do is introduce them to Jim.

As our fifth year of hunting elk approached, I spent some time thinking about the crew that was going with me. My lovely wife, Aline, would be on her third elk hunt. She hunted hard in bad weather her first year and was not successful. The second year, she arrowed a mature cow on the first night and spent the rest of the week butchering the cow and relaxing. Before we left Jim's ranch it was in vacuum sealed meal sized portions in the freezer in the trailer. My long-time hunting partner, Command Sergeant Major Marshall "Mark" Ware, had been with me every year. He arrowed a big 5x5 bull his first year, but since then had been unsuccessful. A close friend, Major Andrew "Quail Head" Caldwell, had never hunted with us and had not bow hunted in years. He paid for a rifle elk hunt with an outfitter the previous year and did not even see an elk.

In those same four years, I killed two bulls, two cows, and a big Pope and Young black bear. Even though we walked off Jim's ranch to hunt the same area of the national forest our success had varied widely. It has been feast or famine for our crew. Last year, there was a drought in the area we hunt, and the bears were hungry, skinny, and aggressive. They were close to hibernating but had not put on enough weight. The drought made mast production, acorns and berries, very poor. The bears had little forage all summer and were aggressively pursuing any food source around the clock. In fact, by the time we got to Aline's cow that year there was a bear eating it. That same year another hunter in camp had to fire warning shots to prevent a black bear from attacking her.

This year, there was an abundance of acorns and berries. The bears were fat and we were not worried. I suppose it is feast or famine for the bears too. Prior to the hunt we decided to hunt elk and black bears. It's really an elk hunt, but black bears usually make an appearance and give one of us a shot, so having both tags is smart. Plus, Mark has been trying hard to kill a fair chase black bear for a long time. The elk tags are over the counter, but the bear tags are a draw. In July, we were relieved to discover we all drew bear tags. I called Jim to tell him we all had bear tags and to make final coordination. He told me the last two months had been dry and most of the water holes were empty. There are about seven water holes, one big meadow, two old established wallows, and four big ridges we normally hunt. Of those seven water holes only three held water and the wallows were dry. After talking to Jim, I decided to insist that Mark, Aline, and Andrew hunt the water. That gave them the best chance of killing an elk or a bear. I had been successful in previous years and thought it was best.

Maybe one of them would kill early and I could go sit their water hole after them. I could also do some exploring. I thought I'd walk twice as far as we ever have and search for a wallow or water hole to sit on. There had to be one we did not know about or one Jim hadn't told us about. In the area we hunt the elk are extremely pressured. We often see other hunters. We hear them drive the roads, get out of their trucks, bugle, get back in and drive away. We also run into game wardens, who want to interrupt our hunt to check our tags. I do not know why they can't show up in camp and check our tags, but I digress.

So, in the area we hunt the elk are not just call shy, they are known to run away from calls. We hunt them the way Jim taught us, by ambushing them, much like you would hunt mature whitetail bucks. Jim tells all the hunters who stay with him, "Leave your calls at home, find an early season wallow or water hole, sit as still as possible with the wind in your face as long as you can, and you'll see elk, probably kill one."

By the good Lord's grace, we arrived at Jim's after a twenty-five-hour drive in good shape before lunch on Friday. Since we had all hunted there before, except Andrew, we set about getting our gear together and discussing strategy. After lunch we were ready to hunt, and general locations were decided. Aline would hunt "Emery's Pond", the draw leading to it, and the meadow above it. Yes, my wife, Aline, hunts public land by herself with a bow. Mark would hunt "Muskrat Pond", the high ground to the northwest and the meadow to the southwest. I would take Andrew to the bottom of

"Dirty Meat Gang" draw above "Beaver Pond" and drop him off. I would hunt "Linda's Wallow", which was dry, but sat astride two well used trails.

About ten minutes before dark I heard movement to my rear and climbed up and looked with my binoculars, it was Jim and Mark. That could only mean one thing – Mark was successful on the first night. I scrambled down the trail and came up behind them making enough noise for them to hear me. Mark said one word with a wide smile, "Bear." Jim was asking about a blood trail, Mark laughed and said, "Don't think you'll need one." I was shocked to see Muskrat Pond, normally about the size of a basketball court full of water, was not much bigger than a kiddie pool. But I was awful happy to see Mark's bear lying dead near the water.

The bear had walked in during the last of the afternoon light to get a drink and Mark put a fatal arrow in him. It spun to bite the arrow like a dog chasing its tail. Mark nocked another arrow and shot it again, it laid dead where the last arrow hit it. I was so proud. Mark finally had his fair chase bear. Back at camp with Mark's bear, we learned that Andrew had seen a cow and calf elk, plus some turkeys. Aline had not seen anything but had a wonderful evening in the mountains. Everyone went to bed with great anticipation of the coming dawn and our first full day of hunting.

The first full day was beautiful, warm, and calm. We all headed out on our own and had a great morning. Andrew saw another cow and calf. The rest of us saw nothing. That evening Aline discussed with me privately, that there was no cover close enough to the water to shoot this year. Emery's Pond had dried up and the pond edge was now over fifty yards from her stand. I asked her if she wanted me to hang a stand on an aspen closer to the water for her. She said, "No, two well used trails go right passed my stand and I can hunt them on the way to the water." That was a good logical call, so I did not encourage the new stand location idea anymore.

The second morning I headed out early in the dark with my climbing stand and went up "Reverend Weiss's Draw." It is a great travel corridor between dark timber bedding and open meadow feeding areas. I got to see a wonderful show of mule deer coming in and out of the timber. I could have arrowed a half dozen or more, but I saw no elk or bear. Mark saw nothing. Andrew saw a cinnamon sow with cubs. Aline had a long fifty yard plus shot on a good bear drinking at Emery's Pond and it did not work out. She was ready to move, but strangely decided she did not want me to hang a new stand closer to the water's edge.

That afternoon we had some intermittent storms and the gorgeous rainbows and clouds associated with fast moving weather at 9,000ft. I believe the sky is the Lord's canvas and he is magnificent painter. Mark had a big bull and cow elk come in together, but he did not get a shot. Andrew saw a whole flock of turkeys. I saw a bunch more mule deer. Dearest Aline saw nothing, again. That evening, I discussed with Jim about letting Aline hunt his alfalfa field, he agreed. He has a ladder stand there and she would at least see mule deer. She had never hunted there before, as we don't normally hunt on Jim's ranch. Aline agreed and the next morning I would walk her into that area and help her find the stand in the dark. Then I would back track down the valley and go up the next drainage to Emery's Pond. I was on a mission to find the right tree and hang a new stand for Aline. After I picked a tree, I planned to sit there a while. If that bear came back and gave me a fifty-yard shot, he might get an arrow for breakfast.

The next morning was still and gorgeous. Aline and I took our time getting to the alfalfa field and were surprised by a distant bull bugling high above us on the mountain. We hunt the early season and bugling bulls are rare. After she was safe up on stand, I started walking toward Emery's Pond at a slow clip and enjoyed watching the sun come up. It was a long walk and I had a climbing stand on my back in addition to my normal load. About halfway up the draw towards the pond, I heard a bull bugle again.

He was far away. The stillness of the morning helped the sound carry a great distance and it echoed down the valley. I wondered how far away he was and thought about calling back to him. I walked on, climbing slowly higher up the draw toward the pond dam at Emery's. As I got to about a quarter mile from Emery's, the bull bugled again. Then rapidly another bugle. I stopped, took a knee, and watched my hands shake. I had never hunted bugling bulls. The bugles had a tremendous effect on me. The heavy load I was carrying had me dripping with sweat. I stayed on one knee resting and then he bugled again. I thought, "I have got to have a call somewhere in my pack."

I dropped all my gear, clawed through my pack, hands shaking. I heard myself say in a whisper, "Please let there be a call in here, please." There was an old dirty reed call in the bottom of my pack. I put it in my mouth and tried to call, nothing. I spit and whispered to myself, "Okay Mr. Wizard, take a deep breath, clean the call and try again". A rough cow mew came out the second try and it was immediately answered by a bugle.

He was probably three hundred yards above me. My heart pounded out of my chest. A better cow call came out the next time. He responded immediately again. I stripped off everything but my base layer, grabbed my bow, and ran for the meadow above Emery's Pond. I got to the pond dam and hid behind it, nocked an arrow, took a deep breath, drew my bow, emerged all at once above the pond dam ready to shoot a bull in the meadow beyond.

He was not there. I stood there dejected and started to giggle. Then a hundred yards above me the thick saplings cracked and thrashed. The bull was working his way through the thick bush into the meadow. I froze and thought, "Way to go, you're busted, sky lined on a pond dam." But the bull did not see me, as he stepped out into the meadow he looked left and right, licked his nose twice and started down the hill toward the pond. I dropped as if taking cover from incoming artillery. I was curled up behind the pond dam shaking and thought,

"Camouflage works. It makes sense, my last calls were 200 yards down the valley behind me. He is not looking for the cow yet. He thinks the cow is way down the valley, not here at the pond."

My hands were shaking uncontrollably. My heart was pounding so hard it was all I could hear. I did not get a good look at him, but I was certain he was a legal bull. When my hands stopped shaking and I could hear again, I could only hear one sound, glug…glug…glug. The bull was drinking on the other side of the pond dam I was hiding behind. I drew my bow on my knees, stood up fast and was facing a giant bull just across the water hole. I put both my 20 and 30-yard pins on him and let the arrow fly. He was hit hard, exploded out of the water, spun about, and stopped to check his back trail. He stood there broadside staring at me and bleeding. I had the good sense to take a range, 54 yards. Still he stood there, bleeding. I nocked another arrow, drew, and let fly. The second arrow also found its mark. The two fatal shots anchored him. He wobbled back to the edge of the forest. He fell and died.

I do not think I walked back to camp. It was more like floating. As soon as I came through the gate, I ran into Mark and Andrew who just finished butchering Mark's bear and putting it on ice. They noticed my quiver was two arrows light and asked what happened. I told them I called in a bull and shot him twice. They did not believe me. But as I recounted the story, they became believers. We were looking for Mark's bourbon to have a toast, when Andrew asked, "Well, how big is he?" I said, "He's a stud, my biggest bull by far, but I'm not sure, my hands were shaking so bad I couldn't count tines, I could barely get a range." We took our time gathering up proper knives, saws, game bags, and some bottled water while waiting for Aline to come back in for lunch. After a quick meal, the whole squad with Jim in the lead set out for Emery's Pond.

The bull was a monster of a 7x6. We took some pictures and then Jim looked right at me and said…

"You got a knife right partner?"

"Yessir I do."

"Good, I'll be back with mules, I'd like to see those shoulders off when I get back."

"Yessir."

Aline stayed with me, helped me skin and quarter the elk, while the rest of the crew went back with Jim.

Jim returned with two mules and his grandson, Ty, to help recover the bull. When they arrived, we had the shoulders off. Jim and Ty made short work of the rest of it. One of the mules was young and had never packed out an elk, which made for a little more adventure. It also caused the older mule to be loaded heavy. Jim decided we should leave the cape and antlers, because the young mule would not carry it and the old mule was loaded down. We would come back later as we had most of the day left.

I said, "No way, I'll carry it."

Jim responded, "Mike it's a long walk and we can come back and get it."

"With my luck a bear will get it."

"Mike you don't have a pack frame and it's heavier than you think."

"Don't care Jim I'm not leaving it up here."

His cape, skull, and antlers were awful heavy and without a pack frame it was no fun, but we all got down the mountain and back to camp safe. We hung the quarters in the tack shed on hooks and spread the skull, cape, and antlers on the cold floor. Then I collapsed exhausted in my hammock. Mark and Andrew were already out hunting. Aline got ready quickly and went out for the last couple hours of daylight.

I am not sure how long I slept, but someone walking down the mountain in daylight startled me. It was Mark, and there is only one reason he came home early, he shot an elk. He told us that he had arrowed a nice bull, probably his biggest bull, about an hour ago. Jim said, "Ground your heavy gear, get your flashlights, pistols, and let's go find the blood trail before it's pitch dark." We scrambled to get ready and headed out. Jim found the blood trail easily, but then started tracking uphill. Mark and I looked at each other, "Running uphill is not good." We crested the summit at sunset and still had not found the elk. Jim stopped shortly after we crested the summit and said, "Man I smell something, I think he's close." Mark and I were perplexed, we could not smell anything. Jim was joking. He could see the bull not twenty yards in front of us, piled up against an aspen stump.

It was Mark's biggest bull. The recovery of that bull at night was an adventure. At one point, Mark left me alone to go link up with Jim who was bringing the cavalry to get the bull out. I stayed with the elk and kept working on it. I do not remember how it happened, but I fell asleep covered to my armpits in blood, next to Mark's dead elk. I am not sure what woke me up. It was pitch black all around. I was groggy and not thinking clearly. But I heard footsteps and a stick crack. I woke up and started talking to myself…

"What, where am I?"

"Man, it's dark and smells bad."

"How long have I been asleep?"

"Damn I'm cold."

"Why can't see anything?"

Then my head cleared, "Oh crap, I fell asleep cutting up Mark's elk and my headlamp's off."

"Where is my headlamp?"

"Where's my gun?"

"Dammit!"

"Okay, found my headlamp," it was on my head.

I turned on the light and found my pistol in its holster. I scanned the perimeter and there was no sign of whatever broke that stick. I made a note to myself, "Sleeping on a field dressed elk at night in the Rocky Mountains is on the wrong end of stupid." In my defense, I had a long morning recovering my bull and was exhausted when we went back out for Mark's bull. The cavalry finally arrived and with everyone's help we got Mark's bull back to camp.

Day four dawned and I dragged myself to breakfast and wished the hunters good luck. Mark was tagged out and exhausted. Aline was going back to Emery's Pond, even though her lazy husband did not hang the stand closer to the pond the day before like he promised. Andrew was switching it up and going to Muskrat Pond. After breakfast, I set to work butchering my elk. At lunch we learned that Andrew saw another sow with cubs and Aline saw nothing again. Mark and I hustled out at lunch and hung a stand for Aline within thirty yards of the water at Emery's Pond. Everyone went hunting after lunch including me. At the end of the day, no one had any luck.

Day five saw some weather rolling in, but nothing we could not handle. Mark stayed in camp to butcher his elk. Andrew went back to Muskrat Pond. Aline and I walked out together on the last day of the hunt. It was kind of romantic. I was amazed to find nothing had eaten my bulls' gut pile. The morning was unproductive for everyone and at lunch we shared stories. Andrew had seen a sow with one cub again. I saw a sow with two cubs. Aline saw nothing. With only one afternoon hunt left we ate lunch quietly.

Aline and Andrew still had both their tags and I still had my bear tag. That afternoon, I decided to go back to Linda's Wallow, its closer, I was tired, and it has the best view down the valley. If nothing else I would have a great view of the sunset on the last night. About an hour into my sit a mule deer doe and fawn walked by at 18 yards. Then, a few minutes later directly in front of me a perfect 6x6 bull broke cover at thirty yards. Oh, dear Lord, why didn't Andrew or Aline sit here? The bull was in range for a long time and although I enjoyed watching him, I wished someone else was sitting there.

When I got back to camp, I found out that Aline saw a huge rutting bull moose! He came in glunking and walked right under her stand so close she could smell him. She got a great video of him. When Jim saw the video he said, "Yep that's the big bull around here, he is Pope and Young for sure." Poor Andrew only saw a sow with cubs again, but was upbeat saying, "Hell I made progress…I didn't even see an elk last year."

Another elk camp had come and gone. It was feast and famine for my crew. Mark and I were successful. Meanwhile Andrew and Aline were going home with their tags in their pocket. Nevertheless, we had an absolute blast and hated to leave, as it's one of our favorite places on Earth. The freezer was near full in our trailer as we pulled out of Jim's drive and headed down the mountain. The hunt was a success and we all knew that, but it is impossible to get rid of a small bit of regret and feeling of failure when you go home with tags in your pocket.

Recipe -

Here's what you need, "soup to nuts" to serve up your own similar elk hunt –

Ingredients:

_____ A willing soul, a semi-stout heart, good legs, feet and hips – priceless

_____ Time Off – (# of days) x (what you get paid daily) until you get it done = ???

_____ CO Non-Resident Over the Counter Hunting Fishing Combo, Elk Tag and Habitat Stamp $661

_____ CO Non-Resident Over the Counter Hunting Fishing Combo, Bear Tag and Habitat Stamp $351

_____ Fee to hunt with someone like Jim $2,250

_____ Gas & Travel $800 (KY to CO and back)

_____ Archery equipment – you should already own it, your deer rig is perfect (fixed blade broadheads)

_____ Clothes and boots – you should already own it

_____ Blind or climbing stand – neither is necessary, but you should already own it

_____ Pack, binos, rangefinder, etc. – you should already own it – deer gear is fine

_____ Food & Water – Included, when you hunt with someone like Jim, but you can always add $$$

_____ Meat hauling – freezer and drop cord $250; zero dollars if you already own it

Total Cost: $4,312

Directions:

The directions for this recipe are strikingly similar to the previous chapter, "Colorado Bear."

Chapter 15 –Turkey and Hogs

I am often asked how we can afford to travel and hunt as much as we do. The truth is that we usually start by purchasing our hunts at charity auctions. These charities are really 501c3 conservation organizations that auction off donated hunts as part of their annual fundraiser. The hunts are originally donated by outfitters, so the conservation organizations make one hundred percent profit from the auction. The secret that I am letting out of the bag is this – the hunts almost always sell for less than their retail price at the charity auctions. Thus, it is a win-win. The charity gets the proceeds and we get a hunt at a reduced cost. This can work in your favor if you have smartly designed your long-range and short-range plans. Some of the hunts at the charity auctions will be for the same year (short-range) and some will be for the following year (long-range). The key is to research each charity auction prior to attending to see which hunts fit into your plans. Then you need to develop your bidding plan. The bidding plan involves looking at the quality of the hunt, the services provided, the location of the hunt and the quality of the species in the area, calling the listed references for the outfitter, then comparing that to the retail price to determine what your maximum bid will be. Our maximum bid is always less than the retail cost of the hunt. Once at the auction, the only other caveat is to be aware if your bidding against a friend. I've been known to let a hunt go and allow a friend to have it, versus bidding against them and wasting both our money.

The hunt in this chapter required us to slog through nasty cold and sleet to attend the local Kentuckiana Safari Club banquet in February. They are particularly good about publishing their banquet program in advance. We had spring break and warmer temperatures on our minds. We also had our eye on a hunt for osceola turkeys and feral hogs down in Florida, that was in their program. The banquet was a wonderful affair that we enjoyed a great deal. When it came time to bid on the Florida hunt, none of our close friends were bidding and we won it for a great deal less than the retail price. All that was left to do was the near-term planning and to dream about big toms, big boars, and warmer temperatures.

Prior to the hunt, we corresponded with the outfitters. They reminded us, "The hog hunting is always good, but the turkey hunting will be tough, because you're coming at the end of the season." We had no choice but to hunt then, because my lovely wife, Aline, is a school principal and as such we were confined to hunt on her spring break. So, most of their birds had been hunted and were educated at this point. Surely that would make for tough hunting, but we thought, "Okay, no worries, if we fail on turkeys, we can fill the freezer with a couple hogs and head to the beach."

The trip was uneventful. We took our normal rig: pickup truck pulling a small cargo trailer with a chest freezer and our gear in it. Upon arrival our guide and his wife showed up and gave us a tour of the camp. It was more than adequate with 3 cabins and an outside entertaining area set three miles back from paved roads in the Florida swamps. Gorgeous trees covered in Spanish moss, alligators, waterfowl, and nature all around added to the atmosphere. The cabin was one large living and sleeping area with a full bath and a screened in front porch. The camp ran off a propane generator and had endless hot water. We were so happy to be out of the cold weather and into this cozy little camp with our new neighbors, even if they were gators and skeeters.

Before dawn the next morning, we found ourselves hiking through the palmetto scrub woods, cypress swamps, and cattle pastures listening for a tom turkey's gobble. We decided to split up and cover more ground, so the guide went to a different area with Aline and I struck out on my own. That morning I saw turkeys at long range, but they were shy. We did get the toms to respond, but they did not want to come out in the open. They stayed just inside the cypress swamps tempting us to come in after them. This wasn't our first rodeo and we knew that trying to sneak into tight cover, especially a swamp where your loud splashing as you waded through the water, would bust the turkeys out and ruin the spot. So, we stayed put on the field edges outside the swamp and remained patient.

About 11 a.m., I called a gobbler out of the cypress swamp and out on to a strut zone. I worked that bird all day and never got him in range. I called three of his hens to me. One of the hens came so close I could have grabbed her with my bare hands, it was exhilarating. Nevertheless, Mr. Tom Turkey never left the strut zone one hundred and fifty yards out into the open cattle pasture.

When I met back up with the guide and Aline, I learned they had no luck either. I told him the story of my day. He said, "Mike that there is a "boss" gobbler and ain't no one had pulled him closer than 200 yards all season." I heard his words as a challenge but kept it to myself. I started thinking about all the ways I could kill "the boss." Bedtime snuck up on us like a mountain lion. We did not hear it coming and before we knew it, lights out. I suppose the previous day's drive and the excitement of hunting today did us in before we could even think about seafood and beer on the beach. We woke up, side by side on the couch about 10:30 p.m. It was the first place we sat down upon arrival back at camp. At least we would be well rested for day two.

The next morning, dawn broke and brought with it an unwelcomed guest, cold harsh rain. The temperature dropped about 20 degrees, the wind picked up and the rain fell with an angry intent. We abandoned hunting and rested. When the rain finally ceased beating on the roof as if it owed it money, we went out for lunch. Lunch conversation immediately turned to hunting and we decided to hog hunt that evening. We had never hog hunted and Aline wanted me to go first, so she could watch it and see what it was all about.

We called the outfitter. He was pleased we had not pushed to hunt turkeys in the rain and was excited to hunt hogs with us that evening. The evening came quickly and as we stalked up to the blind, there were already hogs out feeding in the field. We had no way to get to the blind without pushing them off, so we moved quickly, pushed them off and got set up. The guide said that after we quieted down the hogs would come right back, and they did.

As a novice hog hunter, I was not sure what a shooter looked like. I found myself thinking, "There's no antlers and I bet the little ones taste better," just then a big boar walked out of the swamp and into the field. He was popping his jaws and all the other hogs gave him space. The light was fading fast and my initial impression was that a black bear walked out into the field. I was taken back when I glassed him and saw the frothing mouth and blood on his shoulders. The guide said he'd just been in a fight with another boar. Now, I did not think I'd get excited about shooting a hog, but I was. I slowly moved my rifle to my shoulder and ever so quietly put the crosshairs on its neck, where the guide insisted I shoot, and took the slack out of the trigger. What followed was the most deafening sound I'd ever heard come from a rifle - "click!" I unloaded the chamber of my rifle before climbing up the ladder into the blind for safety but had not put a round back into the chamber.

There was immediate quiet laughter in the blind at my expense. It took a few minutes for the three of us to regain our composure and the light was fading fast. Thank God the sound of the empty gun firing was not loud enough to run the boar off. He did look in our direction, but soon looked away and continued his violent dominant display in the field. This time my aim was true, and the boar's reign of terror ended quickly as he dropped where he stood.

After the shot, we had another good laugh at my expense. Then we went down and inspected the boar. He was tremendous. I continued to giggle to myself about the mistake as we skinned and quartered that hog. The outfitter was blunt about it, "Mike I've had that click thing happen before, and it's always funny, but you made a helluva shot, and honest it made it more fun. Plus, I don't usually get any help skinnin' and quarterin' up hogs, so thanks bud." Mistakes like that are made because of the excitement and anticipation associated with hunting.

There really is something primal about it. If I ever stop getting that excited and killing becomes routine, I will quit hunting.

The next morning, we decided to hunt a different location and met up with a local rancher. We toured some of his property, while stopping occasionally to sneak in a turkey call, in hopes of getting a response from a gobbler. All the properties were a mix of pasture, swamp, and coastal Florida jungle. Some had turkey sign, some did not, but the rancher insisted all held birds.

After the tour, we got a chance to talk to him and man was he a character. He was one of those men who'd done it all: cattle rancher, beekeeper, farmer, general contractor, and a father of ten children. The rancher and I started talking and telling stories and before I knew it, the Outfitter and Aline were looking at their watches and looking at me as if to say, "SERIOUSLY! How long are you going to stand around and chew the fat! There's hunting to do!" When we finally got back in the truck and set out to hunt some more, I said, "I could have listened to the rancher all day. When his generation is gone, we will lose that knowledge." Aline said, "Well, I'm glad you loved the stories because you stood there for 3 hours listening and never turned your head. You're sunburned on just one side of your face." And for the second time in two days, we all laughed so hard we almost burst.

As we were driving away, the outfitter and I talked about not hearing any birds gobble today. He said we'd most likely been around birds, but osceolas live in swamps with bobcats, cougars, black bears, bald eagles, alligators, and monster sized raccoons. Plus, they'd been hunted by humans for a few weeks already. So, unless they are out in an open field where they can see, they keep quiet and don't give away their position to predators. We had a tough time trying to decide where to hunt that afternoon. I tried to convince the outfitter we should try to kill that "boss" gobbler. It took some cajoling, but he reluctantly agreed.

I mean I am the client and it is my hunt, so I gave him the plan too. The outfitter would sit on the opposite side of the field from the strut zone and call with a visible set of decoys. His job was to keep the boss tom's attention. I would slither down into the edge of the cypress swamp, quiet as a bobcat, and try to flank the tom from an oblique angle in the swamp. The plan relied on the outfitters ability to keep the boss's attention to allow me to move. Aline wanted to be away from all the talking men. Apparently, our jibber jabber was having a negative effect on her spring break. She wanted to hunt on her own. So, we dropped her off at an adjacent field on the way, where she promptly took up the base of an old tree and soaked up the afternoon. I wished her luck and we were on our way.

Upon arrival, I snuck into the swamp, just me and my shotgun. The outfitter set up on the field's edge across from the strut zone with his decoys and called. After about an hour of sitting perfectly still and listening to the outfitter call, the boss gobbled. I thought, "Springsteen your mine." The name came out of the cobwebbed recesses of my mind and it stuck. Then Springsteen came out of the swamp into the brilliant sunlight of the pasture. In full strut, his plumage against the brilliant green of that spring pasture was a sight to see. Yet, he stayed loyal to the turkey mating ritual; the hens are supposed to come to the toms. That is why the toms strut and display. He could see the hen decoys and he knew they could see him. So, he never moved closer then three hundred yards to the decoys. What Springsteen could not know, was that I was already one hundred and fifty yards from him watching from the swamp.

I sat down on a stump in the swamp and thought about it. I changed the plan and texted the outfitter, "Keep calling to keep his attention. I'm going to belly crawl flat as a flounder across the pasture and shoot him in the face." The outfitter's calling kept Springsteen's attention, while I moved slow and low, dodging cow patties and getting eaten alive by mosquitoes. Thirty minutes later, Springsteen was still strutting. I was covered in sweat, cow manure and afraid to raise my head too far. Still flat on my belly, I listened to Springsteen's occasional gobbles. They were thunderous and much louder now that I'd crawled closer. I had no real way of knowing how close I was, as I had not raised my head to even look. I knew I was so close that any further movement would waste the previous efforts and make this whole scheme mere folly.

Just then he gobbled again. I was sure I was withing range. I took a deep breath and exhaled. Then all at once, I pulled myself and my gun up into the prone position. Springsteen saw it, quit strutting and stuck his head straight up. I 'let-her-eat' and the blast of the big 3.5" shell rocked my tired body, for a second I lost him. One Mississippi later, I looked up to see Springsteen doing the death dance. I sat up, dripping with sweat, covered in cow poop, swatting mosquitoes, exhausted and yet exhilarated. Then I heard whooping and hollering. I looked back, and the outfitter was so happy he was dancing.

Springsteen was a real trophy. He had a nearly twelve-inch beard and his spurs were just shy of two inches. His spurs were certainly the biggest of any bird I'd ever taken. Aline heard the shot and walked to meet us at the truck. Back together, we told her the story and she marveled in our success. The morning hunt was over. It was time for some food and a change of clothes, for me at least.

Over lunch we decided to give the turkeys a break and go after a hog for Aline. We moved into an area where the hogs "root" around this time of day, in the deeper darker cooler recesses of the swamp. To our surprise there were already hogs feeding. Aline got her gun up on the sticks and was ready to shoot, but alas they were all sows and small boars. She wanted a big boar, so we continued into the stand. I was happy it was a double ladder stand, so we could sit together. The afternoon went well and with the Thermacell working we did not even get a mosquito bite. We also didn't get a hog. They were all small boars or sows. Aline stayed true to her plan and let them walk.

The following day dawned with a new plan. Aline would go with the outfitter down by the cypress swamp, where I killed Springsteen. I'd seen another gobbler in there and we thought with "the Boss" gone that maybe the other gobbler would come out to play. The outfitter asked me to, "Sit in the ladder stand on the big field two-hundred yards away and keep watch. If you see a bird text us." I was happy to help the guide get Aline a bird and the game plan seemed tight. We saw hen turkeys. We saw hogs. We even saw bald eagles. But we did not see a tom turkey all day. Aline was hunting her little heart out and was getting no cooperation from the tom turkeys.

The Rancher was tracking our progress and feeling sorry for Miss Aline. We were the last clients of the season and after talking with the outfitter, he took us to a pasture late in the day that had not been hunted in years. This parcel of land was more jungle than swamp, but it bordered a big cow pasture full of cattle. Every patch of mud or sand had turkey or hog prints on it. There was game sign everywhere. We decided to leave it alone that evening and come back to hunt it the following morning. That afternoon we went back to the same double ladder stand to hunt hogs until dark. Once again, we saw a lot of hogs, but nothing Aline wanted to shoot. The day ended with three exhausted humans having done no harm to birds or swine.

Up early on the last day, we snuck through the predawn swamp. Aline and the outfitter were hunting turkeys. I would separate and hunt hogs.

We set their blind up in thick vegetation on a dry spot no bigger than a tennis court. After helping them get set up, I turned south on a game trail. It was still dark, very swampy and the jungle was thick. I decided to go at least a half mile into the watery thick stuff, so as not to influence the last day of Aline's hunt. I finally found a small patch of sandy high ground out of the water, which was also the confluence of 5 game trails. I tucked my little one-man chair blind into the bush and sat down to rest a minute.

Suddenly I was under attack. The first sign was the enormous buzzing. Then I realized, "Dear Mary Mother of God there's a hundred mosquitoes in here!" I tried to repel their attack. Forgetting my bug spray and Thermocell I swatted to no avail. My hand was no match for these monster blood suckers. They were big enough to stand flat footed and breed a chicken. I could have used a tennis racquet but had not brought one. Swatting was futile. After the first half dozen bites on the back of my neck and face I rummaged desperately for my bug spray. I failed my precombat checks and inspections, the bug spray was still in the truck.

In the rummaging, my hand now deep in my pack fell on my Thermocell. As I scrambled to get my Thermacell running I caught one vampire and smeared his body and my blood down my neck. The time passed in slow motion while my Thermocell heated up. I was outnumbered and losing the battle. In desperation, I broke open a Thermacell pad and started rubbing it all over myself. This was sheer unadulterated stupidity.

"Dear God, that burns. Ahh my skin is on fire!" Okay, even for an infantryman this sucks. Suddenly, I came to my senses and thought, "Breath deep, relax, this will pass, you're a badass, soak it up." I sat back and let it happen, drifting off to my happy place. I even stopped swatting at the bloody bastards. I am not sure how long my skin burned and the mosquitos feasted. When the Thermacell filled the blind with the wonderful pest repelling vapors the hummingbird sized vampires were gone. Relief came over me like a warm wave and my heartbeat slowed.

Mere moments passed in the dark, before God sent his sunbeams through the canopy and illuminated a wonderfully green and vibrant jungle. The sound of the birds was deafening. The jungle was alive with plants, birds, bugs, and lizards everywhere. Dawn seemed to set the entire swamp in motion with an energy I could feel. An hour or so passed quickly after the sunrise as I watched the flora and fauna.

I was shaken back to reality by the vibration of my phone. Aline's text read, "6 or 8 small hogs ran past our blind, but no shot". We exchanged texts and she lamented that there were no turkeys answering their calls. The jungle started to quiet down around 10 a.m. Sitting in the relieving vapors of the Thermocell, I thought about taking a nap.

Just then, I heard a rush in front of me and coming through the swamp was a sounder of hogs. They were on the move and obviously had a place to go. I tried to get my rifle up in time but could not get a bead on the running beasts. I yelled at them to get them to stop, but they could not hear me over their splashing feet and continued to trot on by. Without hesitation or any real thought, I simply lifted the blind, push it off me and ran after them. They were making so much noise they didn't realize they were being followed at a trot. This strange line of runners did not make it too far, splashing through the swamp, before the lead hog stopped. I stopped, raised my rifle, and shot the hog closest to me. It fell dead instantly. The rest bolted for the security of the palmettos and I did not get a second.

Shortly after the gunshot, the outfitter called me to ask what happened. I told him I shot a hog and I was going to sit tight in case the other hogs circled back. I waited about fifteen minutes, they did not. Aline texted me that they'd decided to go back to the truck to get her rifle and then they were going to spot and stalk hogs. I told them which way the hogs ran off and that I was going back to the truck to get my drag harness. I also told them that I would be wearing blaze orange and that I would walk back into the swamp, field dress my hog, and drag him out.

On my way back to the truck, I saw a small red dot in my peripheral vision to my left. My heart started pounding. What luck another turkey! I started to slowly angle towards it and raise my rifle. Still not sure what I'd seen, I continued cautiously, when the jungle in front of me exploded. A cow the size of a

Volkswagen Van almost trampled me. I dove out of the way cursing and watched her red ear tag bouncing as she ran away. Holy shit, what a day so far. I almost lost the "Battle of Mosquito Swamp" and now I almost shot a cow in self-defense.

I made it back to the truck without further incident, donned my blaze orange safety vest and grabbed my drag line. Then I headed back into the swamp to get my hog. The jungle around me was quiet now, except for the buzzing of insects, it seemed as if all the larger creatures had found some relief in the shade and took their afternoon respite. Just then, I caught the ever so small glimpse of red out of my peripheral vision. I thought, "You're not going to get me again you kamikaze moo cow."

Again, I slowly turned in that direction, not sure what I'd seen. Then the red spot moved. Oh my God, it was a tom turkey. I played it cool and kept walking, as if I hadn't seen him. He froze at first, then he turned to walk away, slowly, very slowly, as if he thought he could sneak away. The moment he turned his head away and couldn't see me, I wheeled, raised my gun, and shot.

In the commotion of the moment I'd lost sight of the tom. When I looked where he was standing in the thick jungle, there was nothing. I was sure I'd missed him, because there was silence. Normally, when you shoot a turkey they flap around, like a chicken in a barnyard that has been separated from their head. I'd not planned to shoot a turkey with a rifle, although it was legal, it just didn't seem right. If I'd planned to, then the effort to kill Springsteen would have been moot. I walked to where I'd last seen the tom and sure enough, there lay another mature osceola gobbler. Just then, my phone rings, it's the outfitter and the exchange goes like this:

"Hey, Man, did you need to put another bullet in your hog?"

"Nope."

"Why did you shoot again?"

"Turkey."

"No way!"

"Yep."

"You're kidding me?"

"Nope."

"You shot a turkey wearing blaze orange walking down a trail?"

"Yep."

"At what range?"

"30 yards."

"I don't believe you!"

"Okay, in about 10 minutes you'll see me walk out of the swamp to the trucks. I'll be the guy dragging a pig and carrying a gobbler. You'll know it's me because I'm wearing blaze orange!"

The outfitter immediately hung up on my smart ass.

The hunt was officially over that afternoon. I was sad that my beautiful bride did not harvest a hog, nor a bird. But sometimes that's the way it goes. She had passed on several hogs. She normally kicks my butt during deer season, so maybe I have the family "swamp mojo." There was the normal pleasantries with the outfitter. After we tipped him, he went on his way, asking us to simply lock up when we left camp. Back at camp, I finished deboning the hog and the turkey as Aline packed up our belongings. By the time I had all the meat cleaned, in bags and in the freezer, Aline was ready to leave.

There is always a sense of accomplishment when leaving a hunting camp and the freezer has meat in it. The two hogs would provide wonderful roasts and sandwiches, while the turkeys would be saved for Thanksgiving and Christmas dinners.

I locked up the cabin and climbed in the truck asking, "Where to?" Aline responded, "The beach of course. It's spring break."

Recipe –

Here's what you need, "soup to nuts" to serve up your own pig and bird trip:

Ingredients:

_____ A willing soul, a semi-stout heart, good legs, feet and hips – priceless

_____ Time Off – (# of days) x (what you get paid daily) until you get it done = ?

_____ Florida Non-Resident 10-day hunting license $46.50 + turkey permit $125 = $171.50

_____ Gas $600 (KY to FL and back, plus two weeks driving about 50mi a day)

_____ Turkey and hog hunting equipment – you should already have it

_____ Guided hunt and/or trespass fees to access hunting land approximately $1,500

_____ Clothes and boots – you should already own it

_____ Blind – you should already own it

_____ Pack – you should already own it

_____ First Aid Kit – you should already own it

_____ Food & Water – Breakfast $8; Lunch $8; Dinner $25: $41 per day x 17 days = $697

Total Cost: $2,968

Directions:

Note: It was legal to hunt turkeys with a rifle in Florida when this hunt happened. We chose to hunt turkeys with shotguns, but if while hunting hogs a turkey presented itself, we were not going to pass it up.

The Florida Fish and Wildlife Conservation Commission website is super easy. You can easily acquire your licenses and permits there. There is no fee for hog hunting, if you have a hunting license, you're good to go.

Finding an outfitter is easy, if you start the year before the hunt and not the winter right before you want to go. Some outfitters have flat rates, like $1,500 for 5 days. Some have a $200 per day price for guided hunts without food and lodging and a $300 per day price for guided hunts with food and lodging. The cost is usually lower if you buy the hunt at a conservation organization's chapter fundraiser, so you can save money there. We bought this hunt at the Kentuckiana SCI Chapter annual banquet. Over the years we've bought hunts at RMEF and NWTF fundraisers as well.

I recommend a guided hunt or doing some research and paying trespass fees to hunt private land, because there simply is not that much osceola habitat that is public land. Also, finding an outfitter/guide who offers hog hunting in addition is a good idea, especially if you're planning on spending a week or two down there for spring break.

Feral hogs are surprisingly good table fare and worth the effort. If not hog hunting, then perhaps you'd have a plan to spend the remainder of the week on the beach with family after you harvest your bird.

Since I live in Kentucky, driving was the least hassle and was cost efficient. Flying with firearms is a bit of a hassle and if I can avoid it, I do. Driving gives you the flexibility to do more things if the weather is bad or you tag out early. Plus, it gives you the option of bringing a chest freezer, which is my favorite technique for maintaining my meat on trips and enjoying the days after I harvest an animal, without worrying about the meat spoiling.

Spring mosquitoes in the area are a real pain. I highly recommend you bring lots of bug spray and at least one Thermacell device per person.

The turkey calls you use for eastern turkeys will work on osceolas, but don't expect them to be as vocal. Your normal turkey gear and shotgun will work great. If you want to bring a rifle and turkey hunt with it, it was perfectly legal in Florida when we hunted. Please check the current regulations before you go. Caliber recommendations are different if you also chose to hunt hogs. I hunted the hogs with 7mm x 08 and it had a devastating effect on the turkey.

Patterning your turkey shotgun to figure out maximum range and minimum range is important. Yes, I said minimum range. All too often, turkeys are missed at close ranges, because hunters are using "super full turkey chokes" and a "flight-controlled wad" type shotshell. This combination does not really start to open until about fifteen yards. The closer the bird is when you shoot the smaller your shot pattern. In fact, inside of about ten yards, the shot may still be in the wad. If you do not test it, you do not know. Once you know the minimum range, you know when you will have to shoot at the vitals of the bird versus the head. Meaning, if the shot is still in the wad out to ten yards, you are basically shooting a golf ball sized mass at the bird inside ten yards. That being the case, you should aim the same place you would put your arrow if you were archery hunting turkeys.

Food and water could be more expensive or cheaper, just depends on how you roll. If you decide to do the daily rate, with no room and board, then you need to add a campground or hotel cost. All in all, this is a fun hunt and a great way to fill your freezer if your elk or deer season did not go well.

The turkey is a trophy. The hogs can be shot in good numbers and the meat is excellent. Just make sure you wear latex gloves when butchering the hogs and cook the meat to the temperature to avoid the possibility of illness. It's rare, but hogs can carry trichinosis. If you have a fully guided hunt that includes hogs, your outfitter/guide should do the field dressing for you and offer to take it to a local processor if available.

If you are lucky the beach will be close by as well.

Chapter 16 – Pronghorn

I have a friend who just will not travel to hunt. I have tried to get him to travel out west and hunt with me. He has almost gone a couple times, but so far, he just cannot do it. You might be thinking it is money, time off or any number of the normal reasons that stop folks from actually doing a big western hunt. Nope, it is none of the normal mundane excuses. It's a real-life tangible obstacle, anxiety. You see, he simply cannot bring himself to be more than a few hours away from his family. It's not his fault that he doesn't want to travel, he's earned his anxiety.

My friend is a veteran, who has seen more combat than a man should. He even brought home some shrapnel, that he gets to carry around forever. We hunt together locally in my home state of Kentucky during turkey and deer seasons every year. We talk all the time and in some of those conversations we imagine big western hunts together. Through those conversations, I've learned that pronghorn antelope are his weakness. I doubt we are ever going to travel to hunt, but that does not stop me from trying to get him in the truck when I leave for the West.

I was about to retire from the Army, and it seemed like a retirement present when I drew a mule deer tag in my favorite over-the-counter elk unit. There are other places to hunt mule deer that are not trophy units, places where the tag is easier to draw, but I was familiar with the terrain and had seen some fine mule deer there. So, for four years I tried to draw the tag and now I had it in my pocket. I was already planning to do my annual DIY public land archery elk and black bear hunt and now I also had a mule deer tag in my pocket.

Since I was retired and finally had all the time in the world, I thought, "Why not add pronghorn. I've got the time and I can try to get my friend in the truck." I tried hard to get my friend to go with me. It did not work. He very deftly and graciously changed the subject every time I brought up hunting speed goats together. As the spring and summer progressed, it was apparent that no amount of cajoling, enticement or down right bribery was going to get him in the truck. So, my post retirement hunting odyssey would be archery, public land, DIY and solo.

I would retire from the Army on my 46th birthday. I would drive to Pennsylvania to shoot the International Bowhunting Organization's World Championships in an amateur class. Then drive back to Kentucky, pack the truck and leave to hunt elk, pronghorn, black bear, and mule deer. After a decade of hunting in my favorite elk spots, I believed I could hunt three species: elk, mule deer and black bear all in the same general area. After coming up with primary, secondary and tertiary plans to find a good mule deer buck, with elk and bear as a bycatch, I set that work aside and began planning in earnest to find public land pronghorns.

It was not long before I figured out that hunting pronghorn with an over the counter tag on public land is a bit more difficult than hunting other big game species. Across a great deal of their range, they inhabit flat land that is good for row crop agriculture and grazing livestock, thus most of that land is private. There were a few other places to go, but I focused on the Comanche and Pawnee National Grasslands of Colorado. After further research I realized the Pawnee was highly fragmented and checkerboarded with private land that could complicate my hunt. So, I settled on the Comanche National Grasslands.

The summer came and went in a flurry of retirement preparation and archery tournaments. August arrived, and I retired. I shot well at the tournament, rolled home, packed the truck and I was off toward the Rockies. I was driving across the Kansas prairie, staring at the horizon and a long straight endless stretch of I-70 West, when I had an epiphany. For the first time in 27 years I wasn't in command of anyone. I flashed back to my first day at my first assignment, 1st Platoon Leader, Alpha Company, 3rd Battalion, 15th Infantry, 2nd Brigade, 24th Infantry Division. God I was young, maybe too young, but I was immediately given command of 31 infantrymen in my platoon. I was so proud.

The number of Soldiers assigned to my command grew with each promotion and assignment, peaking as a Brigade Commander and about 3,200 Soldiers. Now, driving across the prairie, staring blankly at the horizon I realized, I was in charge of one person – me. It was a thought I meditated on throughout the hunt and still do sometimes today.

I spent the rest of the first day's drive mentally going through the checklists of all my sets, kits, and outfits. I prepared meticulously for this hunt prior to departing. Four big game species, solo, over thirty days was daunting, even for me. I was sure I had everything, but that did not stop me from making a few notes at each gas stop. Then that night at my first waypoint, a KOA campground in Kansas, I double checked things and put my mind at ease. I was ready.

The second day's drive ended at my pronghorn camp. I set up camp. I reviewed my plan and double checked my maps. Then I went scouting.

Referencing my OnX map app and driving my 4x4 van across the "national forest" roads on the prairie I realized a few things (1) this place is flat (2) this area is used by off road enthusiasts quite a bit (3) the rains earlier this year had produced a sea of tall sunflowers that could help me stalk goats in this moonscape and (4) there were pronghorn here – I saw them. Proudly I returned to camp, it was time for dinner and a beer. I was excited.

This was my first pronghorn hunt ever. Without any help, I turned my internet research and map reconnaissance into success. I found water holes, a long dry creek bed I could use to stalk, a sea of sunflowers and antelope. The question was, how would I hunt them tomorrow? After some meditation and reflection, I decided to hunt the dry creek bed. It ran east to west and provided cover. Over the eons of time, the water had cut through the dust into the bed rock below and although it was dry now, there were pinon and ponderosa pine along it's shoulders extending fifty to a hundred yards in both directions perpendicular to the course of the creek bed. I would be there at sunrise with the sun at my back and use its blinding rays to help me close the distance on a buck. I would hunt them until the sun was overhead and was of no further use to me, take a lunch break and return in the afternoon and hunt with the setting sun at my back, in the opposite direction west to east.

I called my friend and told him what he was missing. We had a great conversation. He wished me luck. Then I tried to sleep.

I parked the van before dawn on the eastern edge of the hunting unit, where the creek bed passed under the state road. Then I waded through a herd of cattle. Public land is multiple use land and I would wade through cattle quite often over the next month. In short order, I was set up on the slightest piece of high ground waiting for the sun to crest the horizon.

It seemed to happen all at once. The sun exploded in a palate of bright shimmering light that lit up the dying night sky into a kaleidoscope of yellow, red, orange, purple, pink and turquoise. I marveled at the Lord's work for quite a while before I regained my composure and started to glass toward the west. Minutes later I was laughing quietly to myself, I spotted a good buck and three does. They were feeding north out into a sea of sunflowers from the cover of the creek bed. I spent the next hour stalking quietly down the creek bed, always to the west. I stopped regularly to look north and check the position of the buck.

The third time I stopped to glass up the buck, I also glassed up some hunters. They were on another road to the north, glassing the same buck from a half a mile away. They did not know they were too late. I was already stalking the buck while they were still trying to get a plan together. At the last bit of cover, I left the creek bed and stepped out onto the open prairie with only sunflowers to hide my movement. The hunters on the road certainly saw me, but the antelope did not - not yet.

Quickly finding myself out of sunflowers I sat quietly and watched the antelope feed north east.

They were approaching a dry rivulet that fed the creek. It was full of huge sunflowers. They would have to cross it. I back tracked toward the creek, then moved up the rivulet, using the sunflowers as cover. The final stalk was over six hundred yards and took most of the morning. The cool prairie was heating up rapidly and starting to look more like a desert. At one hundred forty-three yards I had nothing left to hide behind. I wished for a minute that I had a coyote skin to crawl under like a Native American. Then I remembered I had my Montana Decoy Antelope Buck with me. I slowly deployed the decoy whenever the buck's head was down. Then I crawled toward them behind it.

It did not work. I am not sure what range it was, when their famous six power binocular vision sorted me out. It was close, easy rifle range, but it was not bow range. The buck stood alert and transfixed on me for a few seconds, then with a burst of speed only pronghorn can display, they were gone.

Over the next week, I was blessed with great days, book ended with amazing sunrises and sunsets. I stalked antelope every single day. I got within easy rifle range of good bucks, but never closer than one hundred seventeen yards. Except for the dry creek bed and random fields of waist high sunflowers, the public land I chose to hunt was a moonscape. It was flat, dusty, rocky, and mostly covered in scrub no taller than your knees. I felt a combination of accomplishment, having found pronghorn, and failure, never getting into archery range.

Frustrated, I pulled out my last trick – contact the local taxidermist. I called him and sincerely asked, "If I kill a goat, would you mount it and hold it until I come back to hunt next year?" He agreed in a warm easy kind way. Then he asked where I was hunting and how I was hunting. I shared that I was on public land and that it was a bowhunt. He asked how I was doing and after I explained, he told me that I needed to be sitting water. Further, that if I had time, he would take me out tomorrow morning and show me some lesser known water holes on public land. The taxidermist trick worked.

The next morning, I met Rudy at a local lumberyard. We rolled out onto the prairie in his old Ford. Sure enough, before lunch I was shown the dark side of the moon. It was actually the far corner of a public unit, miles away from where I was hunting. There he showed me a beautiful little waterhole covered in fresh antelope tracks. I was so thankful that I offered to take him out for a steak – my treat. He declined saying, "Not until you kill a buck." He took me back to pick up my van and I agreed to keep him informed on how my hunt went.

Then I drove back out to the waterhole and set up my blind. I was confident I had everything in order. I drove my truck over the horizon out of sight, walked a mile back to the blind and crawled in with great anticipation. Well great anticipation turned into a war of attrition. Nine days passed, with me sitting from dawn until dusk in that blind on the flat open moonscape prairie. It was part wonder and part torture.

In the morning, I would be greeted by an amazing sunrise and cool temps. Then as the glorious orange, red, yellow, and pink rays of the sun warmed the moonscape a vast number of birds would visit the water hole. As the sun reached its zenith and the blind become an oven, a young badger would sneak in for a swim. Occasionally, I would see coyotes trying to run down a jackrabbit as big as they were. But every day without fail, the heat would come, and I would roast. It was in the afternoon that antelope would be seen. Some even came to the water hole, but only once did any drink and they never presented a shot.

I read the entirety of Lewis and Clark's Corps of Discovery Journal. I kept up my spirits thinking about the hardships they suffered and telling myself that day after hot day hunting antelope unsuccessfully was a drop in the bucket compared to how they suffered.

The truth is, I'm not a very good blind hunter. There were times I was sleeping. There were times I was stretching. Hell, there were times I was doing something that might be characterized as a dance. But after a few days, getting into the blind in the morning started feeling like getting into the "the box" from the movie Cool Hand Luke. I lost weight. I talked to myself. I drank two gallons of water a day. I sweated out three gallons of water a day. I still haven't ruled out the possibility that the badger was a hallucination. The snakes and tarantulas were certainly real. But it was the sighting of antelope daily that kept me coming back.

On the tenth day, at 12:01pm as I was debating eating my sandwich when a buck walked by at seventy yards to the northwest and never stopped. I slowly watched him go, dreaming of making a shot on him. I even quietly got out of my chair and gently lowered a closed window to watch him walk out of my life. Dejected and thinking about giving up, I lowered my head and closed the window. The three other tags in my pocket felt heavy as atlas stones. I breathed deeply and slowly exhaled. I decided today would be my last day. Tomorrow I would pack up and head to the mountains. I had just retired. I had all the time in the world, but I had spent enough time on antelope.

For whatever reason, I thought with my head hung low, it just was not meant to be. Maybe it was the pressure of all the other hunters, including the dove hunters that were blasting away on other adjacent water holes. Maybe it was the fact that my blind was positioned wrong. Maybe I set the blind up late and the antelope did not have a chance to get used to it. Maybe, I am just a terrible blind hunter. I quietly sat back in my chair and drifted away to the cool aspen and spruce covered mountains. Finally, raised my head in disgust.

Holy Mary Mother of God!

A young buck was drinking right in front of me. I reached for my rangefinder slowly, ever so slowly and with the greatest care I ranged him, forty-one yards. Then it happened – the slow motion. I was in slow motion.

How the hell did I get into slow motion?

I had to get out of my own head. Day after day in the heat had done strange things to me. I had to focus and get this done. I reached for my bow and he raised his head. He looked right through me. I was sure he was going to be gone in an instant. To my utter surprise and disbelief, he lowered his head and drank again. I drew my bow, settled my pin, and took the slack out of the trigger. The arrow reached him, just as he gathered himself to run.

Then he was gone.

In an instant anguish turned to elation and back to anguish. Days of bowhunting alone on a public land moonscape just turned into my first buck or did it? It happened so fast. Did I hit him? I think so. It took a few minutes for me to regain my composure.

I crawled out of the blind to glass the prairie for him. He was nowhere to be seen, so I moved slowly over to where he was standing when the arrow reached him. Praise the Lord, there was a blood trail Ray Charles could follow, so I did. Very shortly into the blood trail, a buck stood up out of the sunflowers to my left. He was easily in range. Instinctively, I turned and drew my bow. Something stopped me from shooting. This buck was bigger, much bigger than the one I shot. He was not bleeding. I let my bow down. The buck just walked away. Incredible, he was in easy bow range. How did that just happen?

I took a deep breath, sighed, and turned around to pick up the blood trail. Suddenly, there was my buck. I went over to him, knelt, thanked him, and thanked God. Honestly, I started to tear up in that moment of silence, then suddenly and uncontrollably I exclaimed, "I did it!" I stood up and screamed. I jumped up and down. I danced like no one was watching, well hell, no one was watching.

Then it him me, it was almost 1 p.m. and it was ninety-three degrees. I had to get him taken care of and quickly. I hustled across the prairie for over a mile back to the truck. Then I drove my rig down the "national forest" road close to my buck. I still giggle that they labeled the roads with National Forest signs across that dry dusty prairie. I dragged him over to the shade made by my van. I pulled out a plastic folding table and my butchering tools. I turned the freezer on and plugged it into my solar generator. In less than an hour I had the buck skinned, caped, deboned and in the freezer.

As soon as I got phone signal, I called my old friend and told him the story. He was so proud. I told him the only thing that could have made it better is if he were with me. Then I called my new friend, Rudy, the taxidermist. He was ecstatic. We had kept in touch, throughout my journey. He'd never heard of anyone chasing antelope on public ground with a bow for as many days as I had. It called for a celebration, so he was going to grill some steaks.

I stopped and got a bottle of Knob Creek Single Barrel Bourbon and parked the van at his place. He had invited some local friends and we had a wonderful cookout. One of his friends even drew me a map to his elk camp in the Rio Grande National Forest and insisted I meet him there in a week. As the night wound down, I stumbled out to my van thinking about how fortunate and blessed I was. Blessed to have set a goal and accomplished it. Blessed to have a wife who is also a big game hunter and understands the quest. Blessed to have public land to set out on such a quest. Blessed to have harvested a buck. Most of all, I thought, blessed for the treasure of friends.

The antelope was only the first chapter in my retirement hunt. The rest of the trip would see me take a color phased black bear, miss an easy shot on a mule deer, and let a small bull elk walk. Each of those hunts are their own story, but there is nothing like a first. At forty-six years old I had another first, my first antelope. The milestone capped my greatest accomplishment, retiring from the service.

Recipe –

Here's what you need, "soup to nuts" to serve up your own pronghorn antelope hunt –

Ingredients:

_____ A willing soul, a semi-stout heart, good legs, feet and hips – priceless

_____ Time Off – (# of days) x (what you get paid daily) until you get it done = ???

_____ Colorado Non-Resident Over the Counter Hunting Fishing Combo, Tag and Habitat Stamp $399

_____ Gas $800 (KY to CO and back, plus two weeks driving about 50mi a day)

_____ Archery equipment – you should already own it, your deer rig is perfect

_____ KOA Campground for my rig $41 a night for 17 nights = $697

_____ Clothes and boots – you should already own it

_____ Montana Decoy – Pronghorn Buck Decoy - $70

_____ Blind – you should already own it

_____ A couple good books – you should already own them

_____ Food & Water – Breakfast $8; Lunch $8; Dinner $25: $41 per day x 17 days = $697

Total Cost: $2,663

Directions:

The Colorado Parks and Wildlife website is a very informative place to start your research. After that, you simply need to do some looking at Google Earth and onX Maps. Normal maps will not help much, because the terrain is so flat and featureless in the national grasslands. There is some relief and roads of course, but if you buy maps of the area from the USGS or some other source, they are fairly useless. I love their maps for the mountains, but the prairie – not so much. You're looking for relief in the terrain, hills, knobs, creek beds and bumps that might signal a low spot with water in it. Those features are visible using satellite imagery, so your best bet is Google Earth and OnX.

After you do your research, you should get there before the season starts and scout. I recommend setting your blind up as soon as possible on the best water hole you find. After you set your blind up, brush the mud bank flat again so that you can see if there are new tracks when you come back. After that, you go to an adjacent unit and spot and stalk hunt for a few days. That gives the antelope some time to get used to your blind. Go back and check the banks of the water hole under the cover of darkness, when there are fresh tracks, you are ready to hunt out of the blind.

Every morning when you arrive at your blind, give it a hard shake before you open the door and listen to make sure jake the rattlesnake hasn't made your blind his home.

The terrain and weather for this hunt are easily suited to someone who is not quite ready to hunt the mountains. The long stalks and long walks to get to your blind will help your fitness. This area of Colorado, while flat, is actually at about 4,000 feet of elevation, which makes a week of antelope hunting a wonderful prelude to a week of hunting the mountains for a beginner.

You should get there before dawn and walk into your blind in the dark. Depending on which expert you listen to, antelope have 6 or 8 power binocular vision. I believe if they see you get into or out of your blind, you have hurt your chances. Dawn and dusk are when I saw the most antelope. They did come to drink during the heat of the day, but there was so much rain in the area that spring that the sunflowers bloomed, and all the water holes were full. If they thought anything was wrong at all at my waterhole, they simply went to the next one.

You probably will not need 16 days to get it done, but I sure did. Colorado non-resident tags are not cheap, an elk tag is almost $700, so by comparison a pronghorn tag is cheap. You can get it online and it will be mailed to your house usually within 10 days. The decoy is not necessarily a "must have", but the later it gets into September, when the bucks start rutting, decoys are effective.

The KOA campground was a necessity for me. I needed to run the AC in my rig at night to sleep and a daily shower was a must because of the heat. Food and water could be more expensive or cheaper, just depends on how you roll.

Again, if you kill an antelope in the first few days the cost goes way down. Shoot a buck on the third day and this hunt is $1,215. This really is a bargain of a DIY hunt.

Chapter 17 - Friends Family Tribe Nation

Today is day thirty-three. I am so cold. The wind is cutting through me like a razor. It is as if I am naked, yet I am wearing all the clothes I brought to the top of the mountain. I am familiar with suffering. It was my profession in the infantry, but I am retired now, and I suffer only at my own bidding. For the first time this trip, I think, "I'm going home."

The view across the valley from the peak is breathtaking and it is the only thing that keeps me from hiking down the mountain back to camp. So here I sit, praying for an elk or a deer and suffering.

I can see the different bands of spruce and aspen in their green and yellow splendor disappearing into the low clouds across the valley. The mountain top is hidden in the low clouds and it gives the whole view a dreamy sleepy feeling.

I have been hunting alone, first on the plains and now in the mountains, for weeks. Now I have company, lots of company. I do not begrudge the muzzleloader hunters who started swarming all over the mountain yesterday. They have a right to be here too, this is public land, just as much theirs as mine. Truth be told, I am happy they pushed me to the top of the mountain. There is an isolated water hole up here and I am sitting on it. It is a good tactic to move ahead of other hunters and let them, unknowingly push game in your direction.

The fact is that I have been spoiled rotten. I can count on one hand the number of other bowhunters I met or saw this month. Two days ago, the sudden sound of all-terrain vehicles and the sight of orange vests everywhere seemed like audible and visual pollution. The mountains were so quiet before they arrived. I remind myself that they are members of my tribe, my fellow hunters. Still it is too much for me, I cherish the solitude. Between the cold and the new hunting pressure, I think once again, "I'm going home."

The welcome rays of the sun finally burned through the clouds at 11 a.m. and my spirits rise with the temperature. I sit quietly, shedding clothes now and then as the hours go by. Now, it is warm and early afternoon. There must be a thirsty elk or deer nearby. The pressure of the other hunters, fourteen hundred feet below me in the valley, has to push game up to higher elevations. There is very little water up here and I am feeling good about my chances. My anticipation for the last few hours of magical daylight bolsters my spirits, maybe I am not done.

There is a lot of time to think and meditate in such places. I remind myself that I have lost a significant amount of weight and I am tired. I need to be disciplined in my shot selection, if the good Lord sees fit to give me one. Tracking an animal a long distance and adding to my task would be foolish. Packing an elk off this mountain is about all the gas I have left in my tank. I started this trip just after my last day in the Army and I arrived here with four tags in my pocket: elk, pronghorn, black bear, and mule deer. I have a pronghorn and a black bear in the freezer in my van at the bottom of this mountain.

Fifty percent is a success rate any public land bowhunter would be proud of. I had shots at a good mule deer buck, but I saw a great one and my lust for the bigger buck means I am most likely going to eat that tag. I also let a small legal bull walk early in the hunt. It looks like I am going to eat the elk tag too. The old quote, "Fatigue makes cowards of us all," crawls out of the recesses of my mind and I shake myself out of the funk of self-doubt. An elk and a mule deer could both walk into this water hole today, that is a fact.

Then it happens.

Someone crests the mountain top and starts walking right toward me. It is 4 p.m. It is prime time. I think, "This asshole is either obtuse, ignorant or downright rude. He is just going to walk right through the meadow, straight to the water hole."

I stand and wave my hat. He has got to see me. He waves back. He walks right through the meadow and around the waterhole leaving fresh human scent and making an obvious visual presence. Any elk or deer nearby have either smelled or seen him. I take a deep breath and try to remove the angry countenance from my face. I fail.

He speaks first. "Hi, my name is Randel."

"What's up? Is there some emergency you need to tell me about?"

"I usually hunt this water hole."

A silent voice inside my head screams, "Are you kidding me!"

With all the discipline I can muster to be calm, I respond, "It's public land you know that, right?"

He is pointing at the water hole, "Yeah, I know it's public land, but it's where I hunt."

Dumbfounded I sit mute, anger welling up inside me. My baggage from combat very slight. I have brothers and sisters-in-arms with serious post war problems. My only baggage is an almost imperceptible increased tendency towards fight, in the fight or flight response. On top of that, I was not a regular Joe either. I was an Airborne Ranger

Infantry Officer, who in my younger days competed at the All-Army Combatives (Hand to Hand Combat) Championships – twice.

I have always marveled how people fail to realize they could be upsetting a grizzly bear, not a teddy bear when they are obviously rude and selfish. Thank God I packed a climbing stand up to the top of this mountain. The fifteen feet between me and the ground is the obstacle I need to keep my cool and the only obstacle preventing Randel from getting a tune up.

After a long silent pause and some serious direct eye contact, Randel continues. "I guess since you got here first, that I must have been running late."

"I'd say about ten hours late. I climbed this mountain in the dark and got here before dawn this morning."

He looks at the ground, "Oh… um… well I guess I just ruined your hunt."

"Yeah, I'd say you did – Randel," trying not to drag out the pronunciation of his name in disgust.

"I suppose I will just walk over the ridge and hunt there," again he pointed.

I just shook my head in the affirmative and said nothing. My silent inner voice was raging and urging me to question the origin of his mother's canine genetics in a loud and thunderous voice. Years of discipline and doing the right thing, even when it was terribly hard holds me back. I sit mute, breath deep and watch him walk away slower than he walked toward me. He takes twenty minutes to walk four hundred yards. I think, "Now I'm done. If the cold wind cutting through my skinny worn out body was not enough, that inconsiderate thoughtless entitled jerk, that just purposefully ruined my evening hunt tipped the scales."

People like that are not members of my tribe. I do not think I can even call him a hunter. My tribe are generous people who would never do that to another hunter. No, Randel is not a hunter, he is just a person in camouflage. He does not deserve the title "hunter." After a few deep breaths and some prayer my optimistic side wins me over again. I did all the work to get here, quitting while there's still daylight is foolish and stranger things have happened. An elk or a mule deer may yet come into the water. I planned to use the evening thermals to mask my descent to camp on a different route than I climbed for the same reason, thermals. The darkness will also hide my movement. It is the right thing to do, even if I do not come back tomorrow. The last hours were painfully quiet. I climb down the tree and then down the mountain in the dark. When I shed my pack at camp I thought, "Well you're still in one-piece old man." Then without explanation, I laugh and say out loud to no one, "I guess tree stands save lives."

The morning was cold and clear. The two unfilled tags I still had in my pocket felt like heavy. I sit quietly, staring up the mountain into the morning mist and watch the sun burn off the clouds above tree line. God, I love this place. The good Lord outdid himself when he built it, but it's time to leave. I'm gone.

Rolling down the gravel road, still miles from any town, I start to get excited about seeing my wife. Aline is a big game hunter. She endorsed this trip, this odyssey, this quest. Just before I retired from a few decades in the Army, I got my Colorado trophy unit mule deer tag in the mail. I was so excited. It took me four years to draw it. The more I thought about it, the more I realized that I had all the time in the world to fill it. I had the whole season. I was retired. Then I decided to add all the big game tags I could buy over the counter and turn the hunt into something special. I added a pronghorn, elk, and black bear tag to the mix. The plan was to hunt until I filled all four tags. Now, I am rolling home with two tags still in my pocket.

I called my wife, Aline, as soon as I got cell signal.

"Hey baby."

In an excited voice, "Hey baby, you got an elk!"

"No, I'm done. Coming home."

"What? Are you kidding? You're coming home without an elk?"

"Yes, my love. I'm tired and I'm done dodging muzzleloader hunters. The one I ran into yesterday was a total ass."

"I cannot believe you're coming home without an elk. This will be the first year we don't have any elk meat in a decade."

"Well I have a pronghorn and a black bear with me in the freezer. I will kill a few whitetails. No worries."

With disappointment evident in her voice, "It's not the same. I really wanted an elk."

"Well okay, sweetheart I am excited to see you too, goodbye." I hung up abruptly.

A text hits my phone immediately, "Sorry, I am happy to see you. I just wanted an elk, sorry."

Wow, after 19 years of marriage, she is obviously more excited about elk meat than her husband coming home. Just then I look up and before I go through McClure Pass, I am once again stopped dead in my tracks by the beauty of God's creation. I had to stop and take a picture of this view. I'm leaving and won't be back for almost a year or so I thought. After getting home and giving everyone the presents I bought them, I head off to bed, exhausted.

The next morning, first thing, Aline continues, "You can still get an elk."

"Baby, I've got whitetail hunts in three states. I don't have time to go back out west for an elk."

As she walks away, "well that's a shame. I love elk meat and we're out."

I think about it all day. The next morning I call a friend, Larry Richards for help. Larry has been everywhere and done everything. He will know where I can get a late season elk without drawing a tag. Larry points me to an outfitter he knows in New Mexico. I call the outfitter. He agrees to fit me into a week he already has full. He also tells me that he has landowner tags, so a cow elk is no problem with a rifle. He thinks it will take just a couple days, because the elk will be in big herds that time of year. I send him a deposit, and everything is set.

November comes quickly, and I find myself in a lodge outside Chama, NM waiting with six other hunters on the pre-hunt briefing from the outfitter. Just then there is a commotion and the outfitter booms into the room. One of the other hunters says, "How you doing?" The outfitter responds, "Well no one has threatened to kick my ass or sue me today, so it's a good day so far." I shake my head and try to pay attention to the briefing. At the end, he confirms all the hunters cell phone numbers, telling us that our guides will call us tonight and set up a meeting to pick us up for the hunt the next morning. That is when I realize none of the guides are present, which seems strange.

I get up to walk out and the outfitter stops me, "Mike – since you called late and I was already booked up, I had to get an additional guide to take you. His name is Marino. He is young and you two will do good. He is out cowboying right now but should call you tonight." I thank the outfitter and drive back to the campground.

Later that night the phone rings, "Mike? This is Marino. You ready buddy?"

"Yep, sure am."

"Okay, I will be there at 4:30 a.m. Is that okay?"

"Yep, sounds good."

"See you then."

Okay, seems like he has done this before. That is the least I've spoken with a guide before a hunt ever. He must be good. I got five days and my rifle to get a cow elk in this open country on a fully guided trip. I've never been on a guided elk hunt, never shot an elk with a rifle, and never hunted one on private land. I suppose I should not worry. I'm hungry, it's time to go get a steak and a beer.

Surprisingly, I sleep like a baby. Normally, the night before a hunt I am a mess with anticipation. I love my Mercedes Beast 4x4 Sprinter van. I built the interior around two essentials, a full-sized bed and a chest freezer. I sleep well and can always keep my meat frozen. After a cup of coffee, I get my gear together and stand outside. Right at 4:30 a.m. a big white Dodge pickup rolls up to my campsite and I meet Marino for the first time.

He is young, bright, and wiry. We get acquainted a little bit on the drive into town. We stop at the only gas station open. As soon as we pull in, I realize it's where all the guides meet with their clients to discuss the plan for the day. I watch as Marino talks to the other guides and sit quietly.

When Marino gets back into the truck he says, "My uncle Larry has two clients, they are older, and he will need our help."

I said, "Okay, no problem."

But thought, "I am also a paying customer, why is it my problem to help get other clients an elk?"

I took a deep breath, reminded myself to be a better Christian and take what the day brings me. Soon enough we are rolling down the road telling stories like old friends and I find myself thankful that Marino is my guide. The grey light of day is just breaking when Marino gets quiet and starts focusing his gaze out the window into the shadows.

Suddenly, he slows down pulls over and says, "There, there they are."

I am waiting for my eyes to adjust and do not see anything at first. Then just as sudden as Marino stopped the truck, I see them, an entire herd of elk out in the high desert. They are not half a mile away.

Marino says, "Damn. I wish they were on this side of the road. We have permission to hunt this side of the road."

I ask, "Who owns that side of the road, where the elk are?"

He simply says, "It's the Rez." And pulls out to continue the search.

We move on to other vantage points and glass for elk. We do not see any other elk. We do see a bunch of elk urine and scat on the roads. Then we round a bend on the mountain road, and I see Uncle Larry's truck. Marino pulls over and gets out to talk to his uncle. I can hear their conversation. Uncle Larry has seen a lone cow three quarters of a mile to the west, sky lined and lit up by the rising sun. Marino tells him that we drove all the way around that canyon and saw elk urine and scatt on the road. They agree that the elk herd we are looking for must be over the ridge and down in the hidden canyon we cannot see.

Then I hear their plan. It appears I am being volunteered to climb over the ridge into the canyon system and chase a herd of elk out, so that the two older hunters in Uncle Larry's truck can get a shot opportunity. It seems they are too old and feeble to go in after the elk themselves. I say nothing. Marino gets back in the truck and asks, "You up for a walk buddy?" I respond, "Of course." Marino grabs shooting sticks and his binoculars, then jumps out of the truck. I grab my rifle and daypack and follow.

Marino is fast. I've never had trouble keeping up with anyone. I remind myself that it is my first day above 8,000ft elevation, he lives at this elevation, and he is twenty years younger than me. I soon discover that the hidden canyon is three ridgelines away and we hike hard and fast to get there. When we get there, we glass for a while and listen, we cannot see or hear a single elk. Marino bombs off the ridge and drops down into the bottom. As he rolls up the next canyon wall, he stops short in the shade of a juniper and waves for me to follow. Then he points straight up to the top of the next ridge and whispers, "Cow bedded, how far?" I do not see her with the naked eye and halfway don't believe him. Without admitting I cannot see her I pull up my range finding binoculars and scan just below the crest of the ridge. There she is right where he pointed. I take a range, "403 yards and she is bedded." I'm impressed by his skills at this point.

We sit there and develop a plan. Marino is convinced there are more elk in this canyon, we just cannot see them. He starts to make soft random cow calls, as if he is a young cow that has lost the herd. He is hoping to get a response from a mature cow and then we will have a play. The young cow we can see gets nervous and stands up.

Marino asks, "You want to shoot her?"

I respond, "no."

Then I follow up in a whisper, "I have no problem shooting an elk at 400 yards, but I'd rather not on the first morning."

He says, "What range are you comfortable shooting?"

I respond, "I'm a hunter, not a shooter, the closer we get, the bigger your tip gets."

He controls his laughter and smiles at me broadly. The muted laughter is broken suddenly by the bark of a mature cow.

There are other elk here.

Immediately, the young cow we can see crosses the ridgeline and is gone. We are standing there scanning the other side of the canyon for the mature elk that barked at us when we hear, boom, boom…then a few seconds go by and we hear boom, boom, boom. Marino looks at me and says, "The plan worked buddy. The old guys got their shots. We need to move fast and catch the herd." With that and without discussion, he pitches off the canyon wall to the bottom.

We walk, run and slide across the soft dirt canyon wall scrambling to the bottom, across it and up the other side. Marino is moving fast, he stops halfway up and says, "I think the elk are just over the top, be ready." I am climbing hard and still cannot keep up with him. He is fast. He reaches the top about 30 yards ahead of me and drops suddenly. He runs back to me, "They are over the top across a small canyon and they're leaving, we've got to go." I smile and shake my head, but do not respond. I need all the oxygen in the canyon to make it to the top, and purposefully slow my heart rate to make a good shot.

We crest the ridge and there are at least 20 elk across the next canyon on the far side. Marino opens my bipod and sets my rifle down as I range them. It is two hundred seventy three yards to the center of the herd. I am shooting a Christensen Arms rifle chambered in .300WINMAG. My bullet is a 180 grain Federal Premium Tipped Trophy Bonded. It drops less than a foot at that rage and I can take dead aim on the top of an elk's vitals and "let it eat." I settle into the top of the hill and take a deep breath.

Marino says, "Don't shoot the spike."

"I don't see a spike. I do see the herd leaving."

"Shoot the really big cow near the spike, just don't shoot the spike."

I am now looking through my riflescope and respond, "I don't see a spike."

Marino says, "Look lower on the canyon wall."

"Okay got him. He's a 3 point. I see the big cow. Here we go." I take the slack out of the trigger.

My rifle barks and the muzzle brake throws dirt everywhere, damn New Mexico loose dirt. We wipe the dirt off our faces. Marino is back in his binoculars quickly. I'm back on the scope. The cow didn't move.

"How did I miss that damn shot?"

"I don't know buddy. I couldn't see through the dirt. Hit her again."

I take the slack out of the trigger. The rifle barks and throws more dirt on our faces. The herd is leaving with a purpose now. The big cow is still standing perfectly still as the rest of the herd runs off.

"How the hell did I miss twice!"

"Hit her again."

I rack another round into the chamber and get back on her. Just as I level my reticle on the cow, the 3 point bull tries to breed her.

"What the hell," Marino says laughing.

Just as I am taking the slack out of the trigger, she falls dead.

I roll over laughing.

Marino says, "What's so funny?"

I respond, "You know what that young bull thinks?"

"No, what?"

"He thinks his dick is deadly!"

We have a good laugh and then climb over to see my cow elk. Wouldn't you know it, both shots were perfect, and she never moved. She is massive, easily the biggest cow I've ever seen. We exchange some congratulations, field dress her, and decide to walk over the ridge down into the open near the road where we parked to see how the two older hunters did.

We catch up to them and they are looking for a blood trail. They know where one elk is, but they cannot find the other one. We help them look for over an hour. During that time, we get separated. As I am climbing to the top of the next ridge, analyzing every gap and hole in the juniper trees I find mountain lion tracks - shit. I am creeping through this stuff with the scariest apex predator in North America. I take my rifle off my shoulder and chamber a round. I follow the lion tracks to the crest of the next ridge and then find what looks like drag marks.

Suddenly, Marino appears. He is following elk tracks, but no blood. He thinks the drag marks are the elk we are looking for and she is simply dragging her back leg. He is not sure what to think of the lion tracks. We continue together along the ridge and find a mule deer leg that was eaten. We break off the search and head down the canyon wall to meet up with Uncle Larry.

Uncle Larry calls off the search for the second elk and rightfully orders that we recover the two elk we know are down. After the second cow is field dressed, we use good old-fashioned human muscle power to drag them downhill to the bottom. Yes, no kidding, we did not quarter them. Marino, Larry, and I drug them downhill. Then Larry uses his winch to get the two cows into the bed of his truck. My cow goes in second and she does not fit. Her rump is up against the front wall of the truck bed and her head and shoulders are laying on the open tailgate. We drive out of the canyon and park near the main road for Larry to get signal and call the outfitter.

I am eavesdropping on the phone call. Larry is trying to convince the outfitter that the second client should be allowed to continue hunting. The problem is we are sure he hit an elk, even though we did not find a blood trail. The rule is that if you hit an elk, that is your elk. You can search as long as you like, but you cannot hunt for another elk. The client who made a bad shot is almost physically sick at his poor shooting and sits with his head in his hands distraught. We all walk off and leave him with his friend to console him. They decide on their own to walk back into the canyon and look again. I am now a bit upset, because if they can walk to track an elk, they should have been able to walk to hunt. I shake my head and stay out of their business.

Larry does not see them leave. He is still on the phone with the outfitter. Marino and I take a minute to call our wives. Aline is happy I got her an elk. I am happy that I'm off the hook for not bringing an elk home from Colorado. And, since I got it done on the first day, I have more time to hunt for whitetails. Aline and I are talking about it and celebrating over the phone. I am watching Marino, who is kicking the dirt and talking on the phone about a hundred yards away downhill towards the main road.

Suddenly, Marino hangs up his phone and runs to the truck. Something is up, so I do the same. I meet him at the truck, and he says, "I found the other elk. She made it to the bottom of the arroyo near the road. She was shot through the back leg and simply cannot jump the fence. She's still alive." I grab my rifle and run after Marino. We get to the edge of the arroyo and there she is near the fence, still alive. I shoulder my rifle and apply the, "coup de grace." She's dead. We are relieved to have found her. Then Marino says, "Look up there. That's the ridge where we stopped looking. Maybe those drag marks were not a lion and a mule deer, but her dragging her back leg." I agree and turn away to fetch the older men, whose elk we just finished. Marino nods as Larry is headed our way, wondering what the gun fire was about.

I find the other clients and tell them we need to go back to the truck. They say they're not leaving until they find a blood trail or it gets dark. I tell them it's over we found the elk and I shot it. They are dumbfounded. I do not wait for a response and start walking out of the canyon back to the truck. In short order, we get back and Larry and Marino have the third elk field dressed and winched up into the bed of the truck.

We transfer my elk to Marino's truck and are saying our goodbyes when one of the older men walks over to me, "Hey Mike, thanks for all your help today. We really could not have done it without you. Can I give you a few bucks for helping the guides for us?"

I respond, "Nope, you can buy me some beer when we get back to town." He smiles, shakes my hand, and walks off.

Larry is on the phone with his preferred local meat processor. They are willing to take two more elk. He asks them about taking a third, mine of course. The two older clients didn't do anything but wait for Marino and I to push the elk herd to them and one of them made a terrible shot. Now, just because they are older they get precedence at the processor? I bite my tongue at first. Then I get heated and ask Larry, "What am I supposed to do? The outfitter doesn't have a place I can hang my elk and butcher it." Larry calls another processor, no luck. I look at Marino. He shrugs his shoulders and looks at the ground in deference to his uncle. There is a long pause. I am done with Larry. He has used me all day to help him be successful.

I look at Marino and say, "Brother I can debone that elk in the bed of your truck at the campground myself. Then we can throw it in the freezer in my rig." Marino smiles and says, "Let's go." We follow

Larry back to town and he waves for us to stop. Marino stops and we watch one of the old men go into a gas station. He comes out with a twelve pack of Budweiser and walks up to my window as I sit in Marino's truck. In a very sincere tone and with genuine thanks in his eyes, he gives me the beer and says, "Thanks Mike." As I look into his old eyes and shake his hand, I realize what God's plan was. God wanted me to help today. He planned for me to get my elk, but he knew that Larry and Marino would need a little help with the older gents and three elk on the ground. As I watch the old man walk back to Larry's truck, I said a little prayer of thanks for the strength and the opportunity to help.

Marino pulls out and starts driving toward the campground. I am lost in the beautiful scenery going by out the truck window for about ten minutes, just staring glassy eyed at New Mexico, "The Land of Enchantment." Marino shakes me back to reality, "Buddy what if we go back to my house, after we get your van at the campground and you can cut up your elk in my driveway. I do not want to do it at the campground. That might not be a good idea." I had not thought about the feelings of the other campers. I agree.

Before long, I am following Marino and we pull into his driveway. He has a modest house with a great view of the prairie and the mountains. We are not there long before his children come running over to us. He is obviously a beloved father. They are so excited to see him. He beams with pride as he introduces his boys.

We start working on the elk and I am not paying much attention to anything around me when I realize we have company. There are now more children, they are not Marino's, but they are just as cute. The boys somehow negotiate their way into my stash of beef jerky and are super happy when I give them as much as they can eat. Marino thanks me and then says, "Mike, this is my wife Sunshine." I had not seen her walking up. Still focused on my work. I look up from my work to see a young lady with a great smile. I introduce myself and she walks up to the house.

For the next half hour, we work on the elk and are entertained by the kids. Then I hear Marino say something loud toward the driveway. When I look up the neighbors are walking up the walk. Two handsome young couples are interested in what we are doing and stop by to visit. I keep working as Marino visits with them. Then another car pulls in the driveway. It's Marino's dad and an old friend. Marino stops me and introduces me to his Dad, and we start talking. I need a break anyway. I sit on the tailgate and crack a free Budweiser, thanks to the old guys. Marino's Dad pulls out a bottle of whiskey and we pass it back and forth.

It is at this point I realize that the neighborhood is in Marino's yard. I look over at him and he smiles a big warm smile. I am impressed by the warmth and friendship. Marino walks over and explains quietly that they thought my van was a moving van and were worried Marino and Sunshine were leaving. When they realized it was just a hunter cutting up an elk and that Marino and Sunshine were not leaving, they were so happy they stayed to party.

Marino's front yard turns into a bit of a family or tribal reunion. There are family members, tribal members, neighbors, and just regular old friends. We are having a "big time" as we say in Kentucky. Before sunset we finish with the elk. It took us longer than normal, because of the stories and the drinking. About the time I have all the choice cuts off the elk, bagged and in the freezer, Marino hands me the ivories. Then one of Marino's friends opens a folding knife as he walks up to me and says, "Hey brother, are you going to take all that neck meat?" Before I can answer another one pulls a knife and smiles. I need to share the harvest.

I put down my knife. Climb out of the truck bed and grab a beer. Then I say, "Man if you want anything else off the elk, have at it." Family and friends clean her up and take all the remaining edible meat. I watch as this scene unfolds. There are family, friends, and neighbors all sharing the harvest. I am not an Apache, but I am with my tribe. This is how it is supposed to be. Everyone shares in the harvest. Then a warm feeling begins burning in my chest. I whisper to no one, "Thank you, God."

The sun is setting. Children are laughing and running in all directions. Adults are telling stories and laughing as well. The beer and the whiskey are adding to the glow of an amazing sunset. Marino builds a fire. I am soaking it all in when he says, "Hey man, you shouldn't drive. You need to leave your RV in my driveway. You can plug up to my house." An hour passes and some of Marino's family and friends depart. The kids stay. I'm sure two of the boys are Marino's, but I'm not sure where the others are from. They hang out around the fire with us. We tell stories and I feel like I have known these people all my life.

Just then Marino says, "She wants to sing us a song." I am taken back. I look towards Marino and see him pointing toward a pretty little girl, "She wants to sing us a song." I am honored and simply nod. I think it's going to be a Christmas carol or something. Then she pulls out a drum and starts drumming a rhythm akin to a heartbeat. Then she starts singing. It's a native language. I guess Apache, but I do not know, but it moved me to tears. Just as she finishes, before I can ask Marino what that was, Sunshine yells from the front porch, "Dinner is ready."

I say, "Man you have been a tremendous host. I will let you get to dinner. Thanks for letting me crash in your driveway." God has yet another surprise for me today. Marino says, "No brother, Sunshine has already fed the kids and herself. She made dinner for us." I didn't know what to say and was startled when Marino yelled back to the house, "We will go inside in a minute. Let me finish my story." He finished his story. We grabbed the last couple beers and went inside.

I was greeted by Sunshine who explained that dinner was homemade enchiladas. The house was spotless. You could eat off the floor. The kids were running around a Christmas tree. A woodstove provided the warmth. I smiled and thought, "This is what happiness looks like." We ate, finished the beer, and told more stories. Then it was time to say goodnight. Marino invited me to hunt with him again, anytime. I accepted. Sunshine had gone to bed, so I asked Marino to thank her for the wonderful dinner. I shook his hand, walked out to the van and crashed.

To my surprise, I woke up five hours later, bright eyed and bushy tailed, ready to drive home from New Mexico. There was not a light on in Marino's house, so I didn't wake them. I decided to call him later that day on my drive. He had done more for me in one day than any other guide has done for me in ten.

I had a successful hunt, but more importantly I'd been cured of the anger that Randel had planted in my heart. I know God has a plan. I trust that plan. I love him for the plan and am as thankful as a man can be for it. But when God shows you his love through other people. When he demonstrates his love through the kindness of strangers, it is a thing to be cherished. It makes me hope and pray I make it through the narrow gates someday.

Marino, Sunshine, their family, and friends treated me with such warmth, kindness, and respect that I felt like I belonged. It did not matter that I wasn't a member of their family or their tribe or that my skin was a few shades lighter. It mattered that I was a genuine human being and a hunter. Halfway across the country I found other members of my tribe.

Recipe –

Here's what you need, "soup to nuts" to serve up your own cow elk adventure –

Ingredients:

_____ A willing soul, a semi-stout heart, good legs, feet, and hips – priceless

_____ Time Off – up to one week including travel, maybe less

_____ Tag – New Mexico non-resident hunting license $65; private land antlerless elk tag $347; habitat management and access validation stamp $4 = total $416 *note - many New Mexico outfitters include the cost of the tag and license in the cost of the hunt. This can make New Mexico a bargain compared to other states.

_____ Outfitter $1,500 + guide tip $300 = $1,800

_____ Firearm – you should already own it

_____ Gas and campgrounds = $1,016 (2,600mi gas + 3 nights in a campground)

_____ Ammunition - $100 (5 boxes of 20; 4 for practice and 1 for hunting)

_____ Clothes – you should already own it

_____ Boots – you should already own it

_____ Pack – you should already own it

_____ First Aid Kit – you should already own it

_____ Food & Water – $41 per day x 6 days = $246

_____ Hiking Stick(s) – you should already own them

Total Cost: $3,578

Directions:

There are a few different states and outfitters to choose from when doing a late season cow elk rifle hunt. This hunt is usually short and easy too. The elk are herded up and have moved down into lower elevations for their winter range. My hunt was still over 5000ft, but yours doesn't have to be that high. Especially if you choose a location and outfitter with lower elevations in mind.

I drove across the country in my RV because I'd rather do that than get a firearm on and off a plane. Plus, it's much easier to get the meat home in my onboard freezer.

Most of the friends I have spoken with who have done a hunt like this said it lasts maybe 3 days, tops. The outfitter said it was rare that they have someone who hunts for more than 2 days, even with weather challenges.

The tags are guaranteed in New Mexico with their outfitter/landowner program. It is a truck hunt. You drive around scouting for an elk herd. Then you get out and usually, make a short stalk to harvest your cow.

My hunt was an exception and I honestly appreciated the additional work. The truth is, that things are just more precious when you work for them. So, in the end I was happier about the work I did, even though I was a client.

I camped on the way out in Kansas and did not on the way back. So, there again, it's up to you and how you chose to do it. The shorter the hunt, the less expensive and vice versa.

Chapter 18 - Black Death on the Rocks

Buffalo Trace is a fine Kentucky Bourbon and when ordered on the rocks is simply, "buffalo on the rocks." In the African parlance, Cape Buffalo are called, "Black Death". They are called that for good reason. In 2012, the year before this hunt took place, I read an article that said five Professional Hunters (PHs) were killed by dangerous game animals in Africa. It said all five were killed by Cape Buffalo, not one by a lion, leopard, elephant, hippo, rhino, or crocodile. Cape Buffalo are also one of the most abundant of the dangerous game species on the African continent. We were about to learn that "Buffalo on the rocks" isn't just a cool way to order your bourbon, sometimes it's a way to hunt "Black Death."

In late July of 2013, Aline and I arrived in Zimbabwe for the hunt. We met our PH, Jonathan, at the airport. On the ride to the conservancy, we learned that he knew the land very well having grown up there. He was a fifth generation African and learned his trade from his father, Daryl, and older brother, Dion. Their style of hunting in this part of the Bubi Valley of Zimbabwe was to use the large rock massifs or kopjes to glass vast areas and then put on a stalk, much like we do in the western United States. I was unaware of this prior to our arrival, but by the end of the safari I would be quite familiar.

The first day of our hunt was Election Day and to Jonathan's surprise and regret all the staff were gone to vote. It appears his father's love of democracy surpassed the safari booking schedule and he gave everyone the day off. I took the opportunity to discuss Zimbabwean and sub-Saharan African politics with Jonathan. I had studied such topics for my master's degree and found Jonathan's views fascinating. We had a great day, despite the lack of staff. We got close to a bachelor group of younger buffalo bulls and stalked within 35 yards of some zebra. Aline and I really did not care about the slow first day, we were happy to be back in Africa on safari and that was good enough.

Overnight the wind was ferocious, and we awoke to cold temperatures and rain. After a great breakfast we huddled by the large stone hearth, were warmed by the fire, and watched the weather. We finally went out about 8:30 a.m. and drove the roads for a couple hours until the tracker, Sakhile (sa-key-lea), called Jonathan to stop. Off the right side of the truck were fresh buffalo tracks. Jonathan verified the good news and then we bounded ahead a couple miles, rushed into the bush with the wind in our favor and climbed some high ground. This is where I realized that Jonathan's hunting style starts out the same as most buffalo hunters, but then veers off into something normally done in Montana or Wyoming.

We would do this all safari. Cut track or somehow spot game, then move to high ground, sometimes extremely high ground and wait, glassing for a shot. It was not long before we could see six bulls moving up the valley a few hundred yards away. Jonathan immediately decided we were in the wrong place. We backed out, bounded ahead again a few hundred yards, climbed another kopje, and got set up. I was amazed to see the bulls again, within the hour, feeding in our direction. The last bull looked to be a real big old bull, so we held tight. The bulls kept coming and the wind was good. None of us realized the bulls would walk almost right on top of us and into the thicket at the base of the kopje. In tight cover and inside of thirty yards, it was hard to determine which bull was the big bull.

We were all trying to shrink into the rock. I was as low as I could get on the rifle and still shoot. Jonathan was trying to pick out the right bull. We let them feed right by at less than twenty yards and were blessed the wind was totally in our favor. It could have been a very dangerous situation if the wind shifted, but there was no way to know when we got set up that the bulls would simply continue walking right toward us, what a rush. We did however pick out distinguishing features on the big bull. He had a bald spot with an open wound on his rump and red hair on his face. We would know him coming or going from now on.

I asked Jonathan if he was sure that bull was worth taking. I also told him I was not afraid to shoot on the second day of the safari. Jonathan responded, "We were very lucky. That does not happen very often. Michael, I've been hunting buffalo a long time. I know you would be happy with that bull, because I would be happy with that bull."

Jonathan decided to drive to the head of the valley and climb the biggest kopje I'd ever seen and wait the bulls out. If they continued up the valley, we would see them again. While glassing from the bald knob on the end of the kopje, about four hundred vertical feet off the valley floor, Jonathan spied a tremendous old impala ram alone. Aline has taken great animals from multiple African Safaris and is a talented marksman, but the humble impala gives her "buck fever." There have been times while "making bait" on a leopard hunt, that she could not shoot impalas due to the shakes.

I asked her if she wanted to try first, to climb out on that ledge and second to get a shot off on this impala ram to "end the impala shakes." She of course said yes. It was a serious climb. At one point, we had to span a deep fissure and Aline was uncertain how she would make it. So, I climbed into the fissure and let her climb over me. In short order she crawled to the end of the cliff and got set up for the shot lying prone on the edge. I had to stay back and could not watch, only Jonathan and Aline fit on the edge of the precipice. At the report of her rifle I heard Jonathan, "Yes, that's it. He's down." Aline made a marvelous long range shot and had the first animal of the safari in the bag.

We tried all day to get into position on the buffalo again. Three times we climbed to high ground, found them, stalked down to the valley floor, and lost them. Nearing dusk, we were discussing calling it a day, when we unexpectedly caught a glimpse of some buffalo going into a dry creek bed. They were a few hundred yards away and we were not sure they were the bulls we saw earlier. The light was fading, and a dark dry creek bed is no place to be with cape buffalo, so we called it a day and drove back to the lodge in the dark.

The weather on the third morning cooperated and we set out much earlier. We drove the roads near the bulls we left in the dry creek bed the day before trying to cut their tracks. After a few hours, we found buffalo tracks. Jonathan immediately turned the truck around, drove quickly down the valley to the next road the buffalo would have to cross in the direction they were headed. They had not crossed. So, we know they were somewhere in the couple miles of forest behind us. Jonathan turned the truck again and headed for a long low ridge of kopjes that ran parallel to the direction the buffalo were traveling.

The ridge provided us multiple vantage points to peer into the valley at long range. It was also much safer than trying to track feeding buffalo in the thick forest below. We moved from vantage point to vantage point, glassing for the bulls and picking apart the forest. On the third stop to glass, Sakhile disappeared. He returned with a broad smile and said he found the big red-faced bull from yesterday.

We followed Sakhile and upon nearing the buffalo Jonathan motioned for us to stop, while he went forward to assess the situation. He returned and told us that the bull was ahead with three other bulls, bedded at the base of the kopjes we were on. Then he motioned for us to stay low and follow him. We fell in line quickly and quietly. The closer we got, the lower Sakhile moved, until when in range of the buffalo, I would testify that he was slithering over the rock. Jonathan crept close behind, while Aline and I stayed back and waited for another signal from Jonathan.

Then it happened.

Jonathan signaled me to move up.

When I was close enough to hear him, we spoke in whispers. "Stay very low and get to the edge…get ready to shoot."

At the edge, he asked, "Can you see them?"

"No." I replied.

"You're looking too far out. Look straight down."

To my shock the bulls were bedded directly below us. We had to wait for them to move. There was no shot. I took a range while I waited, sixty yards on a very steep down angle. This shot was going to be something akin to sheep hunting.

"Michael, you can see them now, yes?"

"Yes."

"Good…now look carefully and find the boil on the ass of the big bull."

"Got it, but I cannot see his head, are you sure."

"Yes, it is him and Michael, load a solid."

When buffalo hunting the preferred technique is to load a soft or a partitioned bullet in the chamber of your rifle, as the first shot can be planned and measured. The bullets behind that in the magazine should then be all solid bullets because the follow-up shots which are almost always required on a buffalo cannot be planned and measured. I do as I am told and we wait.

There is a curious bird in Africa called the "Go Away Bird." Its call is an alarm to the other animals. To our utter contempt, a Go Away Bird started to call his loud alarm.

"Michael the birds…damn…get ready… make it count… the bull is getting up."

All I can see is the boil on his rump, so I move my cross hairs from there to the top of his shoulder.

There is no time to get nervous. The bull stands. I aim as low on the shoulder as I can without hitting the rocks in front of me or the rocks in front of the bull. I take the slack out of the trigger and my .458 Winchester Magnum erupts. The bulls explode into the thicket below. I recover from the recoil and chamber another round as Jonathan reports, "Michael only 3 bulls ran out of the thicket. 4 bulls ran into the thicket."

We now have arguably the most dangerous task in African hunting. We must go into a thicket after a wounded buffalo. The intrepid and unarmed Sakhile is already climbing down the rocks and into the thicket. Jonathan tells Aline and I to make sure our rifles are fully loaded and to follow him. We pick up safe intervals behind one another and move into the thicket, all rifles at the low ready position. Sakhile is ahead of us twenty yards. I am trying to cover him without allowing Jonathan or Aline to cover my field of fire. Jonathan is at the ready moving slowly into the thicket scanning on the left flank. I am moving and covering his right. Aline is covering our rear. This is where buffalo get their name, Black Death. Wounded buffalo are known to run, hide and lie in wait to purposefully gore and trample their pursuers. Dead buffalo nearly always give a death bellow, we have heard no such bellow.

Our hunting party is tense. I move ever so slowly and scan, check Sakhile's position up front, check Aline's position in back, and do it again. Minutes seem like hours. We find blood but no bull. We can see sunlight ahead. We are nearing the edge of the thicket where it opens onto the plains.

Suddenly, Sakhile exclaims, "Dead! He is dead!" Sakhile is standing arms raised triumphantly over his head. We all move quickly to where Sakhile is standing and find a bull laying on its back, motionless, blood running out of its nose.

Jonathan says with urgency motioning for me to follow him close, "I didn't hear a bellow."

As we get within twenty yards, Jonathan reminds me, "Michael it's the dead ones that kill people. Shoot him again through the spine right between the shoulders."

I put another 500 grain Nosler Solid into the bull's spine. There is no movement. He is dead. We all finally exhale. Smiles, handshakes, and congratulations are shared all around. He is laying on his back and we cannot see the boil on his rump. I walk around to the front of the bull. He has red hair on his face. It is him.

Johnathan and Sakhile are now figuring out how to get the Landcruiser to the bull and walk off to do some planning. Aline and I are enamored with the beast and stand in awe.

After the shock wears off, she says, "The first solid found it's mark." Aline is pointing at the dime sized entry hole where my bullet entered the bull's chest. I had not looked for it. After seeing it, I reply, "Hit the golden triangle." The heart, up to the point of the shoulder, back to the rear of the lungs is the golden triangle. A bullet through there is certain death for any animal. My bullet cut right across the bull's plumbing above his heart.

Jonathan and Sakhile hike off to get the truck. As Aline and I wait, we marvel at the size of the bull and talk about the blessings of such early success. We also talk about how hunting from rocks above the valley floor, glassing for game, and stalking from a point of advantage is awesome. I say out loud, "Bartender, make mine a Buffalo on the Rocks," and we both laugh.

Jonathan and Sakhile are back in about 45 minutes with the truck and I ask, "How are we going to load this giant angry bovine, there's only 3 men?" Jonathan laughs and says, "Watch this!" He cuts two slits about 6 inches long in the buffalo's rump, runs a rope through, and attaches that rope to a block and tackle. Then he runs the winch cable through the block and tackle, attaches the running end to his bumper, and hits the button. Sakhile and I stand on either side, only to keep the buffalo moving in a straight line. I was impressed. The winch flips the beast into the truck bed in a matter of seconds. I'm still smiling when we arrive at the skinning shed.

I am still marveling about our good fortune and falling in love with the red hair on the face of this beast, when Jonathan says, "fourty-one inches."

"What, you're kidding? Really?" I reply.

"Yes Michael. He is quite a big one…told you that you'd be happy."

He is right, a mature bull is classified as over thirty-six inches. Anything over forty inches is a true trophy.

The next morning, we were not sure what to do first. None of us, Johnathan included, believed we would have such early success on a bull of that caliber. We booked a ten-day safari and it was only the fourth morning. Sitting by the big stone hearth after breakfast warming ourselves, I decided it was time for Aline to hunt. As the client who was paying for this trip, it was my place to make the decision and I let it be known, "It is Aline's hunt now." She beamed a broad pretty smile at me. Jonathan said, "Alright then, what do you want to do Aline?" I knew she wanted to hunt at night and call hyenas, we had done that before and it's exhilarating. I also knew she wanted a warthog, but after that, even I was not sure. The diversity of game in Africa is a strange thing to grasp as a North American Hunter. It can seem other worldly, but you must decide what to pursue. African game animals do not all live in the same type of terrain and the techniques to find and kill them are varied. The area we were hunting was well over one hundred thousand acres. Aline and I discussed it. She told Jonathan, "Let's go hunting today and see what happens."

Not long into the morning, Jonathan wanted to stop driving and climb rocks. We followed, and climb we did, kopje after kopje, glassing for game in each pocket, draw, and valley. Sakhile would often move out ahead and would randomly return with news of game over the next ledge or distant ridge. Upon returning from one of his solo excursions he said simply, "Kudu bull." Jonathan turned to me. I pointed to Aline. She smiled and said simply, "Yes."

We crawled up a rock face, over the summit and down into a pocket on the other side. Sakhile was sure there was a big bull in the forest below. Jonathan so trusted Sakhile, that we simply sat for hours glassing and never saw it. It was long past midday when Jonathan sent Sakhile around the pocket of forest we were glassing and over the horizon into the next valley.

An hour later Jonathan spotted Sakhile through his binoculars on the horizon, signaling for us to follow. When we got there, we crawled up the rocks two hundred feet above the valley floor. This time Jonathan could see the bull, but there was no shot. Once again, we glassed and waited. I stayed above and to the rear of Aline, to be out of the way. After hours of waiting, it happened.

Aline and Jonathan started moving slowly and pointing. Aline's face got serious, her finger went to the trigger and her .300 Winchester Magnum barked. Jonathan said, "You hit it, good bull that." We moved quickly down the rocks and into the forest. Aline's kudu bull was dead the instant the bullet hit it. The sun was setting as Sakhile drove us home. Jonathan, Aline and I were all in the back of the truck still talking about Aline's big kudu bull and what a great shot she made. We were hoping to see game in the dwindling light, but we were not very seriously looking.

Just then, Jonathan stops talking, as if something is certainly wrong. To my surprise, he says, "Bushpig…big bushpig…grab your rifle." Then Jonathan knocked on the roof of the truck for Sakhile to stop. The truck was still moving when Jonathan said, "Right we must go, jump…Michael Jump!" I am not sure why I followed his command to jump out of a still moving truck, but I did. To my surprise, when my feet hit Mother Earth I did a pretty good combat roll and my rifle never touched the ground. I came up ready to shoot, when Jonathan caught up to me and grabbed my rifle, "No! That's the female." The light was fading to darkness, only dim rays were penetrating the forest. I could not tell which was which. He let go. I swung to the other pig and my rifle erupted. The .458 knocked the pig off its feet.

What a contrast of the two hunts today. We spent hours of waiting and Aline made a long-range beautiful shot on a big handsome old kudu bull. Then a mad scramble out of a moving truck, combat roll on a dirt road, and shot a boar so ugly it was pretty.

The next day we try hard to get Aline a bushbuck and saw quite a few, but none old enough. We also saw a great deal of game and spent a lot of time climbing rocks and glassing terrain, but the day was uneventful. That was fine by us, because we were sure looking forward to going back out after dinner to call hyena. Aline has always wanted to take a hyena and we have had a lot of fun trying to call them before on previous safaris. Most people discard the hyena as a game animal, but they are challenging to hunt without baiting them or killing them as a "bycatch" on a big cat hunt. Also, most people don't realize that an old male hyena can be five-foot-long and weigh up to two hundred pounds. It is a thrill to call in a pack at night and we do it every chance we get.

As we are loading up to go out, the first thing I realize is that Jonathan's audio system and calling equipment are far superior to the other PH's who have taken us hyena hunting. His plan is similar, we will go to locations near hyena dens just before dark and set up quietly, hopefully without being detected and wait for sundown. As soon as the sun goes down, we will start calling, sounds simple, but it never is.

We get to our first location, set up and wait. The sun goes down and Jonathan turns on his calling system. From the pitch black forest returns an immediate loud bloodcurdling "Whoop." Shivers roll down my back. The night is still and starlit, without any moonlight, perfect. Jonathan uses his calling system and a dialogue of sorts begins with an entire pack of hyena. Suddenly, there is a pack running in the black forest all around the truck. I thought to myself, "How did they get here so fast? It is as if they grew up out of the ground." Jonathan tells Aline to get ready, she does, and he throws on the spotlight. But there is no shot. The hyena are too clever and move out of the light each time. Mere minutes pass and they are gone. We were surrounded, if only one would have stood still for just a heartbeat, I'm sure Aline would have done her part. We try multiple set ups over many thousands of acres throughout the night and get multiple answers, but no hyena. We get back to camp in the early morning and collapse exhausted.

The next morning at breakfast, without prompting, Aline reminds Jonathan that she wants me to shoot a zebra and we are not just on a bushbuck hunt. He replies, "Yes ma'am." During our morning driving and glassing from kopjes we see baboon, waterbuck, a herd of cow buffalo with young males, wildebeest, and impala. We've yet to see zebra or bushbuck and it's getting to be time for the midday repose and repast. When a herd of zebra cut the trail in front of us and drop into a small valley on the other side.

We jump out of the truck and head up the rocks. Sakhile, Jonathan, and I play chess with this stallion in the rocks and small draws for the better part of an hour before we get the wind and terrain to our advantage. We crawl behind a small outcropping of rocks down off a main ridge onto the valley floor. We can see the zebra herd ahead through holes in the bush. When we get to within one hundred twenty-five yards the wind starts to betray us and Jonathan knows it's now or never. The problem is that we are too close, pinned down hiding on our knees. Only Jonathan can see the herd.

In whispers once again… Jonathan asks, "Can you see the stallion?"

"No I cannot."

"I'm going to stay on my knees and put the shooting sticks straight up, you stand, get on them, and if you can see the stallion, shoot him."

"Got it."

Jonathan puts the sticks up. I cautiously stand and get my rifle on them. I can see the stallion.

"Jonathan I've got him."

No reply.

"Jonathan I've got him."

No reply.

"Jonathan I've got him."

No reply.

Finally, I look down. Jonathan has his fingers in his ears. I chuckle to myself. Breath, relax, aim, squeeze, boom! The bullet makes an audible thud when it hits the stallion's chest. To my surprise he thunders away at a gallop bleeding hard. We follow him immediately.

We track and find the stallion quickly, but the stallion catches movement and gathers himself to run. Jonathan is putting up the shooting sticks, but he is too late. Without permission, I raise my rifle offhand and put a good shot through his neck. He drops. As we walk up to the stallion, I marvel at how beautiful and tough they are. Then I remember how much I love zebra. It is one of my favorite game meats in the world and we were treated to a wonderful meal just a few days later. We take the zebra to the skinning shed and head back to the lodge to rest up, eat dinner and prepare for another long night's hyena hunt for Aline.

Nothing of consequence happens on the way to the first calling location. I am still amazed at how good Jonathan's calling set up is: speakers, amplifiers, CD player, and remote control. We stop the truck and let the forest settle down, it is quiet and clear, no moonlight again. Jonathan starts the calling sequence using an individual hyena calling to find his mate. There is an immediate response. Jonathan switches to the sound of a feeding frenzy and they come running. He tells Aline to make ready and he throws on the spotlight. Aline can see eyes and is about to shoot when the hyena runs. In fact, the whole pack spooks. Frustrated and exhilarated, we talk about what went wrong. Jonathan thinks they do not like the truck and tells us to dismount and get into an old empty concrete cattle dip tank nearby that hasn't been used in decades. Then he tells Sakhile to drive off. While we are waiting for the hyena to make the next move it gets so quiet, the quietest I have ever heard anywhere on Earth.

I stop staring into the forest for hyena and look up at the night sky. I can see more stars than I have ever seen before. There are so many wonders to behold on the Dark Continent. We wait silently for a long time, but the hyena did not return. The silence is broken when Jonathan whispers, "time to go." I ask if I can try calling them back, he laughs and says, "With what? Your voice? (Chuckle) Sure, right, go ahead." I let out my best "Whoop!" It was immediately answered, "Whoop!" Jonathan is shocked and encourages me. For another twenty minutes, I "talk" to a hyena with just my voice, but our efforts were in vain. When the hyena did not return, Jonathan radios Sakhile to bring the truck. When the truck arrives, Jonathan says, "I've never seen someone talk to a hyena." That causes Aline to break into a fit of laughter and we are all smiles as we climb into the truck.

The following morning, we are tired and moving slow. The plan is a bushbuck for Aline and so we start off in a whole different direction. We are not yet a mile from the lodge when we see that a huge animal has been dragged across the road. Jonathan stops the truck and we follow the trail. We find a dead yearling giraffe surrounded by huge leopard prints. I was able to put an entire .458 shell in the pad of one of the leopard's footprints. It is a monster of a cat. One of the giraffe's hindquarters has been eaten. We are confounded about the size and power of a predator that can successfully kill a small giraffe and drag it off.

Jonathan decides we need to anchor it to a tree and put up a trail camera. It took all our strength, all four of us, to drag the giraffe about ten yards to a forked tree. Sakhile and I pull on the trunks of the tree until they stretch apart. Jonathan struggles to lift the head and pushes it through, and we let go. The two small tree trunks snap back together, and the giraffe is solidly anchored. It took all of us to drag the giraffe. The power and size of such a cat is not lost on us. The giant leopard is probably in the area. We are all appropriately tense, until Jonathan has the trail camera up and we drive away. As the day wears on, I find myself trying to imagine the cat that did that, what a beast.

Soon we are back on the hunt for bushbuck. We check all the likely areas around the lakes and kopjes nearby. We find two small bushbucks, but no old males. Jonathan decides we should climb the highest kopje on the concession and glass for them. Once on top, Jonathan shows us the ancient ruins of a bushman's village. The top of this kopje is flat and probably seven acres in size. I imagine it was a wonderful place to live. There are small stone walls, pieces of pottery and other evidence of a village. I almost lose myself in an Indiana Jones type archeologist's fascination, when everyone walks away to continue hunting. When I catch up, everyone is glassing an immense expanse of forest all around this massif.

We spy a great deal of game, but nothing mature and worth pursuing. When Jonathan spot's bull eland nearly straight down below us and walking toward the rock out of sight. Aline encourages me to follow Jonathan out onto a ledge where we can see almost straight down, but she is staying on top for safety. I am a retired Airborne Ranger qualified Infantry officer. I have parachuted out of planes and helicopters. I have also repelled out of hovering helicopters. I am not scared of heights, but this ledge is small, and I would fall for about two minutes before I hit the ground. I was nervous to climb out on that ledge. I took my time climbing over the edge and down to the ledge. Finally, out on the ledge I find a crack with a small tree growing out and I lean back into the crack and use the tree as a rifle rest. Taking a deep breath, I try to relax and range the valley floor straight down, one hundred forty-three yards. I settle back, breath deep and find the old bull eland in my binoculars. There is not an ethical shot, we must wait.

Three hours later, I am still standing on a ledge looking four hundred twenty-nine feet or roughly the height of a forty-story building straight down to the valley floor. We can still see the old bull and his younger companion bulls feeding in thick forest below. We keep tabs on them waiting for a shot. Minutes turn to hours. They finally start moving, but it is right toward us. Now they are directly below us in the shade of this massif, bedded down and we cannot see them. We climb back up to the top and discuss strategy. We decide that I should take Aline's .300 Winchester Magnum for its greater range and that Jonathan and Sakhile should scout for another vantage point.

Aline and I sit and soak up the view, we can see for miles. We are resting in the midday sun when Jonathan returns and says, "You're not going to like it." We move down the massif losing altitude to where he wants to climb over the edge. It appears to be a right angle straight down. If this was a military operation we would be, "roped into the rock." This time, Aline forbids me to climb over the ledge. Jonathan insists we climb over the edge. He looked and there is a ledge we can stand on below that is about two feet wide, from there he says we will be able to get a shot. It is near vertical and I tell Jonathan, "I'm not dying to kill an eland, pun intended." A few minutes pass, while Aline and I discuss it, and Jonathan looks on anxiously. Then, over her protests, I climb over the ledge with her rifle slung over my back.

We make it safely down the ledge and shuffle along it. I am thankful Jonathan is wrong, the ledge is three feet wide. I find another tree growing out of a crag. I wedge myself behind it and use it as a rest. The bull is standing two hundred four yards away now and the angle is not straight down, but the shot will be severely vertical. There are some zebra moving toward the eland. Jonathan sees an opportunity and starts pitching small egg sized rocks off the ledge at the zebra. He only has to throw them about thirty yards horizontally, they then drop about one hundred fifty yards vertically near the zebra. He wants the zebra to spook the eland out into the open. It works.

The zebra run. The eland run. Jonathan, now spotting from his binoculars says, "Get ready...the big bull is moving... he is the one on the right." There are four bulls total. I relax and try to breath. They are moving away quickly. The zebra change direction suddenly. The eland are confused and stop. I settle the reticle and take the slack out of the trigger. The bull's back legs buckle. He is hit. The young bulls run and my old bull follows. Jonathan implores me to make follow up shots at the moving bull. I never take shots on running game. He implores me again, "Before they are gone… Michael shoot!" I hesitate and then comply. I shoot at my bull until the gun is empty, then realize the cardinal sin of rifle hunting. I have no more ammunition.

I switched rifles with Aline. The .458 rounds in my ammunition pouch are worthless. Jonathan realizes I am empty before I ask. I watch in amazement as he climbs the rock face sideways with his .300 Winchester Magnum in one hand and completes a traverse a baboon would be proud of. He gives me his rifle and says, "Hit him again." I respond, "It's not zeroed for me, just give me two bullets." Jonathan complies as the bull stops in the open. The zebra and the shooting have confused the young bulls who normally follow the old bull. The old bull is hit and it caused them to circle back. The bull has stopped at three hundred twenty-one yards and looks sick. Jonathan and Sakhile are talking, asking each other if I hit him while he was running. I have time to breath and make a good the last shot. At the report of the rifle, the bull falls where he stands. We all exhale and smile as the adrenaline passes.

Like spiders, we climb back up and then carefully over the ledge onto the top of the kopje to find Aline. She could see nothing. The multiple gunshots have her sick with worry and she is relieved to have me back on top. She tells us that she has been worried and praying. We all must catch our breath before we can tell her what happened. It takes a long time to navigate off the massif and get to the bull, but when we do, I am very proud. He is huge and very old. He has a thick shag carpet between his ancient old ivory tipped horns. I hit him twice. After dropping the bull at the skinning shed, we go back to the lodge to rest up for another night of hyena hunting.

As we are unpacking the truck, we are discussing the two shots on the running bull. Jonathan and Sakhile disagree about what happened. I disagree with them both. Jonathan believes I hit the bull on the initial shot and the last shot, but that I shot a different bull when they were running. Sakhile believes I missed the first shot while he was standing still, then hit him once while he was running and the last shot. I believe that I was aiming at the running bull, but not leading it. So, the running shots fell harmlessly in the dirt and I hit him the first and last shot. The only ethical thing to do is go back and track the other bulls to see if any of them were hit. We put our gear back on the truck and drive back to where my bull fell. Sakhile finds the tracks of the other bulls and we begin. We track the other bulls for nearly a mile. There is no blood. Sakhile and Jonathan stop for a conference. There is no blood and from the eland's tracks none appear to be limping or dragging a leg. They concede, that I was right. I have never been happier to miss an animal.

After dinner Aline wants to hunt and we decide to try to catch a bushbuck before sunset and then stay out and hunt hyena. Jonathan also decides that we need to bring some of the guts and bones from the zebra. He thinks we should leave some each place we get a response from hyena in hopes that it will keep them close. We get down to the largest kopje near the lake without incident or anything of note and begin glassing. We saw four bushbuck but nothing old enough to shoot. We climbed down off the rocks and prepared for the night's hunt. The hyena come running into our first set up as soon as we turned on the call. Aline is getting ready to shoot. While Jonathan is set to turn on the light.

It is immediate pandemonium. The giant dogs are howling and barking all around the truck. Jonathan switches on the light. Aline sees the eyes and just as she is ready to shoot, the dogs run. This happens multiple times. The adrenaline rush is real. The entire team is a mess with excitement. Alas, Aline gets no shot. We leave an offering of zebra guts and bones, then move on to the next set up. This time we are in a wide canyon with kopjes on both sides. Jonathan turns on the call. It echoes down the canyon, "whoop!" echoes right back. I am baffled by another sound, echoing towards us in the still night air. Then I realize it is the footfalls of the running hyena. We scramble to get set up amongst the whoops and howls surrounding us as they bounce of the canyon walls. The pack approaches the truck with great speed, but at the sight of it they break and leave with a similarly impressive haste. It is past midnight when we get to our third set up and begin calling. We hear a distant response and wait. Nothing comes in. We leave the remainder of our zebra offering and depart.

As dawn approaches, we finish breakfast tired but with great anticipation. We are all making preparations to get Aline a bushbuck. As soon as the grey predawn light illuminates our path we depart for the old dry lake. The lake is about a half mile wide with a small one acre patch of tall reeds near the center, in what used to be the deepest part of the lake. As we approach the dam, we spy an old bushbuck and the hunt is on. Before we can get into position we are busted and the bushbuck slinks into the one acre patch of reeds in the wide open center of the dry lake. Sakhile climbs a tree to watch the flanks of the reeds with a radio and Jonathan decides we should simply wait the buck out. After a long while, I volunteer to stalk around to the other side of the reeds and push my way through, certainly this will cause the buck to leave and give Aline a shot. Jonathan agrees and I am off.

Jonathan gives me hand signals as I stalk up to the reeds and I enter at the point he directs. I am only a few yards deep into the tightly packed reeds when I hear the bushbuck flush. I freeze. I wait. I hear no shot. I back track out of the reeds and walk back to the truck. When I get there, I wonder why Aline is looking at me in a strange way. Before I can speak, she says in a very spooky voice and points at me, "Jonathan um…" Jonathan looks at me and says, "Oh shit man!" I look down and it appears that my clothes are alive and moving. I freeze, horrified.

I have hundreds of ticks covering my body. Jonathan leaps out of the truck and begins beating me with his hat. Aline yells, "Take off your clothes!" Who am I to resist a woman as pretty as my wife screaming, "Take off your clothes!" Jonathan understands and stops beating me. I strip down to my underpants and get into the back of the truck, as Jonathan speeds away.

In no time, we are back to a road and flying. I am in my early 40s now and have always been an athlete. I am certainly less impressive naked than I used to be. But all the Africans we pass along the road appear quite impressed by me. My ego would like me to believe it is my physique that was impressive. The truth is that they have never seen a nearly naked white man, standing in the bed of a safari truck, who has been made a brilliant rosy shade of pink because of the cold winter air. We were in such a hurry, we didn't think to get me a blanket or anything to ward off the wind.

By the time we get to camp I am a very nice shade of red. Aline requires me to lose even my underpants and now I am standing naked as the day I was born outside in the cold. Aline does a tick check all over my body. Jonathan puts my clothes into a trash bag, which he fills with something to kill the ticks. The vampire bug crisis is averted and I shake as I put on clean clothes. That is the very last time I pretend to be a bird dog and flush game in Africa.

An hour later, we are back on the hunt for a bushbuck. We start by checking all the likely areas the small secretive antelope normally frequent. Another small lake is empty of bushbuck as well as water. A big lake is empty of bushbuck, but full of water. We are unsure what to do, but not surprised when Jonathan wants to climb the tallest kopje that leads to the west side of the big lake. We glass for a while in all directions but find nothing. I realize that Sakhile is gone, just about the time he returns with good news. He has found an old buck bedded. We stalk over to where Sakhile found the buck and I cannot see it with the naked eye at all and struggle with my binoculars. The ability of African trackers to see game with their naked eyes never ceases to amaze me.

We wait for hours and the big buck never moves. We sit tight and keep our vigil. Sakhile is acting funny, crawls over to Jonathan and points. Jonathan looks where Sakhile pointed and smiles. Then he whispers, "A younger buck is walking towards our buck." We all sit tight and watch the drama unfold. First, a female bushbuck we had not seen stands. That explains why the old male was holding so tight. When she starts to move away the old buck stands and moves between her and the young buck. The young buck stupidly continues toward her and then it happens. The forest explodes with energy as the old buck crashes violently through the forest after the young interloper. We watch the show as they twist and turn through the forest and then disappear. All we can do is wait and hope the old buck wins and returns to his lady. He does and they bed down in the same fissure in the forest floor.

So, we wait. Another hour goes by and we are baking on the rock. Even in the winter in Zimbabwe, the afternoon sun is strong. There is no respite from the sun on this bald rock face. Jonathan and Sakhile have both stalked away and back again multiple times, trying to find a better angle. They cannot. Aline sits like a statue. The doe stands and begins to slowly feed. A few moments later, the buck follows. Without guidance or provocation Aline quietly repositions higher up on the rock face, gets behind her rifle and says, "I'm going to take him." Jonathan and I simply exchange surprised looks as she took charge of the situation. Aline's rifle barks. The old buck sprints downhill toward the road. For a moment no one is sure what happened, then suddenly the buck tumbles to his death mere feet from the roadside. Aline has her buck and a magnificent old buck he is.

We try again that night for hyena. This time we bring Jonathan's nephew, Ian Andrew. Our first calling location produces no response. We move on. The second calling location produces one short tentative, "whoop." We move on again. At the third calling location we get a powerful response, and everyone quietly does their job. Jonathan and Aline move out in front of the truck seventy-five yards into the dark forest. I suggested this tactic, because every hyena that came in so far turned and ran when it saw the truck. Ian Andrew's job is to follow them with a sack of rotten meat, dump it on the ground and return to the truck. I am running the caller. Ian Andrew returns at a sprint and is sure he was being chased by hyena. He was wrong, but I don't blame the young lad. The dogs are close. I never saw Jonathan turn on the spotlight and 45 minutes later they return to the truck, no shot.

We try one more location and no hyena, but when Jonathan throws on the spotlight, he sees a grysbok, a big one. He hands me his varmint rifle, chambered in .22 Winchester Magnum. It takes a moment, but I find the grysbok in the sights and the .22 barks. Jonathan is terribly excited, but I do not understand why. The grysbok fell where it stood, and Jonathan runs over to it. They are a species of small antelope, so he simply carries it back to the Landcruiser. At the truck Jonathan is visibly excited, "Michael this is the biggest grysbok I've ever seen. It is certainly a record, maybe the world record." I am happy, quite happy with the chance encounter and the blessing of such a kill, but I am skeptical about its record book status. Nevertheless, the ninth evening finally turned up an animal for us in the darkness.

Dawn on the tenth morning was late. I was lying in bed waiting for it. When I finally saw the grey light creep into our lodge and heard the first birds began to sing, I dressed and went outside. The camp staff were already beginning to move and there was coffee. I poured a cup and watched a fire being built in the hearth. The last day of a hunt like this is certainly bittersweet. A few years of saving money. An entire year of planning. The travel to Africa and the first nine days of hunting seemed, now, at this moment to have gone by too quickly. They passed almost like the smoke from the fire, slowly at first until they just disappeared up the chimney.

Aline quietly strode into view and I was brought back to reality, just as the sun crested the eastern horizon. Warthog was the order of the day. This was our third safari and Aline has always wanted to harvest a mature old warthog. She had marginal chances at old boars before, but to her credit she held off. She has also had easy shots at young boars, but to her credit held off. She is serious about the ethic of harvesting the oldest males from a population. We are in Africa, but the conservation model and ethic still apply. The oldest males are often no longer breeding and quite often have been kicked out of the herd by the younger stronger males. They are simply waiting for the specter of death, which usually comes when they slow down. Whether it is an injury or old age that slows them down, eventually they can no longer outrun the many predators here. When that happens, they are chased down and eaten – alive. They fight, but death in nature is a far crueler option than the hunter's "coup de grace."

We go through the normal tactics Jonathan has in his bag before lunch. Driving to likely spots warthogs live, climbing kopjes, and glassing for them. We spot no hogs, none. We then retreat to the lodge for lunch and Jonathan decides we can glass a water hole near the lodge. We are all tired, including Jonathan, although he will not admit it. We have hunted day and night for the last nine days and sitting by a water hole, close to the lodge seems like a fine idea. I especially like the idea because no one hunts this close to the lodge. Less hunting pressure means we might get it done this afternoon. Shortly into our sit, I remind Aline that the last time we "sat water" she napped, while I stood watch. I told her that the first shift we were doing the opposite. So, I nodded off. I wasn't out long when a wisp of wind washed over me and I woke.

I noticed Jonathan was gone. Aline explained he walked back to the lodge. I sat up, looked toward the water hole, and said, "Are you going to shoot that hog or what?" Aline was startled and grabbed her binoculars, "I didn't see him come in." A good warthog was just then kneeling to drink. Aline whispered, "Go get Jonathan." Shooting any animal in Africa, without a PH is a bad plan. I sneak off quickly and quietly and return with Jonathan. Who looks the hog over and says simply, "too small." Aline must have agreed because she did not argue. Jonathan disappeared again.

Aline and I watched the hogs finish drinking and move back into the forest. Aline put down her binoculars and sighed. Just then a big solitary male stepped out of the forest and surveyed the waterhole. Looking through my binoculars, I said, "Are going to shoot that hog or what?" Aline thinks I am joking, but I did not say anything else. She picks up her binoculars and says simply, "Find Jonathan." I leave and immediately bump into Sakhile. It appears we were not totally without supervision, as PHs sometimes do, he left Sakhile to watch us. Sakhile has seen the big old hog and is already on his way to get Jonathan. Mere moments pass when Jonathan returns, looks through his binoculars and says, "He will do."

BOOM! Not one second elapses between Jonathan's pronunciation that the hog was old enough and Aline's rifle barks. She was ready the instant Jonathan gave his approval. The hog is dead where he stood. We hike down to the waterhole. Aline is beaming with pride standing over her old boar. It was a fitting end to a magnificent safari. The warthog is a classic African animal that Aline's been after on three different safaris. At the skinning shed, dropping off the boar we again felt the bitter sweetness of the end of our trip. For those who have fallen in love with Africa, the terrain, it's people, and the hunting you don't need much of an excuse to start saving for the next safari as soon as you get home from the last one.

We have unfinished business with the giant whooping dogs that respond to our calls in the darkness. That is reason enough to return and we will.

Recipe –

Here's what you need, "soup to nuts" to serve up your own black death on the rocks –

Ingredients:

_____ A willing soul, courage, a semi-stout heart, good legs, feet and hips – priceless

_____ Time Off – (# of days) x (what you get paid daily) until you get it done = ???

_____ Booking a dangerous game hunt: $1,000 per day for the dangerous game hunter and $250 per day for your plains game hunting companion is $1,250 per day x 10 days = $12,500

_____ Flights for two to Africa and back economy class, roughly $5,000

_____ Dangerous game rifle chambered in at least .375 Holland and Holland or better at least $1,500

_____ Budget grade ammunition to practice with prior to going on the hunt 10 boxes x $100 = $1,000

_____ Ammunition for the hunt itself 2 boxes of Custom Nosler Solids $320 and two 2 boxes of Federal Trophy Bonded Bear Claws in .458WINMAG $320 total = $640

_____ Ammunition for Aline's .300WINMAG; practice + hunting 8 boxes of Barnes X $45 = $360

_____ Air Service to help get you, your weapons, and bags through customs in Africa $700

_____ Clothes, binoculars, and other gear – you should already own it

_____ Overnight in Johannesburg before flying to Zimbabwe $200

_____ Tip 20% of the safari, plus tracker and camp staff - $3,000

_____ Trophy fee for the buffalo - $3,000

_____ Trophy fees for the other animals depends on what you shoot.

_____ Shipping of your animals home to the United States - $2,000

Total Cost: $29,900

Directions:

Okay, most folks first thought is, "Oh my God, thirty grand!" Well yes, that is about right. And that is why it takes us three years of discipline to save up and go on this type of adventure. This was the first and last safari we ever paid retail for. Every safari before this one and every safari after this one we have bought at a local chapter of Safari Club International's annual charity auction and banquet. The hunts at these local chapter auctions are vetted by the leadership of each club and especially at our local club, they are high quality. The money from the auction goes partially to fund the missions of Safari Club International and partially to fund our local chapter missions. Our biggest mission with the local chapter is a summer camp for kids who want to learn to hunt. The other great thing about buying safaris at venues like this is that they are often sold well below their retail value. This can help anyone do their first African safari.

This safari was particularly expensive. Hunting "black death" is not cheap and should not be cheap. Especially, wild big country free roaming Zimbabwean buffalos. After you purchase your safari at the auction, you will want to contact a travel service in Africa. They will help you get your paperwork approved before you arrive in Africa. They will meet you at each plane and get you through the airport until you are at your final destination, where your PH and his people should pick you up. I highly recommend this and trying to do it without help, especially if it's your first safari is a fool's errand.

Next, you must search for the best price throughout the winter and spring before your hunt for plane tickets. This is best accomplished by an experienced safari travel agent, but you could do this on your own. Either way, I highly recommend you fly to Atlanta and take the Delta 201 flight direct to Johannesburg and back. You can overnight easily in the City Lodge Hotel, which is safe and part of the airport complex. Then get up the next morning and catch your next flight to your final destination on the continent. We have tried other methods. The worst is going through New York, then refueling in Senegal, and arriving early in the morning in Johannesburg. You must immediately catch the next flight to the destination. Where you arrive spent, exhausted and not ready to hunt. And because the New York flight leaves early in the morning, you will probably have to overnight in New York, which is actually worse than City Lodge in Johannesburg.

Check before you leave to see if your transfers (rides) to and from the airport are included in the cost of the safari. Some outfitters and PHs charge extra, some include it. Tips are interesting, as the safari is already expensive. But honestly, tipping is worth it. The PH, trackers, and staff really earn it. You will be treated like royalty the entire time you're on safari, especially by good reputable outfitters and PHs. The staff prepare all your meals, do your laundry daily, and take care of all your wants and needs.

The landowners, outfitters and PHs are responsible for managing their land and the animals on it. They use the money to keep their entire conservancy (ranch) running. These are huge tracts of land, so big it is for most Americans to imagine. Keeping poachers off the land and protecting their animals is a huge expense. It is hunter's dollars that do that, not government money or animal rights groups.

Hunting the animals is what gives them value, without it the locals would simply kill them and eat them, all of them. I realize it is counterintuitive that hunter's dollars save the animals, but that is the truth. We take only one or two representatives of a species from the herd. The herd lives on as a protected resource.

So, the safaris cost pays for a great deal more than just the PH and outfitters costs. Also, many of the rural people in African have no jobs, none whatsoever. They are usually subsistence farmers and have a diet almost void of protein. A safari outfitter provides local jobs and a great deal of protein from the animals harvested to the local people.

A safari rifle is an interesting subject and I am not going down that rabbit hole. The rifle you are most confident with in the minimum legal caliber for dangerous game, which is .375H&H, is the best choice. Your comfort and confidence with the rifle mean much more than anyone else's expert opinion.

Only hits matter, and an animal's life is held in the balance. Make sure you know what ammunition the rifle "likes" and practice before you go. You could also rent a rifle and purchase ammunition from the PH or outfitter. This is becoming a more popular solution as African Nations make traveling with firearms more and more difficult every year.

Trophy fees are based solely on what you chose to shoot. There are places in Africa, mostly South Africa, where the conservancies (ranches) are small, and the hunts are not completely fair chase and wild. I do not hunt at such places, but they are less expensive. We like to hunt big wild tracts of land for truly wild animals. But the thing about Africa, especially well-managed conservancies in Africa, is that the game is plentiful. You will see game all day every day.

You must be ethical and disciplined in what you chose to harvest. Some PHs are liberal with their age classifications and will let you shoot younger males. This can get expensive quickly. You must know what you want to hunt and what you are willing to pay. Also, when paying for trophy fees you will need to decide if you want to travel with tens of thousands of dollars in cash or ask if the outfitter will let you wire them the money after the safari. Either way, you will need to research the animals you want to hunt and hope to harvest in order to be able to pay the trophy fees and not get yourself in too deep.

Finally, what do you do with your animals after you harvest them? Great question. The PH and the trackers will get the animals from the field, back to the skinning shed where they are skinned and butchered. They will salt your hides and clean your skulls, that is included in the safari. The choice cuts of meat are prepared in camp for you and your hunting party. The rest of the meat and I mean all of it, every morsel, will be eaten by the camp staff and any surplus will be distributed to the other villages locally. Nothing goes to waste.

The PH or outfitter will also get your hides, skulls, and horns to a local taxidermist in Africa to be mounted and shipped to the United States or simply "dipped and packed" and shipped home. Either way you have choices to make. If you had time to visit the taxidermist in Africa and are happy with their work, having them mount your trophies, crate them, and ship them home is the least expensive option. If you would rather have your local taxidermist do the work, then have them dipped, packed, and shipped. We've done it both ways and it works, either way.

Shipping by plane is very expensive. Shipping by boat takes a little longer, but it is significantly less expensive. Finally, do not have your trophies sent directly to you or to your taxidermist. Most ports of entry into the United States are not familiar with African animals. If you ship them directly to your local hometown taxidermist from Africa, there is a good chance the local U.S. Customs Agents will not know what to do. They quite often will leave them sit until they figure it out. While they sit, they could rot. If you are unlucky, they will eventually give them to you. If you are very unlucky, they will ship them back to Africa at your cost.

The best plan is to hire a customs brokerage service that brings things like this into the United States all the time. Ask the leaders of your local Safari Club Chapter who they use. The customs brokerages are usually in Dallas, New York, or San Francisco. They will get a limited Power of Attorney (POA) from you, allowing them to act as your agent to import the shipment. When you give them the POA, you will want to step back and simply answer their questions and pay their fees. They will use their contacts and professionally move your shipment through customs. Then you'll want to ask your taxidermist what tannery he uses and give that address to the customs brokerage. They will send your trophies to the tannery and arrange final disposition from the tannery to your taxidermist. They start by tracking the shipment from Africa. Their services are well worth the money. Then all you must do is work with your taxidermist to have them mounted and figure out where you will hang them in your home.

Be careful, Africa is addictive. If it were politically stable, Aline and I would live there.

Chapter 19 – Great White Bear

Lewis and Clark called the grizzly bears they encountered on their journey west to the Pacific, "great white bears." They had never seen grizzly bears before their quest. Along the way, they discovered many large aggressive bears that were blond or silver haired in color and called them simply "white bears." It is believed that they did this to distinguish them from black bears. Their journals are replete with stories of their sometimes deadly, but always dangerous encounters with the white bears. After reading their journals, I dreamed of hunting the great white bears. But truthfully, I had never hunted Alaska and was not ready. The other hurdle was the cost of such hunts. The cost put a "white bear" hunt out of my reach. So, over the years I put it out of my mind.

Then in late 2014, I learned that grizzly bear populations in some areas of Alaska were booming. After speaking with someone at the Alaska Department of Fish and Game, I discovered that there were so many bears, grizzly and black bears, that biologists significantly increased the harvest objective to try to get the populations back in balance. This meant hunters could get two grizzly bear tags each. I was dumbfounded. When I originally investigated hunting them years ago, the tags were hard to get.

Many species from rodents to apex predators, across the globe, have population ebbs and flows. Some as regular as the snowshoe hare, which has a peak every seven years. It seemed that the population boom of grizzlies was happening at a fortuitous time for me. A non-resident of Alaska must have with them a relative who is a resident or hire an outfitter to hunt grizzly bears. I have no Alaskan relatives, so I started calling outfitters. After speaking with multiple outfitters, checking their references, and calling friends who have hunted Alaska multiple times and are familiar with the reputation of the top outfitters, I found one I really liked. While talking to the outfitter, I learned that the Department of Fish and Game needed the bear populations to be brought back into balance quickly.

In the affected areas, the bears were eating themselves out "house and home." That was the reason the Alaskan officials not only increased the tag numbers, but they also allowed grizzly bears to be hunted over bait, a technique normally reserved for their smaller ancestral cousins, the black bear. This made the hunts more successful, less costly, less dangerous, and more accessible to regular guys like me. I have hunted over bait in the past. It is not my preferred technique, but there are times when I think it is a "necessary evil." If the local ecosystem is out of balance and any game species needs to be culled, in order to prevent a trophic cascade or other calamity – then count me in when hunting over bait. I would much rather see hunters pay to hunt, which puts money into our wildlife management and tourism systems, than having tax dollars used to pay government hired "sharpshooters" do it. Plus, hunters will use the resource. The hide, skull, horns, and meat are all used by hunters. That is not the case when government paid sharpshooters are called in. So, in certain situations, I will gladly do it and this is one of those situations.

I booked the hunt and the planning began in earnest. The hunt would take place from a small cabin on a lake south of Denali National Park. Each day, weather permitting, the outfitter would fly a pair of us, hunter and guide, into a bear stand on a remote lake using a tiny little float plane. Since it never gets truly dark at night in Alaska during the summer, we would hunt bears overnight and be picked up the next morning. If the weather did not permit us to be flown into the remote lakes, which was our best chance to kill a grizzly, then we would take long ATV rides through the forest to hunt black bears along the rivers near the cabin. The local hunts would be simple out and back trips and we would be sleeping in the cabin at night.

The hunt included a grizzly and a black bear for each hunter. I had to have two basic kits (1) overnight grizzly kit and (2) out and back black bear kit. My standard first aid, communications, and kill kits would be the same. The overnight float plane kit would include food, water purification, simple shelter, extra clothes, and survival gear. Planes crash every day in Alaska and being marooned for a few days in grizzly country required thoughtful planning. Yes, I was being guided, but that never means to trust that your guide will have all contingencies covered.

I would be taking my Winchester Model 70 Alaskan, chambered in .375 Holland and Holland. I would be shooting a 260 grain Nosler Partition out of that very heavy and very accurate rifle. The pistol decision was a long and winding road. I am of course a combat veteran. I am also an Airborne Ranger qualified career Infantry Officer. So, I am comfortable with a full-sized side arm versus bear spray. I am well trained and have used a side arm many times in training and combat. I am not trained, nor familiar with bear spray. My proficiency with bear spray was and is zero. It was an easy decision to bring a side arm for me.

The question was, which side arm? I dove into the research. The experts all talked about having "knock down power" and "one shot kill" strength. They advised that you would, "only get one shot, so you have to make it count and have the power to kill." I was suspect of their tactics, but they were long time Alaskan residents or bear guides, so I investigated their recommendations. Their recommended bear defense calibers were terribly heavy for pistols. The .44 Remington Magnum, .454 Casull, and the .480 Ruger were the most popular. The experts also recommended nothing but revolvers. There was even a custom bear defense pistol they claim, "fit in a grizzly's mouth."

The first drawback was weight. The revolvers were all very heavy. This was a slight benefit, because it helped tamp down the extreme recoil, but a heavy pistol is not a comfortable pistol and fatigue makes cowards of us all. A tired hunter is likely to put a very heavy pistol in their pack, versus on their hip. A pistol in your pack is a liability. It is as useful as a small boat anchor unless it is on your hip. The second drawback was recoil. The final drawback was the heavy double action trigger on all the recommended revolvers. Sure, you could pull the hammer back and have a fine single action trigger, but in an emergency that is one second you do not have.

I settled on a lightweight Smith and Wesson revolver, chambered in .44 Remington Magnum. I dove into the testing and training. My Army training was with autoloading pistols, not revolvers. I knew I needed some work with my new revolver. So, I designed a simple drill that incorporated the expert's advice. I drew a twenty-inch diameter circle, roughly the size of a grizzly's skull, on a target and started at fifteen yards. The drill was simple (1) yell very loud "whoa bear!" (2) draw the revolver and (3) put two shots into the circle as I walked backwards. The idea was to somehow slow the bear with my yelling, increase the distance by walking backwards, and get two shots off (in defiance of the experts who said you can only get one shot off). Anyone who shoots pistols routinely knows that fifteen yards, forty-five feet is no easy mark, while standing still. Trying to hit the center of a twenty-inch circle while backing up was challenging but became routine. After a few weeks of practicing, I could reliably hit the circle, center of mass on the first shot.

The problem was that the second shot seemed to take forever. The recoil of the pistol lifted my sights off target. I had to push hard down and focus to get back on target. Then the heavy double action trigger became a real liability. It required me to aim left of center, as I am a right-handed shooter the trigger pull on a fast follow up shot while walking backwards caused me to pull to the right. I was starting to agree, that one shot was all you could expect. The idea of that did not set well with me. I was starting to believe that both the revolver advice and the tactics of the "so called experts" were flawed.

After a great deal of thought, I decided to stick with their advice through another series of drills, but this time I asked my wife to time me. The best I could do with the revolver, was three seconds to draw and fire the first round. The second was much less accurate and the best I could do was an additional five seconds. Eight seconds to get off two rounds was not going to cut it. Out of frustration I went into the house and got my Glock 21. It is a full sized .45 ACP that is much closer to the type of side arm I used in the Army. I asked my wife to give me the same eight seconds. I got the first round off in three seconds again and then five more on the first try. By the third try, I got off eight rounds and seven were hits. The standard Glock 21 magazine also holds thirteen rounds, with one in the pipe, that's fourteen total. So, I could reliably score five to seven hits with the pistol in the same time I could unreliably hit twice with the revolver. I would also still, worst case, have five rounds in the magazine to pump into a bear that got to me at point blank range, even if I missed every time on the move. The decision was made.

The year flew by. The hunt was paid for and so were the plane tickets. I kept my marksmanship training up. I double and triple checked all my sets, kits, and outfits. I kept in communication with the outfitter. When the time came for my first big Alaskan adventure, I was ready. The plane ride from Louisville to Anchorage went smooth. Then there was a long drive to the outfitter's home lake north of Anchorage where we caught a large float plane. That float plane took us another few hours north, where we arrived at the base camp. It was a nice cabin on a big lake that put us in proximity of our bears. There were three hunters and we each met our guide on the dock.

My guide was named Johnny and my first impression was not favorable. After that we got our stuff stowed and the outfitter called us to a meeting to discuss the hunt. There were no changes to what he told me over the phone when I booked the hunt. We would go out one at a time by a small float plane to isolated lakes every evening, hunt all night long, and be picked up the following morning. If the weather did not support it, we would hunt along the river for black bears. Then the outfitter showed us trail camera pictures from each of the three stands he planned to put us into. There were grizzlies and black bears at each stand all night long. I was terribly excited but tried to play it cool. The hunt I dreamed of for years would start the following evening and I could not wait.

The weather the next afternoon was the opposite of our bright anticipation for the day. Wind and rain prevented anyone from flying anywhere, so after dinner we mounted the ATVs and drove down to the river stands for black bears. They had only seen one grizzly this far south all season, so no one expected to see a "great white bear." In Alaska in the summertime, it never really gets dark. The northern latitude is such that the sun never really sets. It just hides behind the horizon. So, there is plenty of light to hunt at night. But hunting all night is difficult. You must try to stay awake, make as little sound as possible and move as little as possible.

We were on stand about 7 p.m. Despite my normal discipline, the first night I fell asleep sometime after midnight. Johnny woke me only once to show me a wolf that was moving through. Try as I might, I could not stay awake. When the grey light of night began to grow into the yellow of sunrise we climbed down and rode back. As we bounced and shook, down the trail the shades of grey blew away and gave way to a bluebird sky. I tried to sleep during the day. I knew I had to switch my sleep cycle to be effective, but my body was not ready to stay up all night and sleep all day. It did not help that I was anticipating seeing a "great white bear" either.

Shortly after lunch, we got our gear together and the outfitter told the guides in which order they would be flown out. Johnny and I were last. When we finally got to our stand, Johnny pulled two five-gallon buckets of bait from the float plane's pontoons. He instructed me to leave all my gear on the bank of the small lake and make my rifle ready for action. I did. Johnny then picked up both buckets of bait and told me to lead him down the trail to the stand. Johnny needed to "freshen up the bait" with the contents of the buckets and he expected a bear, black or grizzly, to be on the bait when we arrived.

"What if it's a grizzly Johnny?" I said.

"Shoot it buddy," he replied.

"Okay pretty simple, but seriously we are going to walk right into the bait knowing there might be a grizzly on it?"

"Well we have to get to the stand."

"Okay, I'm ready - let's do this."

We set off at a measured pace. A quarter mile down the trail I stopped… "Johnny, there's a bear on the bait," I whispered.

Johnny set the buckets down and looked over my shoulder, "He's a small black bear, just walk right at him and he will run. If not, you'll fill your black bear tag."

"Right, got it."

We walked right at the bear. It was a rush. The bear ran away. I was thankful. I had no idea what the bait was going to be and let my imagination run wild: horsemeat, beaver carcasses or salmon remains. To my surprise it was old trail mix. Johnny poured out his two five-gallon buckets and we backtracked to the lake and got our gear. Back at the stand we made ourselves comfortable for the night.

In short order there were bears everywhere. Johnny explained in whispers that these bears have probably never seen a human. Further, that our outfitter is the only one hunting bears in this area, because he uses his smallest float plane to get into isolated unnamed lakes. I sat and watched the show, there were bears around us all night long. Near dawn, after watching many small boars and sows with cubs feed on the bait, there was a ruckus and the bears scattered. "Get ready Mike, this might be a grizzly," Johnny whispered. It was not a grizzly. It was a giant black bear boar. I had seen a few bears in my life and knew instantly this was a giant.

As I made my rifle ready, Johnny put his hand on it, leaned close and whispered, "You're not going to shoot this bear." I looked shocked and he said without hesitation, "Just watch it. If there is a grizz in the area and you shoot, you'll never see the grizz." I lowered my rifle and with it my hopes. The black bear was a true giant. Nevertheless, watching the bears all night was something special. I was on cloud nine when the float plane came to pick us up.

The next day I realized my initial impression of Johnny was wrong. He was a damn good guide. Smart, cool, calm, collected and sat all night watching like the best guard dog. The anticipation welled up in my chest, as I squeezed myself into that tiny float plane that afternoon. The plane landed, we disembarked into waist deep water, climbed ashore and made it to the stand without incident.

The night was calmer. The quiet grey light was broken only by the random visit of a few black bears for the first eight hours. I was dozing off, half watching a small black bear boar eat, when Johnny slowly and gently elbowed me to attention. "Grizz," Johnny whispered. I raised my rifle into position and the adrenaline took me from drowsy to alert in an instant. There was nothing. I could see nothing except that same small black bear boar eating. I thought, "Johnny is full of it." Suddenly, "Whoof!!!" came from the dense willows on my right. The small black bear boar ran off as if electrified. Then I saw it, the great white bear. "It's a big blond boar Mike, get ready," Johnny whispered.

I said nothing and took very deep breaths to steady my hands, my head, and my heart. The grizzly came in at a trot, not a care in the world, obviously the dominant boar of either species in the area. When he stopped he was close. I had to remind myself that I was the apex predator. "When you're ready, take the shot," Johnny whispered. I took one last deep breath, let it half-way out, took the slack out of the trigger and my great white bear fell dead where he stood.

The kill is always a strange feeling for a hunter. A counterintuitive narrative of joy and melancholy plays in your head as you approach the animal. I was lost in that narrative as we climbed down and walked up to the bear. "Oh dear God, Johnny!" I was shocked at the body of a partially eaten young black bear, that we could not see from the stand that we had to step over. "Yeah, I bet this grizz killed and ate part of 'em. Chances are that he was hunting the bait too. Meaning that he wasn't eating the bait, but that he was killing and eating the young black bears that were eating the bait." I was shocked back to reality not by the grandeur of my bear, but by the rotting maggot filled carcass of the small black bear that laid only yards from my grizzly. The story of that bear probably ended when the grizzly ambushed him and snapped his neck. Nothing in nature dies a peaceful death. Life as a wild animal ends when you are not looking, you're attacked, killed and eaten or when you're too old or too sick to run, you're pulled down and eaten alive.

I stood both engrossed and grossed out by the scene. Mother Nature was turning what was left of that bear into insect larvae and nitrogen for the plants. I am a biologist by schooling and I appreciate the overall biota of a place, but thinking about how the apex predator in North America, the grizzly killed and ate this bear, just to leave a large portion of the carcass to the smallest creatures and their larvae gave me pause.

"Mike, what are you doing man? Come look at your bear!" Johnny exclaimed and so I did. For the next few hours, we kept watch for other bears, while we skinned and butchered my bear. Taking the time to move the meat in carefully wrapped meat bags back to the lakeshore for transport out. When we were all done, it was still about five hours before the plane would arrive. So, we took a minute to rest and eat.

"Mike, I'm going to put up a tarp and make a fire. We can stay warmer that way and enjoy the next few hours until pick up."

"You do what you like Johnny. I'm going to put on another layer and climb back up into the stand. We are covered in blood up to our elbows and there's now a grizzly carcass to attract more bears in addition to everything else."

"Mike, I've been doing this a long time. I'm sure it will be…"

"Holy shit! Go, Go, Go!"

Suddenly, a huge black bear sow with three cubs came through the willows right in front of us. She postured and clacked her teeth at us, then huffed a signal to her cubs to climb a tree, before she charged. I beat Johnny up the tree, back into the stand. The sow's spit blew onto the ladder when she slid to a stop. Johnny was still trying to turn around as I watched her. Her breath visible and ominous, like a dragon's smoke billowing. Her chin dripped spittle and her gaze deadly. I could not stop looking deep into her black eyes.

"Mike," Johnny said panting, "I left my rifle."

"No worries brother." Johnny did not see I had my Glock.

"Oh, good you've got your pistol."

"Yep, if she tries to climb the stand, I'll put a warning shot in the ground before I shoot her."

"I hope we don't have to."

She stood there clacking her teeth, looking back at her cubs, and then up at us, just twenty feet away for what seemed like forever. When she finally moved off, she did not leave. She simply called her cubs down the tree and they all fed quietly. She never looked away from us except to take a few bites of food and randomly clacked her jaw shut to remind us who she was. We watched her for three hours. Finally, she huffed, and her cubs disappeared into the willows. She looked back over her shoulder one more time at us, almost as if to say, "I would have ripped you apart." Then she disappeared.

The sun was coming up and we had work to do. We moved the rest of the gear to the lakeshore and stood guard until the plane arrived. Back in camp, we celebrated and then I collapsed into a deep daytime sleep. The camp cook, Carly, woke me up to eat and after a fine late lunch I walked down to the lake, thankful and reflective on having taken my own "great white bear." I was interrupted by one of the other hunters, Rob from Pennsylvania. Rob is one of those guys you cannot help but like.

"Hey Mike, the guides are up fleshing your bear."

"Thanks Rob, let's go."

I was still in awe of the big blond boar and beaming with pride.

"That's a good one Mike, hope I get one like it."

Rob was bowhunting and his stand locations were only thirty yards from the bait. I considered bowhunting, but kept my rule, "If what I'm hunting can eat me, I carry a gun."

The afternoon weather turned sour, but we still took off on the ATVs and tried for our black bears down by the river. The rain stopped overnight, and the wind picked up, which pushed the ever-present mosquitoes, off us. I was able to stay up all night for the first time without dozing off, but it was to no avail, because we did not see a single animal all night long. Still, the idea that bears were in the area was exciting.

The weather the next day was spectacular and we were all excited to fly out and hunt. Having stayed up all night yesterday, I was able to sleep most of the day. By dinner time I had a spring in my step and was ready to go. We gathered at the dock, 3 hunters and 3 guides, waiting on the outfitter. He landed the tiny float plane and said, "Mike and Johnny, you're up." We scrambled for the door and got set, anxiously anticipating the night's hunt.

We landed on a postage stamp of a lake, more of a pond to be truthful. We were ashore easily and there were no bears on the bait when we moved in to "refresh it." Things were quiet in the stand for hours, neither Johnny, nor I spoke. It was spooky. If you have ever been to Alaska you know "the quiet" I'm talking about. It seems impossible that you can be out in the wilderness and there is not a sound.

The silence was broken when Johnny spoke, "Mike, get ready."

"What is it?"

"Giant black."

"Right."

I got my rifle into the pocket of my shoulder and took a deep breath but saw nothing. I knew having hunted with Johnny for a few days, that he had seen something. Yet, I saw nothing. Moments passed that felt like hours. Then it happened. A giant jet-black boar stepped out of the thick willows into full view. He was impressive. I made myself ready.

Johnny spoke in a whisper, "Mike that's a great bear. I don't think you'll do any better. It's your call."

"He will do."

"Okay, take your time."

I studied the bear and knew he was not yet comfortable. He was pensive and checking the wind. I sat quiet and waited for an opportunity. Eventually, the big boar started to feed. But he stopped often and checked the wind and looked around. I waited. Finally, he relaxed and started to feed in earnest. Still, I took my time. When he turned and showed me his flank, I took the slack out of the trigger. The hit was mortal. Yet, he bounded to our left into the willows. I looked at Johnny with a question on my face, saying nothing.

Johnny spoke first, "No worries, you hit him hard."

"He's down you think?"

"Maybe not yet, but he will be dead soon."

We took our time getting our gear together. An hour passed before we moved to see about the bear. When we hit the ground, we went to the last place the boar was standing. As often happens with black bears, initially there was no blood trail. Their hair is terribly thick and even with a perfect hit, it takes a long time for the blood to soak through and drip on the ground. Nevertheless, we knew which way he went. This was the first time that Johnny insisted on anything.

"Mike, the bear went to the left. I don't think he's far. You hit him good. I'm going to be in front. Watch my flanks as we walk into the willows, but don't shoot me."

"I can do that."

Johnny led the way. We pushed into the willows, scanning, and trying to see the bear, hoping to see the bear lying dead. It was tense and I did as Johnny asked, watched his flanks. Suddenly, Johnny laughed out loud as he said, "Aw hell, he's right there. You got 'em." We were both relieved, but still approached with caution. With any species of dangerous game, it is the "dead ones" that kill you. Johnny arrived at the bear first and poked the bear's eye. There was no movement. It was dead. We celebrated. What a great bear he was.

After we took a few pictures, we set into the skinning and butchering. We had been working about a half hour when, suddenly, Johnny stopped…

"Mike, what was that?"

 "I dunno."

"I heard something."

"Okay, I'll check."

Johnny stood stock still for a second. Then put down his knife and moved very slowly and quietly to get his rifle. I looked back through the willows.

Johnny whispered, "There's another bear."

"Grizz or black."

"Black."

"What do you want me to do?"

"Watch him and I'll keep skinning your bear."

An hour passed as Johnny skinned and quartered my bear. The other bear sat and looked at us, yet never advanced. Johnny was done and cleaning up his knives as best he could when the other bear simply walked way. We were grateful. I helped Johnny get the meat into the meat bags and haul it to the lakeshore. We had a few hours until light and no idea when the plane would arrive. I sat and watched the mirrored surface of the lake. There was not a puff of wind. The lake surface appeared to be a perfect mirror and the mountains in the distance reflected as a perfect photo negative jagged image off the surface. As I finished the last of my food, a dark form emerged from the opposite side of the lake. I reached for my rifle.

Johnny was too far away. I dared not speak any louder than a whisper. My binoculars were with my pack. As I watched the massive black shape stroll down the far lakeshore, I thought, "My God what a beast." Just then, Johnny walked up behind me and whispered, "That's a big bull, eh?" I struggled to make it out in the gray light, but he was right. It was a bull moose. I'd never seen one with my own eyes and what an impressive creature. Realizing I had nothing to fear, I sat my rifle down and got my binoculars. I watched the bull feed along the far bank of the placid lake for what seemed like hours. Then we heard the tell-tale sound of an engine and knew our ride was imminent. The bull heard it too and disappeared.

Back at camp, we learned that Rob had killed his grizzly. A beautiful chocolate brown bear. Most impressively he did it with his bow at close range. I could not decide who I was happier for, Rob or me. I was tagged out and still had a few days in Alaska. Rob had a great grizzly and still had his black bear tag. It seemed as if we were blessed on this hunt. I realized that being tagged out meant, I could get some rest. The prospect of resting seemed entirely luxurious. When I woke the next morning everyone else was already stirring. A couple guides were working on fleshing bears, while one was doing laundry in a bucket down by the lake. Carly was cooking something that smelled like heaven. I was bouncing as I walked. Tagged out in Alaska, with a few days to spare. It was success beyond my expectations. I sat on the dock and watched the clouds roll by until Carly called the entire camp to eat.

While we were eating the jovial mood was broken by the early sound of the outfitter's plane. The guides all dropped their forks and rushed to the lakeshore. Their mood went from happy to pensive. Rob gave me a foreboding look and I shrugged my shoulders. The outfitter almost leapt from his plane and started barking orders. The third hunter in our group, Joel, had little to no success thus far. He was not even seeing bears. The outfitter yelled for Joel's guide. Rob and I stood at a fair distance and watched the drama unfold. Joel's guide was told to pack his stuff and be ready to leave in an hour. The next hour was a strange tense rollercoaster of ups and downs in the camp.

When the outfitter flew away with Joel's guide, we rushed to ask Joel what was going on. He reluctantly told us that his guide was sleeping most nights and was no help. Joel hesitated to tell the outfitter, but with only a few days left in his hunt, Joel had to come clean. The anger of the outfitter was clear, and camp was awful quiet and tense the rest of the afternoon. Johnny alone was still wearing a smile. He had guided every client this bear season to a grizzly and a black bear and was awful proud. As he moved around camp, he seemed to be the only person immune to the outfitter's anger. He was cleaning his gear and smiling at everyone. Before dinner things had settled down. Rob and Joel were preparing to go out. Johnny was sleeping in a chair at the front of the cabin when we heard the plane.

The guides hustled down to the lakeshore. Rob and I stood mute and waited. Joel was working on his gear. When the outfitter burst through the door of the cabin, I heard, "… I know Johnny… I know. It doesn't matter. Get your shit ready you're taking Joel out." I stood back and watched the world turn. Johnny, the triumphant guide, who had achieved a full season's success, was being told to saddle up and get back into the game. His previous success dictated that he now had to take Joel out and make it happen with only a few days left. Johnny's countenance changed, but he did not argue. In short order, he was kitted up and talking to Joel about the coming night's hunt. Rob had been ready to go for hours and as I watched them walk down to the lakeshore, I said a little prayer for their success.

While I felt bad for Johnny, the truth was, he was damn good at what he did and now stood the chance to make even more money. If he could get Joel a bear in the last two days, he would not only be a hero, he would earn Joel's money. In the short time I'd known Rob, I grew to respect his skills and thought any black bear that came within archery range tonight was in trouble. I retired to my little humble bed in the cabin to read a book and dream about Rob and Joel's success.

The next morning, I moved around camp before anyone else was up. I started doing chores. If anything looked like it needed to be done, I did it. By the time everyone else was awake, I'd got a bunch of work done. After the late morning meal, I went down to the lakeshore and read my book. When I was tired of reading, I sat and listened for the plane, praying for Rob and Joel's success. The first one to arrive was Rob. He had seen bears but was waiting for a giant black bear. He did not shoot. Rob decided to wait with me for Joel. When Joel got off the plane, he was smiling ear to ear. We assumed he had taken a bear. When he approached, Rob said, "You get one buddy?" Joel replied, "No, but we saw bears all night. I couldn't be happier." All was right with the world.

As Rob and Joel collapsed into a midday nap, I slid around camp doing chores. I was bored. I am not good at sitting still. About the time Rob and Joel woke up and we were called to dinner, the camp foreman said, "Mike, we need to talk outside."

Feeling like I was being called into the principal's office at school, "Yeah what's up?"

"You're a client. You have got to stop doing chores around camp."

"Well I'm bored and not good at sitting still."

"Yeah, I can see that. See the yellow ATV?"

"Yes."

"It's gassed up and ready to go. The keys are in it. There's some old fishing poles and tackle in the shed. I figure you can make one good pole out of that mess and find some lures. Do you remember where the river is?"

"Yes."

"After we eat, you grab your pistol and make up a fishing rod. Then you go down to the river and fish. I can't have you working around camp."

"Wait a minute! You're going to let me loose in Alaska with an ATV, a pistol, and a fishing pole?"

"Yes, eat and get the hell outta' here."

I was on could nine. I ran up to the cabin. Carly was not happy when I had only a few bites, apologized, and ran out the door. I stopped long enough to wish Rob and Joel luck. In the shed I found the truth. The fishing tackle was old and a mess. I shook my head and dove in. It took about an hour, but I had the best of what was in there and was on the ATV headed to the river. It is hard to explain the feeling of freedom when a guy from the lower 48 is told to just get the hell out of camp and go fishing in Alaska. Yet, that is what happened and that was what I was doing. The smile on my face acted as a bug catching device as I drove to the river. I did not care and halfheartedly remembered my survival classes, bugs are a great source of protein. I sucked my teeth clean, closed my mouth, and drove on.

The river seemed somehow prettier and more pristine now that I was here alone. I slowly stepped off the ATV and secured my fishing pole and meager tackle box of spinners and spoons. I tied on a small white in-line spinner and started walking the bank. At first, I had not a care in the world. I was simply looking for the deeper pools that might hold a trout or salmon. Then I heard a rustle in the brush. The fact that I was alone in grizzly country came rushing back to me like a wave. I know most Alaskans would think me silly, but I am from Kentucky. Any rustle in the brush along a salmon river was a grizzly in my mind. I checked my pistol. I checked my nerve. I sent my first cast into the river.

I lost count of the rainbows that fell prey to the spinner. That old spinning rod and reel had availed itself. The trout showed me no mercy. Each one raced across the river and turned their silver, pink and blue body into the current for leverage and tried to break me off, but none did. When the sun started to set and I saw the grey light of night, I knew I was late in leaving. I secured the pole and the pauper's tackle box to the ATV. I threw my leg over the ATV saddle like a hero in a cowboy movie and sat mute for one last moment studying the river. "My God, how blessed am I?" Then I turned the key and headed for home.

As I climbed up the riverbank toward the forest, I had an ominous feeling. Then I entered the forest. I knew immediately, I had spent too much time on the river. The easy gray light of the riverbank evaporated and was replaced by the darkness of the forest. I let off the throttle and my ATV coasted to a stop. Three deep breaths passed into and out of my lungs, before I steeled my reserve, unholstered my pistol, turned on my headlamp and rode for home. I arrived late. It was pitch black. The camp foreman and Carly greeted me with anger and relief. It was obvious that I was a rogue element in their camp. My apology did little to ease their pain. They were sure I had drowned or worse. I explained that I had simply been catching trout after trout and lost track of time.

That is when Carly became incredulous, "Wait a dang minute! Not only did you worry us to death, you caught fish and didn't bring any back for me to cook?"

I had little to say other than, "I'm sorry."

I could not sleep. I was praying for Rob and Joel to be safe and successful. I tossed and turned all night, knowing they were on stand hunting bears. I was up early again. I wandered down to the lakeshore and realized there was work to be done. The water jugs were empty. The source of fresh water came from a spring across the main lake. There was a little twelve-foot boat and the guides would motor across the lake and fill the five-gallon water jugs every other day. I had nothing better to do, so I went back to the cabin and grabbed my pistol, the fishing pole and the pauper's tackle box. I climbed into the little boat, pulled the motor into a hum, and started across the lake.

It is hard to explain. If you have been to Alaska you understand it. If you have not, you will not. There are times when you are so awestruck by the beauty of the landscape, that you simply get lost in your own thoughts. That is where I was halfway across the lake. The silence was broken by the first songbird of the morning bellowing their melody. Rocked back to reality, I remembered that I wanted to troll the spinner for any fish in the lake as I rode to the spring and back. I cast the spinner off the starboard side of the little boat and continued toward the far bank. Then I laughed at myself because I did not actually know where the spring was. It mattered not. I would find it.

I was lost in thoughts of how to find the spring when my rod was almost torn from my hands by the strike. I let go of the tiller handle of the small outboard to secure the pole. I forgot the motor was running. In only seconds, the motor listed to the port side and spun the little boat in circles. All I could think of was, "Don't you lose this fish." It took a minute, maybe two, to switch hands with the fishing pole, and lean back to cut the motor off. I was sure it was too long. I was sure I was going to lose this giant fish. The whine of the drag coming off the reel was utterly amazing and unforgettable. I was not prepared, not ready to manage the boat, the pole, and a giant fish. Nevertheless, I found the net with my free hand. I played the fish and did my best to pretend I am a skilled angler. Seconds turned into minutes. Then it happened, I saw the biggest rainbow trout in my life on the end of my line. I took a deep breath and set the net in the water. As I extended the pole behind me to draw the giant into the net. "Pop!" My pole went limp, as the lure broke clean from the fish's mouth. "Oh shit, no!" I watched my spinner leave the water's surface and fly past my head through the air.

I dropped the pole to the bottom of the boat and my head fell between my legs in abject disgust. I remained there for what seemed an eternity. Then I started laughing uncontrollably, "What a fish." I smiled and sat up. I turned to start the motor and go on about my business to fill the freshwater tanks. Wait, in my peripheral vision I saw movement on the lake's surface. It was my fish. The fight had almost killed it. It laid struggling on the surface thirty yards away. In a weird, almost surreal moment I motored over to the giant trout as it floated exhausted and near dead on the surface. I lowered the net and giant fish was mine. As it laid in the bottom of the boat I marveled in disbelief. Then I saw a wound in its mouth where the hook pulled out. It was my fish. I came to my senses and finished my chore of filling the freshwater tanks with a smile on my face.

When I arrived back at camp, the foreman was upset with me. He saw the freshwater tanks full and realized I'd been up early doing the chores his guides were supposed to do.

He questioned me as I landed the boat, "Why the hell won't you listen? Look Mike it's not your damn job to fill these tanks. Can't you relax?"

As he finished his sentence, I held up the giant trout.

"Mike, what a fish!"

"Yep, I was fishing, not doing chores."

"You're full of shit, but Carly is going to be happy."

"I sure hope so." Carly was happy.

She prepared the big trout with some eggs and other sides for breakfast. I had never had trout and eggs for breakfast, but Johnny assured me it's a staple in his home state of Maine. The trout was so big, it did not fit on the grill. Carly had to bend it to close the lid and I smiled in satisfaction.

An hour later, our bellies full, we all set about our business. Since I was tagged out and had caught the biggest trout of my life, I thought my business was sleeping and I set to it. I woke before Rob and Joel left and wished them luck. Later that morning, I took the ATV back out to fish the river. The sense of freedom is hard to explain when you're in what seems like an endless inexhaustible wilderness with a fishing pole. I caught a few more trout and brought them home to Carly. Then I simply sat on the lakeshore and thought about my good fortune.

With the coming darkness I retreated to the cabin. I had a fitful rest. I could not stop hoping and praying for Rob and Joel. The sound of the plane woke me the next morning. I rushed to get dressed and down to the lakeshore. It was Rob. Once again, he had seen a pile of bears, but nothing he wanted to shoot. We talked as the outfitter took off to go get Joel. Carly made Rob and I a quick breakfast and then we hustled back to the lakeshore to wait for Joel. The hum of the plane's engine in the distance gave Rob and I a charge and we anticipated Joel's triumphant return. Once again, Joel and Johnny looked like they'd won the lottery, but didn't have a bear to show for it. Joel said they saw great black bears all night, but no grizzlies and he was here for a grizzly.

The weather turned sour. The skies blackened and the rain beat upon the roof of the cabin like it owed it money. Rob and I were the only one's awake and we played cards and talked. Rob told me about all the black bears he had killed. He was not going to settle on a small black bear, and he was not about to hunt in a driving rain for one either. When Joel woke and joined the group, he looked disappointed. This was the last day. The rain was pounding his hopes into oblivion. Near dark the rain let up and stopped. We sat waiting on dinner from Carly. Then we heard it, the plane's engine. Joel sprang to his feet. Johnny followed him. It was almost sundown and the light was fading, but the outfitter wanted to give Joel one more shot. He got out of his plane on the lakeshore barking orders. In mere minutes, Joel and Johnny were loaded up and gone.

An hour later the rain started again. It hit the roof like an angry jilted lover. Rob and I played cards and talked. Then we heard it, the plane's engine. We put on our raincoats and ran to the lakeshore. We were surprised to see the outfitter and his plane. We secured the plane and he stepped out, "Damn rain is too thick. I'm staying here tonight." We all rushed up to the cabin and shook off our wet coats like a lab just back from a retrieve.

Well we played cards until we were too tired to play cards. Then we all went to sleep in our own little corner of the cabin. The rain went from angry to light to angry again. All I could think about, as I tossed and turned, was Joel and Johnny out in this mess trying to kill a grizzly. The fitful rest I got was mercifully broken by sunrise. I walked past sleeping friends and the outfitter onto the porch of the cabin. The rain was gone. It was going to be a beautiful day. I walked down to the lakeshore and looked up, wondering how Joel and Johnny were doing.

Rob and I ate our breakfast without a word. The outfitter spent the morning pacing around camp on his satellite phone. After our morning repast, Rob and I went down to the lake and talked about all our hunting adventures. The sun was full up when the outfitter walked past us and got into his plane barking orders. We untied him and away he went. It seemed a decade past before we heard the plane. As it circled the lake preparing to land, Rob and I smiled in anticipation and relief. Joel and Johnny had been out overnight in a terrible storm. They had to be on the plane and in one piece. Their safe return was all I cared about.

As the plane's pontoons cut the surface of the lake and it slowed to a an idle, I thought I saw a smile on Johnny's face through the window. The first person off the plane was Joel.

Rob said, "Good to see your safe brother. How'd you do?"

"I got my great white bear."

Recipe –

Well there's multiple hunts in this chapter, so the directions are longer.

Ingredients:

_____ A willing soul, a semi-stout heart, courage, good legs, feet and hips – priceless

_____ Time Off – (# of days) x (what you get paid daily) until you get it done = ???

_____ Alaska non-resident annual hunting and 14 day fishing license $265

_____ Alaska non-resident grizzly ($1,000) and black bear ($450) tags $1,450

_____ Outfitter's fees for lodging, guiding and flights $12,000

_____ Flight to Anchorage and back $700

_____ Rifle, scope and ammunition – if you own a .300WINMAG or bigger rifle you're good, otherwise you'll have to buy one or borrow one. I used a .375H&H

_____ Clothes and boots – you should already own it. I actually recommend your best late season whitetail hunting gear, because it's quiet on stand

_____ Pack, binoculars, rangefinder, etc. – you should already own it – again deer gear is fine

_____ Meat, hide, and skull prep and transport to the lower 48 - $700

Total Cost: $15,115

Directions:

This hunt is expensive. However, the overpopulation of grizzly bears on the landscape at the time I took this hunt, made it more reasonable. Once again, big dreams require saving up your money. Put some money aside for a few years or like I advised in previous chapters, keep the old truck running and after it's paid off put the previous payment in savings. There are many ways to do it, but if you're a "regular joe" you'll have to save up. In the end, the memories you make hunting grizzly bears will be greater than the love you feel for a new truck or the money you miss in your savings account.

The next issue is bear spray versus firearms for bear defense. If you have a guide or friend backing you up with a 12 gauge slug gun or .45-70 lever action, then you have nothing to worry about. I have already addressed what I believe is a very poor tactical decision with regards to handgun calibers for self-defense from bears. I do not agree with the idea that, "you will only get one shot," and "it must be a caliber capable of killing a grizzly bear." I am very comfortable with my Glock 21 in .45ACP. I can deliver up to seven aimed shots with my Glock 21 in the time it takes to deliver two aimed shots with a big bore pistol. In the scenario where my life is on the line, seven chances is way better than two.

Now, the eternal question of whether you should use bear spray or a pistol? The bottom line is proficiency. If you have zero experience and proficiency with a handgun, please choose the bear spray. Proficiency and confidence with a handgun takes thousands of rounds and countless hours of practice. I cannot remember ever qualifying anything less than "expert" with my pistol in the Army. When you add in the Close Quarters Battle live-fire training and such, my proficiency and comfort with a pistol is unquestionable.

Bear spray is designed to be, "spray and pray." However, there are drawbacks to bear spray. You must practice with it. Some companies make practice canisters, but I suggest you use the real stuff. If you use the real stuff in practice and the wind is not 100% in your favor, you will get some of the bear spray in your own face. I believe that is an important lesson in the use of bear spray. That leads me to the first drawback with bear spray. In an emergency you will not have time to gauge the wind and will not care. If a bear is charging you, you will be lucky to deploy the spray. If the wind is blowing in your face, you are going to spray yourself. The good news is that you will also spray the bear. Their sense of smell is exceptional and bear spray will certainly deter if not disable them. The challenge is not disabling yourself.

The next drawback to bear spray is that the canisters have been known to go off in the worst places at the worst times. Your bush pilot will most likely ask you to put your bear spray in an ammunition can strapped to the wing of their float plane or put it in the pontoon of the float plane. If it were to accidentally go off inside the plane, there is a chance you are going to crash and die. If you are in your tent at night and there's a bear outside, you cannot spray them. You will have to open the door and try or you will have to wait until the bear cuts his way into your tent. If a bear is pawing at your tent and you believe they are trying to get in, with a pistol you could certainly make a small hole in your tent and an equally small hole in a bear. If your bear spray goes off inside your tent you have huge problems. Your tent and most likely your sleeping bag are worthless at that point. Not to mention, you've bear sprayed yourself.

I am not recommending a pistol over bear spray. I am simply trying to point out the pros and cons. Obviously I am a fan of handguns. If you asked me to give a definitive answer, I would ask a question. "Are you proficient with a handgun?" I am not asking if you are familiar. I am asking if you are proficient. If the answer is yes, I recommend the handgun. If the answer is no, then I recommend buying a couple canisters of bear spray and practicing with it. Remember, practice makes perfect. In the heat of the moment, you must be ready and proficient.

After you find your outfitter, ask questions and more questions. Work on your packing list and keep refining things as you go. There are too many variables to plan for everything, but you can learn a great deal by asking questions of the outfitter or the people on their reference list. Take notes and make sure to review them. This type of hunt is expensive, and you will be wasting your hard-earned money to show up anything less than totally prepared.

Flights to Anchorage are easy. Outfitters who fly their hunters directly out of Anchorage into the wilderness should be asked a great deal more questions. While there are some amazing fishing locations within the range of a small float plane from Anchorage, the best places to hunt normally require more travel.

You will need to incorporate a certain amount of salt into your fly-in packing list. Hides that are not fleshed and salted in the field usually "slip" and are worthless as mounts. Some decent work in the field to skin, flesh, and salt your animal's hide is necessary. If you're being outfitted, this is 100% their job, you just need to be aware of it.

Once back in Anchorage, all good outfitters will get you hooked up with a reputable licensed taxidermist. The taxidermist will flesh and salt your hides and skulls again. Then they will get them sent to your local taxidermist back home.

The outfitter should also take you to a "meat company" or a "butcher shop" that will process, freeze, and send express overnight your meat home to you.

None of this is cheap and it should not be. Think about it and prepare for success. Do not simply say, "Well if I'm lucky enough to get my bear I'll figure it out." That is a plan for failure. A hunt for the "great white bear" is truly something special. The fundamentals listed in earlier chapters of this book should be studied and the recommendations heeded.

Chapter 20 - Man Plans, God Laughs

Finding a hunting partner can be as difficult as finding a spouse. There are always folks who want to go bird or rabbit hunting locally if you have good dogs. You will turn people away if you have great deer and turkey habitat on your farm. The exact opposite is true if you are going to journey to the ends of the earth for big game in country with dangerous predators. You will not be turning people away. You will be searching for the right partner. No regular Jimmy, Joe or Jane will do and their willingness to try means little or nothing if they are weak and unskilled. True adventures require partners that are not liabilities. They must be capable, skilled, strong, and level-headed to begin with. Then they must have the resources and be willing. These people usually start out as friends, but if you do it right, they end up as family.

I wanted to hunt Alaskan moose ever since I saw one during my Alaskan grizzly hunt in 2013. A mature bull appeared on a lake shore as if he had grown up out of the Earth. We were waiting on the bank of an unnamed lake for a float plane the morning after I killed my black bear. It was grey light and quiet, impossibly quiet, the kind of quiet only Alaska gives you. The lake's surface was a perfectly flat oil slick calm and as the bull ambled along the shore on the far side, there were two of him, one right side up and his reflection, upside down. The whole scene was framed with mountains that rose into the grey sky like the edge of a serrated knife. The bull certainly could smell us but acted as if he owned the lake and his rolling gait was royal. Sitting here now in my warm dry office, I can still smell the bear blood on my hands as I watch that bull walk across the lakeshore in my mind.

That memory visited me, on and off, for years. Each time the memory ambled into my consciousness I thought about hunting moose in Alaska. The hardest part remained, finding someone who wanted to go with me. This could not be just anyone. They had to be a hunter. They had to be smart, skilled, strong, capable, reliable, and have a level head. They also had to want to do it the hard way, on a Do-It-

Yourself (DIY) remote drop camp, like I did. Many folks want to kill a giant record book animal and I will never turn that opportunity away, but I am turned on by the adventure. So, the moose hunt was a means to an end with me. I really wanted to see how being dropped off by a float plane in the middle of the Alaskan wilderness felt, to experience the feeling of the float plane flying away and knowing that I was on my own. I wanted not only to survive but I wanted to thrive. That was my goal. That was to be my trophy.

Another year went by, but the memory did not fade. During quiet moments, that bull moose would amble into my consciousness on his ever-present silent lake shore. Yet, I still had no partner. I am a career infantryman, moreover an Airborne Ranger. I could do it myself. So, I went so far as to ask the outfitter if they would drop me in by myself. The answer was short, "No, absolutely not." I figured as much. The silent search continued. There is no smart phone app for it, like dating. There are no arranged marriages like they do in the far east. You simply keep a quiet, vigilant lookout for anyone you run into at conservation organizations or in hunting camps. You watch them and think, "Could they do it? Would they do it?" You quietly evaluate all your current hunting buddies. They have no idea you are doing it. If you are lucky like me, you have two or three who could do it. The problem was they did not want to. So, the search continued.

That summer, my new friend, Dave Roesler decided to go elk hunting with us for the second time. Dave had a good hunt his first time, arrowing a bull on public land. I knew he was capable. I took stock of Dave on the drive out to Colorado. He is a pilot, a self-made man, a father, husband, strong, smart, and a good hunter. I decided that at some point in the future I would ask him to do the moose hunt. I am not sure why I did not just come right out and ask. I think maybe the prospect of having a friend who could do it was so good I didn't want to ruin it by hearing him say, "No."

When Dave didn't get an elk that year and I saw how cool and level-headed he was about it, I was convinced he was the guy. On the way home from Colorado to Kentucky there was a period where we were the only two awake. The twenty-five-hour drive took its toll on my wife Aline and our other buddy, HB. They were sleeping. I took the opportunity to tell Dave about my moose, the one that walked across the lakeshore during my grizzly hunt. The one that still walked through the lakeshore in my mind. I explained that before I saw that bull, I did not want to hunt moose. But now, it was something I had to do. When I was done, Dave said, "I'll go with you." I smiled ear to ear and said without thinking, "Well all right then." The next few hours, driving through the darkness in Missouri, the discussion was all about moose hunting.

Things got rock solid after we sent in our deposits and started planning in earnest. We decided to hunt the second and third week of September to hit the start of the rut. We also decided to rent a boat and motor as part of our drop camp. We would stay at a fixed camp, but we would hunt along the river. We spent the spring going over packing lists and getting the gear together. We also arranged all the travel from Kentucky to the little town of McGrath, Alaska. By the time summer rolled around, we were dumping our bags and going over equipment in extreme detail. The last thing we did was sight in our rifles out past three hundred yards. That day I knew Dave was a damn good choice, because he managed to get a nasty "scope bite" right between the eyes. It was deep and bleeding bad. Dave just laughed, took his shirt off and used it to apply pressure to the gash. When the bleeding stopped, he continued practicing with his rifle. Every shot from his rifle opened his forehead back up. Each time he just laughed, took his shirt back off and held it to his forehead.

Earlier in the summer, while working on our first aid kits, I told Dave that in the backcountry I did not bring sutures, but superglue. I explained that I often get so dirty, that poking a needle deeply through the skin multiple times brings as much risk of infection as the wound itself. So, when we were done shooting, I joked that I could fix the gash in his forehead with superglue. To my surprise, Dave agreed. When we got back to his house, with his lovely wife Jenn watching, I disinfected the gash thoroughly and carefully applied pressure to both sides to have the smallest scar possible, before I applied the glue. As I closed the hole in his face, he never flinched. After it was done Jenn reminded us that we were, "Not right." The next few weeks passed quickly, and Dave's forehead healed nicely.

Travel to the little town of McGrath was uneventful, but we were inspired and ready for the adventure. We made a deal that we would hunt every day until we got Dave a moose. I made it clear that my aim was to have an adventure and that if I got a moose, that would be "icing on the cake." Dave was thankful and nothing more was said of it.

Just as we planned, we were in McGrath a day early and did our final packing and weighing of our gear. We were allowed 150lbs of gear and provisions each. We used the scale in the tiny little flight terminal to make sure we were "on the money." That afternoon we left the B&B and went over to the McGuire Tavern. I still wonder why it is not the McGrath Tavern. McGrath is a stop on the world-famous Iditarod Dog Sled Race, but this time of year it is a ghost town, except for moose hunters. We were the only two guys in the tavern for a long time and I asked the bartender about the bar itself. It was covered with inscriptions. "What do you have to do to carve your name in the bar?" He replied, "You need a knife." The bartender was not much for conversation. But I had a knife, so I carved my initials into it.

The next morning, we had a tremendous breakfast at the B&B and spent the morning talking with the other moose hunters. We were not scheduled to leave until the following day, but the pilot told us to be ready. The normally wet weather in this part of Alaska was dry and the skies were clear. They were getting everyone lined up to get into the backcountry, so we got our stuff together and waited. We watched other groups get ready to go and realized the pilots had their own scales. The group in front of us was thirteen pounds overweight. They got rid of some potatoes, onions, and Canadian whiskey. We were underweight, so we took their stuff. Even after that we were still six pounds under. Then the pilot said, "Let's go." Dave and I could not believe it. We were going in a day early. We were going to get an extra day in the backcountry for our hunt. We each brought twelve days of food for a ten-day hunt and now we had extra potatoes, onions, and whiskey. We jumped in the back of the little rusted pick-up and sped off to the river.

The feeling of flying over the Alaskan backcountry is unexplainable. You are exhilarated, yet there is a foreboding feeling. It is beautiful country, but the enormity and remoteness of it is also striking. If the plane went down and we survived, there was no option to walk back. It would be near impossible with the number of river crossings and mountains. Your only choice would be to wait for help. Still, I was smiling ear to ear, until I was shaken back to reality when the plane suddenly turned and slowed down. It only took a moment to realize we were okay. We were at our destination. The pilot was slowing down to land and doing so by flying circles around the small lake he intended for his aquatic runway. The pilot explained that our camp was on the small rod of land that separated the little unnamed lake and Iditarod River. The little plane slid across the lake's surface and bumped to a stop. We jumped out. We off loaded our gear. The pilot helped us assemble the little boat and just like that, he was gone. It was real. We were on our own.

In Alaska, you cannot hunt on the same day you fly. So, there was no rush to make camp. We took our time and did it right, taking all the normal precautions against bears to insure we could sleep easy with both eyes closed. We established a sleeping area a few hundred yards separate from out fire pit, meat poles, and cooking area. We scouted the bank and found a good place to get our boat into the water as the bank of the Iditarod River was steep and slick. We even made a little dock-like area where we could keep it secured overnight. Then we double checked our rifles were still accurate and got our gear ready for the next morning. With great anticipation we retreated to our tents.

I wish I could say we slept, but we simply waited there until morning. We sprang into action the next morning. Launching the boat and running up-river. Then cutting the engine and drifting for hours back to camp. You must run up-river in case the motor fails or breaks, then at least you can drift back to camp. If you run down-river and have engine trouble, well then you are in trouble. We took our time and enjoyed the entire day. We marked where we saw moose sign and let ourselves acclimate to the river. The day came and went in a quiet splendor that is hard to explain. Our satisfaction having survived the first day was compounded when we arrived back at camp to find it unmolested by bears or wolves. We ate well and slept even better.

The next few days came and went in similar fashion. We saw moose sign and wolf sign, but no moose and no bears. We had tags for moose and bears. We could kill wolves without a tag because they were over-populated in the area. But we did not actually see any game animals, just beavers, ducks, swans, and porcupines. We hunted hard, using all the techniques we knew, and some the outfitter taught us before we left McGrath.

Every day we motored up-river in the pre-dawn light, stopping to hunt where we saw good moose sign. Then we got back on the boat, found a place where the wind would keep the bugs off us, and cooked a hot meal on the boat. After that we would drift home listening and calling for the three or four hours it took us to get home by dusk. Back at camp, we would call until it was dark and then we would eat a cold dinner and collapse in our tents. We hunted so hard I noticed we were not even eating all our daily rations. Nevertheless, our hopes and motivations ran high.

We were undaunted by the lack of moose, the mosquitoes, the biting flies, and the daily grind. Finally, we heard our first cow moose call. We were excited. We were sure that cow calls were what we were missing, but they did not help. The next few days were more of the same. We heard a few more real cows calling and one bull grunting, but the dense forest in the river bottom limited visibility. There were no hilltops to glass from. There was no other way to hunt than to find small openings, bogs or ponds and try to call a moose into us. We kept at it and never once lost hope.

Our positive attitudes coupled with proper planning and the right gear meant that camp was efficient and pleasant. We just needed a legal moose. Halfway through the trip, the little boat motor started to sputter and quit. We did some initial troubleshooting and made one small fix but decided not to waste hunting time. We adjusted our plan to hunt the best moose sign close to camp. We would take the boat and the weak motor to local spots and hike into an opening to call for a bull.

The following day, Dave took the motor apart and cleaned everything, then reassembled it. The next morning, we made it about a mile up-river when it sputtered and quit. We drifted home in silence and hunted near camp until dark. As we hiked back to camp it started to rain. The rain continued into the next day, steady and unyielding.

We were hunting in ultralight chest waders and wading boots, with our wet weather coats on top. We hunted in this gear every day regardless of the weather. It works great on a river hunt. You are not constantly taking hip boots off and putting on your hunting boots to get in and out of the boat. But even in this gear, we were getting wet. Rain on the river just has a humidity to it. Eventually a drop runs down your neck and you know it is over, you are wet. It is just that simple. Dave and I were both wet when I recommended we go back to camp. I suggested we sit under the tarps we put over the empty meat poles and call moose from camp. Dave agreed.

It rained all night. The next morning it was hard and steady. We stayed in camp and called. The hunt was nearing its planned conclusion, so I called the outfitter on the satellite phone. He said the pilots were backed up due to the rain. He was still working his, "First hunters in, first hunters out" plan. Hunters that went in before us, were already waiting to get out due to the rain. We knew our return trip was going to be delayed, but we remained hopeful. A bull just had to appear across the river from camp at some point. We did our best to remain positive.

As we told stories I thought it would be great to have a smaller fire under the tarps. When the rain abated from a deluge to just a gentle downpour, we decided to hunt on foot, up the riverbank. We tried hard for hours but found no moose. Instead, we found an old moose camp. In the detritus of that camp, we found an ax, some halfway serviceable tarps, and a coffee can. We brought our treasures back to camp. After we strung the old tarps over our tents to provide another meager layer of waterproofing, we went back to the tarps over the meat poles and called for moose, nothing.

In a smile of disgust, Dave left the shelter of the tarps with the ax and began to chop out the dry center of a dead tree for firewood. While he chopped, I turned the coffee can into a little woodstove. I was trying to get some twigs burning in it when Dave showed up with birch bark. Eureka, birch bark burns wet. That evening we laughed and finished the whiskey as we sat warming ourselves by our birch bark "wood stove" made out of an old coffee can.

So, there we were, our hunt was technically over, but we were not going anywhere. We sat under the meat pole tarps, burning bark in our little coffee can "wood stove" and calling moose from camp. We debated going back out in the rain to hunt, but we decided against it. It was a hard call to make. We would have hunted in the rain earlier in the hunt. Now, we were already wet and had a sketchy motor. Now if we were successful, there was a chance we would have to paddle our little boat in the river current, in the rain, multiple trips up and down-river to recover a moose. It was simply too risky. If we were to get a moose, it would happen from camp.

We started to lose track of the days. Every day we woke up in the unending rain and called the outfitter on the satellite phone. We were told the same thing, "We are way behind. You'll just have to make do." Staying busy was good for our mental health, so we would get dressed to hunt and move up to the meat pole tarps and call for moose - nothing. We told stories and played simple games. We rationed our food and pretended we were not hungry. We were positive and strong, but the rain has a way of beating that out of you. Over the last day and night, the rain was just a steady slow beat. The little woodstove was no longer enough to keep up our spirits.

The desire to hunt was still palpable and we discussed how we could do it. We decided the motor was utterly useless, but the fuel we had left was not. We took turns chopping the dry center out of standing dead trees and bringing it back to the tarps. The plan was to make enough dry wood that we could start a fire with the remaining boat fuel that would burn even in the steady slow rain.

I was chopping wood when Dave said, "Mike! Mike! Moose!"

I ran to the riverbank and right across from camp was a bull. Dave grabbed his rifle and I grabbed my binoculars.

Before I could give Dave the bad news, he said, "He doesn't have four brow tines on either side."

I added, "Yeah brother, he isn't fifty inches wide either."

Dave sat his rifle down and through a quiet laugh said, "Well damn."

We spent the next twenty minutes standing on the riverbank, with a bull moose directly across the river from camp, not one hundred yards. We called to him and he became furious. He raked a willow. He grunted. He rolled his head and shoulders. He even pawed at the ground like a raging bull. When he tried to leave, we threw a cow call at him and he came back. This was confirmation that our calling was good enough to get the job done. We simply had not had a rutting bull in range of our calls, until now. It was great fun, but it was time to let him go and we did. That evening we decided to break out the onions, potatoes, and bacon bits. We had been saving them for a moose kill, but just seeing this bull was cause for celebration and we were hungry.

The rain never stopped. It continued day and night. It was as if rain was normal and anything else was abnormal. The next morning, as usual, we called the outfitter. He said, "I'm gonna try to get you out, be ready." The rain abated late in the morning. It stopped for the first time in days but the clouds were still very low in the sky. It was enough to lift our spirits and we pulled the boat out of the river, disassembled it, and put it on the lakeshore. We moved all our gear up from the tents to the meat pole tarps and waited for the sound of a plane. We never heard a plane. When the rain started again that afternoon it was serious. I scrambled to get our extra tarp over the gear, as the rain was blowing in sideways under the meat pole tarps. We were not going home.

Later that afternoon, the rain slowed, and we discussed going hunting. Dave abhors failure. He is a self-made man who applies himself in layers of hard work until he wins. The discussion circled back to the same point – the outfitter will always fly the moose meat out before us, as spoiled meat brings a hefty fine from the State of Alaska. We were also not number one on the list to get out, remembering the rule, "First in, first out," if we had a moose down it might be a few days until we got out. We agreed that discretion is the better part of valor. We once again agreed that we would only shoot a legal bull if he showed in camp or across the river from camp. Putting the boat back together to cross the river, then butchering and ferrying the moose back to our side of the river in the rain was as far as we were willing to go. We resigned ourselves to burning birch bark in our woodstove and waiting under the meat pole tarps.

The next morning, midday, afternoon and evening came and went. The rain never ceased. We kept our spirits up and tried to remain positive. We were out of whiskey and coffee, but we still had a little food. We were mostly dry and we had plenty of gasoline to keep the fire going, thanks to our sketchy motor. We told stories and retired to our separate tents randomly to read and nap. Pitter patter, tip, top, splat…pitter patter, tip, top, splat. There is no need to look outside when you are living in a tent to know if it's still raining.

The next morning, I called the outfitter to get the inevitable bad news. After he told us that no one was flying, he asked, "Have the guys from the remote float showed up yet?" I replied, "No haven't seen them." He said, "Well your camp is the end of their float, so keep an eye out." I told Dave the news. We were going to have company. Then we went about our routine of telling stories, burning birch bark in the coffee can woodstove and trying to stay dry. When we lowered our food bags out of the tree that morning, we took stock. We were trying mightily to keep our spirits up, but the lack of food was now serious. It was time to begin rationing. Today's total ration per man would be: two cereal bars, one ramen noodle packet and two quarts of soup made from tabasco sauce and garlic powder.

The only good news, was that we were almost done with our books and could exchange them, so we still had something to read. I was reading Mutiny on the Bounty. The following morning our patience finally ran out. We both became a reincarnation of the mutinous leader Fletcher Christian. Screw the outfitter! Screw the pilots! We are hungry and want to go home! A better pilot could fly in this! We complained for the first time and we were loud and raucous about it. Had Captain Bligh been there we would have set him in our little boat with the sketchy motor and forced him to drift down the Iditarod River alone. Suddenly we were both laughing hysterically. We really needed to get that out of our system.

After our poor meager little breakfast Dave retired to his tent to read. Shortly thereafter, the rain stopped. I wanted to enjoy the breeze and the big fire, so I moved over to the firepit and began to stoke it. As I sat facing the river, a welcome breeze blew across the lake from behind me. The smoke billowed up toward the grey sky of the same color. Just then, a human head popped up over the riverbank and looked right at me.

The face of exhaustion belonged to Orrin. I stood and immediately said, "Welcome to camp." The expression of relief was instantly evident on his face. I moved to shake his hand and saw his partner Jesse climbing the riverbank. As I shook their hands I said, "The fire's warm, why don't y'all take a break." They were both soaked to their bones and exhausted. As I looked down the steep riverbank to their fourteen-foot inflatable raft I saw two moose racks lashed down tight over a tall pile of meat bags. The two young men moved to the fire and slowly, as they warmed themselves, you could see their energy return. Dave heard their voices and joined us.

We learned that they took their moose on the third and fifth days of their hunt and had been rowing hard in the rain to get to our camp. About the time the color returned to the faces of Orrin and Jesse, they decided to get to work. All four of us pitched in and we soon had their raft unloaded and tied fast.

They had successfully taken two bulls in probably the most physically demanding type of hunt possible. Their float trip covered well over one hundred river miles. One of them had to man the oars and keep the raft in the middle of the river, while the other called and glassed for moose. They had to make camp every night and tear it down every morning. After they killed a moose, they would have to load and unload five or six hundred pounds of meat, in addition to their gear. In the evenings, before pitching their tent, they had to build a meat pole and tarp it, to hang the meat. They had two moose, which means over one thousand pounds of meat was now part of their cargo. The work required cannot be understated.

However tough it is to float a river for moose, it is also one of the best ways to be successful. You cover so much country and finding at least one rutting moose is almost a certainty. They were happy to see us and we were happy to see them. We had a semi-dry camp, with tarped meat poles already up and a warm fire. They had food and we were hungry. Jesse oversaw cooking for them and still had some Mountain House dehydrated meals to trade for sweets to ease Orrin's sweet tooth. All we had left were a couple cookies and a few ramens. So, the trading began in earnest. Jesse was also nearly out of cooking fuel. They had been boiling their water, not filtering it. So, they were rationing the remaining fuel to make drinking water. We had an eight-liter filter system and plenty of water. We also had enough cooking fuel to last another two weeks for all four of us. Their first real complaint was, "We ain't had coffee in a couple days." I fired up my stove and put an end to their coffee problem. As Jesse pulled his steaming coffee cup from his mouth he said, "You guys help yourselves to any one of the Mountain House meals you like." Dave and I were not starving, but we were damn hungry. We did not hesitate. Orrin said, "Mike I'd be grateful to have one of your cookies with this coffee." I replied, "Orrin eat them all," as I chewed my Chili Mac Mountain House meal. Jesse and Orrin had their coffee and sweets. Dave and I had a real meal. In short order, we were all sitting around the fire as content as we could be, ignoring the drizzle.

That night around the campfire we learned all about them and their hunt. They were accomplished young men in their mid-thirties, easily a dozen years younger than Dave and I. Jesse was a surgical technician. Orrin was a logger who owned his own company. Both were career hunters and tough guys. They never once complained about the work and hardship associated with their float hunt or the rain. They described a river that was hot and cold, night and day different. They floated sections of river that were teaming with life. They saw seven legal bulls and harvested two of them. They also described sections of river that were quiet and devoid of life. They asked us how far up and down river we hunted. We explained that we never hunted down river, thanks to our motor. We told them we made it about five miles upriver on the good days. They said the last moose they saw was more than ten miles upriver and the only thing they had seen in the last two days was wolf tracks.

With the hunting stories complete the conversation shifted to eating and Dave, who is a good cook, volunteered to help them cook some moose. That night we shared a true hunter's camp. A scene that has played out for thousands of years of human history. Hunters sitting around a fire, grilling meat, and sharing stories. Dave and I were nearly out of stories and food, so we were grateful for both. Orrin's stories of being a logger the old-fashioned way and running his own company were almost as cool as Jesse's stories of assisting in surgeries to amputate human limbs. Somehow, Orrin and Jesse also brought a break in the rain that lasted all evening. I fell asleep and it was quiet. For the first time in days, there was no pitter patter of rain on my tent. Sometime during the night, the rain started again, but I had a full belly and could not care less.

It rained all day the next day. Yet, the morale in camp was high. We really enjoyed each other's company. We talked of hunts, family, and our personal histories. It was hunting camp like our ancestors experienced. I had a weird feeling that day about my hunt. I started to feel successful. I was no longer angry at being stuck in the Alaskan bush for days. I'd made a life-long friend with Dave and had a hunting partner I knew I could count on. Now, we made new friends and were talking about hunting with them in the future. The rest of the day we shared camp chores between the four of us and did so without having to ask.

The two biggest tasks were meat management and gathering firewood. We had to take the meat bags off at night to help the meat cool and develop a rind. Then put the bags back on during the day to keep the flies off. We had to search further and further from camp to find standing dead trees for their dry inner wood for the fire, but we succeeded. The grizzly bears, black bears, and wolves left us alone, and since our hunting licenses were expired by this point the feeling was mutual. Camp ran well and we ate well.

Late in the day, we took an inventory of gear and made plans to leave Orrin and Jesse all the additional gear we had that they could use. If the outfitter finally showed up to pick us up, he could only take Dave and I. Leaving Jesse and Orrin would be bad but leaving them well provisioned would make it tolerable. The day came and went quickly, not unlike the previous days. Before I knew it, we were grilling a rack of moose ribs over the fire and laughing like mad men. We ate like kings, told stories, and retired content for the night.

I am always up early. I suppose a couple decades in the Army burns certain behaviors into the marrow of your bones. I said a little prayer and moved up to the campfire meatpole area, a couple hundred yards down river from the tents. I said another prayer of thanks, as I took stock of our gasoline that helped me start a fire in the ever present rain. I spent a great deal of time the previous day peeling birch bark and showing Jesse how I fed it into the little coffee can woodstove under the meat pole tarps to keep warm and our spirits up during the rain. I had a large quantity of the bark left over to build the morning fire. I chopped out some dry wood from the inside of a dead birch and put that in after the bark, then covered it with a large quantity of green spruce bows, added the gasoline and lit it. The plume was glorious, and I smiled from the inside out.

Slowly my hunting comrades emerged from their tents and as they gathered around the fire something happened. The sky opened and a brilliant sun shone through. The rain completely stopped. The clouds rose. The ceiling, a pilot's weather term Dave educated me about, was lifting. When Dave reached the fire he looked up, smiled, and said, "We are getting out today Mike." I smiled and kept working on the fire. We knew the pilots rarely fly first thing in the morning in this region. They must wait until the ground fog burns off in McGrath, so they can see the mountain passes to the west. So, I kept working on the fire and did not get motivated to pack my stuff.

I was making a hell of a racket trying to fan the fire, when Dave said, "Mike shut up. Mike shut up! Mike shut the hell up!"

I stood and said, "Man what's your problem? I'm trying to keep the fire going."

He said, "I hear a plane."

I shut the hell up.

It was a plane. It was our plane. I dropped everything and sprinted down to my tent. After striking our tents, packing involved throwing everything into bags. It did not matter what went into a bag or what bag it was. Then we hustled to the lakeshore. By my second trip, the plane was gliding across the flat calm water toward shore like an archangel coming to avenge our bedeviled situation. By my third trip, the pilot had the plane stopped on the shore and Jesse was holding the mooring lines. Orrin was helping us get our stuff loaded, as I made Jesse aware of the things we were leaving and where they were. I scrambled into the plane behind Dave and bid our new friends, "Good luck, hope to see you again soon."

Before I knew it, the pilot was pushing the throttle forward and pulling back on the yoke. We were airborne and on our long journey home. The sense of relief was real. We were not successful hunters, but we survived and under the circumstances I would even say we thrived.

Recipe –

This is a longer more complicated dish to prepare:

Ingredients:

_____ A willing soul, a stout heart, courage, prudent judgement, good legs, feet and hips – priceless

_____ A good hunting partner – priceless

_____ Time Off – up to three weeks, start to finish, including travel, obviously weather dependent

_____ Alaska non-resident hunting and fishing license, black bear and moose tags $1,515

_____ Hotels in Anchorage $400; split two ways $200

_____ McGrath B&B; room and meals $700 (everything is flown in; thus everything is expensive); split two ways $350

_____ If you don't have proper gear already for a hunt like this buy the very best gear you can; Alaska will test it and you'll need it; plus it will last a long time; cost unknown

_____ Round trip plane tickets from Kentucky to Anchorage $600

_____ Round trip plane tickets from Anchorage to McGrath including a "cargo block" for 300lbs of necessary gear $900

_____ Per person outfitter costs $6,800; includes flights in and out of the bush, plus any additional flights to move moose meat and antlers back to McGrath

_____ Satellite phone and bear fence rental $250; split two ways $125

_____ Twelve days of food, fuel, and provisions $225

_____ Rifle and ammunition; you should already have it; .30-06 and larger calibers with good bullets will do just fine for moose and black bears

_____ Transport of moose meat and antlers to Kentucky $850

_____ Processing of your moose meat in McGrath $350

Total Cost: $11,690

Directions:

We were never in any real danger. We did not have any bear or wolf trouble that we know of. There was only one night we know of that an animal prowled around out tent or campfire areas. The rest of the time it was raining, and we could not hear them if they were there. We made smart and conservative decisions after the pilot dropped us off. There was a real risk of hypothermia, certainly. But proper gear choices and finding a way to keep a fire going, even in a coffee can under a tarp helped.

You must have the basic skills of a woodsman to attempt something like this, if you are not capable, I do not recommend you try, unless you are fully guided. When things go wrong in Alaska, they can go very wrong. Alaska is beautiful, but it can be brutal and ruthless. A single slip into deep cold water could be the end of you. It does not have to be a grizzly bear or plane crash. I went on a mountain goat trip right after this one, and that story follows. While I was on that hunt two pilots crashed their planes. Everyone killed, everything lost, and the cause was rumored to be, simply overloading the plane.

The big hurdle for most to attempt this adventure will be cost. You can save money on hotels in Anchorage and cut some corners, certainly. But the fact is, adventure hunts are expensive and there is no getting around it. You'll pay the outfitter over an 18-24 month period. So, it will not seem like it's that expensive, but when you add it all up – it is. When people ask me about doing hunts like this and say something like, "$6,800 for an outfitter to just fly you in, drop you off and provide a boat and motor seems expensive." Well it is not expensive. The outfitters are working in dangerous remote country. They must have the best equipment they can afford for your safety and theirs. In Alaska, guides and outfitters must be licensed. Their licenses are on the line when they make decisions, so be prepared for them to make very safe and conservative decisions. All in, all done you should expect to spend 100% more than you pay the outfitter. So, if the outfitter charges $5,000, plan to spend $10,000 for everything.

There was a time when we could have hunted in the rain. We chose not to, but it was the most tension we ever felt. The desire to succeed was reduced to anguish by the following facts:

(1) Our motor was not working.

(2) We were already wet, and the chance of hypothermia was real.

(3) Rain washes away blood trails, which means you will need a clean easy shot, any mistakes could mean the tragedy of hitting, but not recovering your bull moose.

(4) We were out there so long our licenses expired.

We tried to fish in the dirty brown river and stained dark lake… seemed there was nothing but beavers in either body of water.

Travel planning to Alaska is long and messy because it's weather dependent. Here is what we did: home > Anchorage > McGrath > Bush flight to hunting area > McGrath >Anchorage > home. Seems simple right? Wrong. You must plan for weather after Anchorage, which means adding days to the plan.

You should buy your food, fuel, and other items you cannot take on a commercial plane from home in Anchorage. There is no guarantee that what you will need will be available in little remote towns like McGrath. Even if they have it at the local general store it will be very expensive. That means you should plan at least one day in Anchorage to shop and repack, prior to taking the flight to McGrath.

Some hunters chose to send supplies and gear ahead of themselves to the Hotel McGrath. The manager of the hotel is happy to receive and secure your packages for a small fee. It's a great service, but it should be obvious the risks associated with such tactics. Things that are outside of your positive control are outside of your positive control. It's that simple.

You must also be cognizant of the weight of your gear and provisions when leaving Anchorage to McGrath and McGrath to the bush. Remember, the planes only get smaller. There is a science to it and if you are a first timer the only way to get it right is to check, recheck, and check again. I highly recommend you give up some comfort items to have salt available to salt your game animal's hide. If you are choosing between the fourth pair of socks and coffee, take more coffee. If you are choosing between the fourth pair of underwear and whiskey, take more whiskey.

So, here's what a daily plan might look like if everything goes well:

Day 1 – Travel to Anchorage

Day 2 – Anchorage day to shop and repack

Day 3 – Fly to McGrath

Day 4 – Day in McGrath to make final arrangements and prepare

Day 5 – Fly into the bush…weather dependent

Days 6 through 13 – 8 day hunt

Day 14 – Fly back to McGrath…weather dependent; arrange for the butchering and transport of your moose to the lower 48

Day 15 – Fly back to Anchorage…weather dependent

Day 16 – Overnight in Anchorage and repack for the commercial plane

Day 17 – Fly home

When the weather gets bad, like it did for us a 17-day trip can turn into 26 days quick. Your travel plan must be just as well thought out and flexible as your hunting plan.

There are more and certainly better ways to do this. This was the way we did it.

Chapter 21 - Four Days Late

Thank God we got out. This was the seventeenth morning of a eight-day hunt. The last nine days of unrelenting rain were brutal. We very smartly started rationing our twelve days of food on the tenth day. On the fifteenth day, we were down to very meager rations and our sense of humor was failing. Then two moose hunters, Jesse and Orrin, floated into our camp in a downpour. We were not in any real danger of starving, but our stomachs were empty and in knots. They killed two moose and had freeze dried meals left, but they were out of fuel, sweets, and clean water. We had a few cookies, a couple ramen noodles, fuel, and filtered water. They shared the extra food they had, and we shared what we had. Thanks to Jesse and Orrin, the last couple days before we got picked up was quite bearable.

The plane ride out of the bush was over a hundred miles of the most remote wilderness in the world. Yet, it took only a few hours. In that short span, we witnessed the beautiful day turn foul. The Carolina blue sky and the green, orange, and violet mountains were swallowed up by the hazy grey and white of another coming storm. It was almost as if we were flying out of the mouth of a giant beast that was slowly trying to swallow us whole. The pilot skillfully flew threw and around the weather and the mountain peaks. When we slid out of the foul grey skies east of the mountains and saw the hamlet of McGrath, the relief finally set in.

When we landed on the Kuskokwim River, the support crew hustled hard to get the plane tied off in the current. As I stepped onto the floating dock and looked at McGrath a wave a relief coursed through my body. I was shocked back to reality, "You boys are damn lucky, look!" The grizzled leader of the ground crew, who bore the worn leathery skin and unkept beard of a frontiersman, pointed. I turned to see our backtrail and watched a wall of clouds close in behind us like the drawbridge on an ancient castle. The intrepid pilot left just after dawn and used the smallest of weather windows to climb over the mountains to our camp along the Iditarod River and back over those same mountains with the storm on his heels the whole way.

We stowed our gear and shuffled into the only restaurant in town. While waiting for our food we learned that multiple typhoons (Pacific hurricanes) were battering the coast of Alaska. We took it personal, thinking those storms crossed the largest ocean in the world just to maroon us in the bush. It was hard not to believe they had some evil intent to ruin our moose hunt, as one after another pushed rain inland for days and days. But we were out now and thankful to be discussing the mythology of storms in this small café on the Alaskan frontier.

The cook, waiter, and owner brought us our food. Then he gave us the news, "There are still thirty-six hunters stuck out in this mess. Pilots are using any window they can to get them out. The first-in, first out rule is the only fair way to do it. The lucky ones killed moose and have food. The unlucky ones are hungry." We stared blankly at each other not knowing what to say. We knew which hunters we were – the unlucky ones. The cook, waiter, owner walked away talking to himself, which I suppose is a valuable trait in a lonely place like this.

We relished our meal in silence, with the news that there were thirty-six hunters still overdue sitting heavy on our shoulders. The pilots "first in, first out" policy, meant it was just our turn to come home. Nevertheless, we felt a bit guilty to be back in this meager version of civilization, while so many others were stranded.

Back at the lodge, I took stock of our current situation and made some calls to the air services. So, many hunters had missed their flights that the normal flights back to Anchorage were overbooked. Alaska Air Transit would hold the seats of those who reserved and paid for them, then fill them at the last minute with those on the waiting list. My gratefulness for being out of the bush was tempered by the stark reality that I was now three days late for a ten-day mountain goat hunt.

The original plan went something like this:

8 day drop camp moose hunt,

2 extra days for bad weather,

1 day to fly to Anchorage, eat a steak, repack for the goat hunt,

1 day to rest,

10 day mountain goat hunt.

Well it worked out like this – 15 day moose hunt and I'm already 3 days late for the goat hunt. We were stuck in McGrath, because all the flights were backed up. My hunting partner, Dave, is a pilot and had to get home or risk losing his flight status and maybe even his job. Whilst I had a mountain goat hunt hanging in the balance, his career was hanging in the balance. I went downstairs in the lodge to call my wife.

During the call, a gentleman approached me… "I simply cannot sit here. Too much going on at home.

I bought a charter and there's one seat left on it. You want it?"

I replied, "Absolutely."

I ran upstairs to give Dave the news, "Pack your shit right now, you're going home."

Dave was ecstatic but broke the bad news to me, "Mike even if I get back to Anchorage, I have to jump seat to get all the way home."

"Okay, so what you can do that, right?"

"Yeah, but brother I cannot take any prohibited items, because I have access to the cockpit."

"Right, so what does that mean?"

"We're going to have to split the gear. I can take all the non-prohibited items, but you're going to have to take my rifle, pistol, ammo, knives, etc."

"Holy shit? Really? Well then, you'll have to take my tent, sleeping bag and some of my clothes. We better get started repacking, the charter will be here in three hours."

"Mike, I know you're missing the goat hunt so I can get home and not miss my mandatory training. I cannot tell you what that means."

"It's just a hunt. You screw up your flight rating and it might mean you're back to flying cargo planes full of rubber dogshit out of Hong Kong."

Dave laughed and ran downstairs to call his wife, appreciating my "Top Gun" movie reference.

I was happy for Dave, certainly. But I needed a minute alone to wallow in the fact that I was going to miss my goat hunt. Upon Dave's return upstairs, we got him repacked and down to the tiny little terminal to get his bags weighed and on the manifest. I stopped the Alaska Air Transit agent to ask about getting out and they told me I could not get out of McGrath for another five days. Well hell. I am already three days late for a ten-day hunt and now I'm not getting back to Anchorage for another five days. The goat hunt is over before it began. I set off to the bar to drown my sorrows. Dammit! The bar doesn't open until 3pm! What kind of hunter's purgatory did I get stuck in? I remind myself there are men still stuck out in the bush and head back to the lodge.

When I got back, I called the mountain goat outfitter, "Steve, buddy I'm stuck in McGrath."

"Mike, yeah I know. I have been getting your satellite texts off the Garmin. I let the packer for your hunt go home as this is the last trip of the year. I am personally going on your goat hunt as the third man now. We are all sitting in Anchorage waiting. The fact that you agreed to hunt new country, that we've never hunted before, has us all excited. If you can get here tomorrow or the next day, we can still get this done."

"Steve, no man. I'm really stuck in McGrath. Alaska Air Transit is backed up for another five days. There are another 36 hunters stuck out northwest of here and it's a mess."

"You're kidding?"

"No, wish I was."

"Well Mike, this is Alaska and things change quick. So, we will wait another couple days here in the house in Anchorage. Call the moment something changes."

"Steve, can we reschedule to next year?"

"Yes, but let's cross that bridge when we have to."

"Steve, I don't want to give myself only a couple days to get a goat. This is a bucket list hunt for me."

"Mike, I know man. If you can get here in the next two days, I think we can get it done."

"Seriously?"

"Yes, tomorrow you're four days late. That gives us six days left. I have my best guide, Jason, we call him Conan, on the hunt with you. I am personally going. I have got my logistics guy, Dan, who will help with the gear and the boat. I think we can get it done in a few days."

"Okay Steve. I will try to get out of here in the next 48 hours."

"Right, talk to you soon."

I went straight to the room, then later the bar and the next thing I knew the sun was up or at least the grey sky was visible through the window. I went downstairs and stared quietly out the window, slowly eating my eggs. The two gents at the only other occupied table were rambling on in a slow southern drawl. I could hear their conversation. They were moose hunters too. I started to wonder how long they were stranded in the bush.

Then one spoke to me, "Hey partner, you okay?"

I responded, "Yeah, brother I, will be okay."

"You look like someone took your lunch money."

"Feel like that too. I cannot get out until the 29th and was supposed to start a goat hunt on the 20th."

"What? You're kidding."

"No, wish I was, my name is Mike – nice to meet you."

"I'm Jason, this is my buddy, everyone calls him Scooter. We are from Texas."

We exchanged moose hunting stories over breakfast. Scooter got a nice bull moose. They had a similar hunt and I was glad to meet them. They seemed to be tough and resourceful guys, the kind I run with and admire.

When we finished up the hunting stories, Jason asked, "What do you do for a living partner?"

"I'm a retired Army Officer."

"Really, well I was going to wait and talk to Scooter, before I offered, but now I'm going to give you the last seat on our charter."

"You're bullshitting me?"

"Nope, I wouldn't bullshit a veteran. The seat is yours."

"Jason, you've made my day brother. What do I owe you?"

"Nothing, just get on the plane. It's my treat."

I tried to argue about paying my way, but Jason, nor Scooter would listen to it. They wanted me to get to the goat hunt and they were Texans. A stranded Soldier, albeit a retired one, seemed like a rescue mission to them and they were happy to have the mission. Their plane was arriving in three hours.

The next three hours were a mad dash to get what was left of Dave's and my gear together. I thought I had a week and left it in piles in the room after Dave departed. After I got the gear shoved into the bags and weighed, I called Steve and gave him the good news.

He was stoked and said, "Mike, we can totally get this done in six days. Just get to Anchorage and we will figure it out."

I said, "Steve, I love it, but man I'm short a bunch of gear."

I explained why and my pilot hunting partner's challenges.

Steve said, "Man, just get here, we will do a bag dump, figure out what you need, go and get it, and then go hunt goats."

The next thing I know I am airborne on Jason's charter and smiling ear to ear. The plane touched down in Anchorage under a partly sunny gorgeous sky. I was beaming as I hit the terminal. I could feel the slowness in my legs and the tiredness in my back. The fifteen-day moose hunt took its toll, but I was mentally strong and so grateful to Jason and Scooter. We were standing outside the Alaska Air Transit Terminal in the small parking lot, soaking up the warm sun and taking a few pictures, when a Ford F350 Superduty rolled up and Steve yelled out the window, "Mike!" I said another thanks to Jason and Scooter and threw my gear in the truck.

As we rolled down the road, Steve and I got acquainted. He introduced me to the quiet fellow in the back, Dan the logistics man. Before long we were at the house in Anchorage and that is where I met Jason, AKA "Conan." He walked up, shook my hand, and said, "Good to know you mate." Conan was a twenty-something Kiwi who guided in Alaska during the New Zealand off season. We wasted no time in dumping my bags and emptying my cases. Conan and Dan watched every move. Steve seemed less concerned.

When it was all said and done, he gave instructions: "Conan, do a load of Mike's laundry while we go buy some gear."

"Dan, make sure the tent is dry and get it loaded."

"Mike, get in the truck, we've got some shopping to do."

Just like that we were rolling through Anchorage. We made stops at REI, Cabela's, and Mountain Warehouse. Steve's advice was key, as I replaced the gear I'd sent home with Dave. If Steve recommended it, I bought it. In short order we were back at the house.

I am an experienced outdoorsman, Soldier, and big game hunter but having two Alaskan Guides watching me pack was a little unnerving. Nevertheless, with their help I was ready in less than an hour and we were on the road to secure Steve's jet boat. Once we were on the road, I was out cold, asleep. The toll of the last three weeks had to be paid and I was exhausted.

When I woke, we were rolling down the coastal highway heading southeast. It was nearly empty, except for moose. I thought, "Damn you moose! Where were you a week ago?" We stopped for gas, coffee, and something to eat before pulling over in a gravel pit to sleep for the night. We all made do with whatever cover we could find and at first light we were up and moving. Conan got some coffee going and Dan found some donuts.

After a hasty breakfast, Steve took charge: "Dan, get the food secured."

"Conan, put a target at the end of the gravel pit."

"Mike, grab your rifle we need to confirm the zero."

Just like that I was following orders. It did not matter that I'm a retired Colonel. This was Steve's show and followership is part of leadership. By the time Conan got a target at the end of the gravel pit, I loaded my rifle and made ready. Truthfully, I was a little self-conscious. My rifle and I had been weeks in the bush on the moose hunt and had a whirlwind of travel to get here. Plus, I just slept in the seat of a truck. Now, with everyone watching I had to make shots count. To my surprise, I put the first two rounds very close to the bull and Steve said, "That will work. Let's get rolling."

Just like that we were headed southeast toward the Copper River. The towns along the way were deserted. It was readily apparent that it was the end of the season. There was literally nowhere to get supplies, fuel, or help. I took a deep breath and told myself, "You're not in charge. Just listen and do what you're told for once." The mountains, forests, streams, and wildlife rolled by my passenger window like an old movie. I rested and listened to the stories, trying to conserve my energy and praying I had enough left in the tank to accomplish this mission. They say that you climb through sheep country to get to goat country and I'd agreed to help Steve and Conan, "open some new country." We were literally going into an area they had never been. I did not let on or say anything, but I was worried if I could make it.

The Copper River is something to behold. If you have never seen it, it is hard to explain. The river is bound on both sides by vertical mountains. The riverbed is wide, but it is fractured across its width by gravel bars and channels. If you were able to float a thousand feet above it, it might appear to be a circulatory system chart from an anatomy textbook. The salmon runs were long gone and so were the fishermen. The river was devoid of life except us. The challenge was that the water levels were twelve feet lower than normal and the boat ramp was a boat cliff. Steve and Conan conversed and decided to drive upriver to a bridge. At the bridge, we circled down to the water, drove across the flats that are normally covered by ten feet of raging river and put the jet boat in off a gravel bar. We loaded the boat with our gear. Then Steve, Dan and I waited, while Conan drove the truck and trailer back up to high ground near the road. Once Conan was back, we jumped in and Steve took off.

If you have never been on a jet boat traveling at a high rate of speed down an Alaskan river with mountains on either side, well let's just say – you've not lived. Steve drove like a pro. I sat and watched like a giddy tourist. Conan and Dave dozed off. About halfway down the river to the planned campsite on a beach below the Chugach Mountains, it started to rain. The rain was hard and unrelenting. It made navigation dangerous and we stopped multiple times to let it subside. One of the stops was at a State of Alaska Salmon Research Facility. It was abandoned for the season, but we still walked through it as if it were ruins and we were archeologists. Steve decided to continue down river versus sleeping at the research facility.

Just before nightfall we were on the beach Steve planned for our camp. There was just one problem – grizzly bears – lots of grizzly bears. We sat on the boat, safely out in the river and discussed options. Steve was lamenting that I did not have a grizzly bear tag. In Alaska, you can downgrade a tag, which means that if you buy a grizzly bear tag you can use it to harvest any other animal. Some guides recommend their customers buy a grizzly bear tag, even if they are hunting moose. Because if you do not see a moose, but you do see a grizzly or a caribou or anything else smaller, you can tag it with your grizzly tag. Unfortunately, I had a moose tag and a mountain goat tag in my pocket.

Steve decided to drift down river a mile or so and check out another isolated beach. There were no grizzly bears or even tracks on the new beach, so we decided to camp there. Steve slept on the boat with a rifle and a magnum pistol. Conan, Dan, and I slept in the tent on the beach. The long day took its toll on us all. Grizzly bears or not, Conan and Dan were snoring in minutes. I thought, "When in Rome, do as the Roman's do," and promptly passed out, cuddled up to my Christensen Arms .300WinMag rifle.

We all slept happily and woke from a bear free night. At gray dawn, our camp was buzzing with movement. In short order, we were packed and back on the jetboat. Steve took the boat back upriver to the grizzly bear infested beach he intended to camp on the night before. That beach was the planned jumping off point for the hunt. There were no bears on it this morning, yet Steve took his time to scout it from the water. When he beached the boat and looked around, he apologized to Dan:

"Dan, I know you wanted to go on this hunt, but the boat is our lifeline to get home. You're going to have to stay on the boat and make sure the grizzlies don't get it."

"I figured as much, this sucks."

"I will leave you with my rifle and pistol."

"Mike, we will be going up the mountain with only your rifle."

"Conan, let's get ready to roll."

Conan was supposed to be the guide and Steve was supposed to be the packer, but the truth is that they were one hell of a team. It was obvious that Conan was the mentee and Steve was the mentor, but they also shared a mutual respect and admiration that was akin to father and son.

I did my best to get ready and the last thing I wanted to do was slow them down. The next few hours were a blur of activity. Steve and Conan were making ready to climb. I was trying not to look worried, as I got my gear ready. I have heard sheep hunters in Montana complain about climbing 3,000 vertical feet off the Flathead River. We had to climb straight up 4,500ft off the beach to get above tree line. Once above tree line we'd make a base camp, but we didn't expect to find goats until we were up around 6,000ft straight up off the river. Whilst that is not that high compared to some locations, the challenge in Alaska is that you start up the mountain from sea level. The sheer volume of elevation gained over such a short distance is what is challenging in Alaska. It is steep, so very steep.

I took a deep breath and tried to relax. Dan was securing the boat with a double anchor system and putting a tarp over it so he could sleep on board. Conan walked over to me and handed me a heavy bag, "Here's your food mate. Secure it in your pack." That was the only discussion. I was shocked at how much they trusted me to be squared away and ready to go on such an adventure. Steve and Conan were ready and with only a, "Take care Dan," we were off.

The half mile walk down the beach was a stark reminder of what I was getting myself into. My legs were already tired. The moose hunt, days of effort and lack of food, wore me out. Yet, as I walked down the beach the weight of my terribly heavy pack grew lighter. Somehow the roar of the river, the feeling of not wanting to let Steve down, and the regular footprint of a grizzly bear in the sand had a weird way of motivating me to keep up.

There is literally no way to explain the following seven hours. We went straight up the mountain from the river. The vegetation was as thick as Medusa's wig of snakes. I climbed and never complained, but twice I did call a halt. It was not because of the evil thick cloud of swarming black flies. It was not because of seemingly impenetrable vegetation. It was not because of the vertical terrain. It was because I was tired. The moose hunt had sapped me, and my tank was already empty. We halted about ten minutes each time and seven hours later, we popped up into the alpine highlands above the tree line.

The difference in terrain, vegetation, and bugs was otherwise otherworldly. We had left what felt like a triple canopy jungle of tangled vegetation and evil parasitic biting flies that belonged in hell, to a windswept mossy rock-strewn alpine nirvana. It was not long before Conan picked us a base camp.

It was obvious that Steve was excited. He had been guiding up here for decades but had never hunted this mountain. While setting up base camp, I apologized to Steve for how slow I climbed and volunteered to go fill the water bladders. Steve responded, "Are you kidding? We rarely have a client that makes it up with fewer stops. Thanks for volunteering to fill the water. Conan and I are going to glass the rocks above before dark."

I hobbled over to one of the many crevasses that was filled with clear cold water and filled all the water bladders. Steve and Conan climbed all over the rocky rim above camp and looked for goats. Finding none, they returned to base camp. We had dinner, told "sea stories" and piled into the tent after dark. They are called "sea stories" when you hunt with Steve because he was in the Navy. We Army guys call them "war stories." Nevertheless, they are fun to hear for the first time and if someone has not heard them, well they are fun to tell for the thirty-seventh time.

Morning dawned clear and cold. Looking out the door of the tent across the Copper River basin to the mountains on the southeast side was breathtaking. There was a small glacier in a deep crevasse directly across the river valley from us. As Conan warmed water for coffee, I played tourist and marveled at the scenery. Once coffee was made, we ate a simple cold breakfast and I listened as my compatriots discussed strategy. One thing was apparent in all the scenarios they discussed – we were going to climb higher.

Everything was done in a measured way, there was no rush and no clamor. I remember thinking, "These guys are professionals." As we packed for the days hunt, I found myself just staring off into the vastness of the Copper River Basin. My God it was beautiful. Seventy-two hours ago, I was miserable in McGrath. Were it not for the generosity of the Texans and the flexibility of Steve and his team, this would have been impossible. There were so many things that had gone right to get me to this point – large and small. I took stock of the situation and I knew what I had to do. I had to listen and do my part, no more and no less. So, I left my ego in the tent, took a deep breath, and followed.

We left base camp and wound our way up and up and up. At every opportunity and every promising vista, Steve and Conan stopped and put in serious time behind their binoculars and the spotting scope. I did my level best to help, straining my eyes to find a mountain goat in the vast beauty of the alpine. The crystal blue skies and velvet blue mountain lakes were framed by the yellow, red, and orange lichen covered black rocks. The beauty of the palate God used to paint the scene was striking. The excited dialogue that Steve and Conan kept up about this, "new country" suddenly stopped. They grew quiet and started whispering. I knew they found something. My heart raced and I thought, "A goat already?" It was a giant bear making its way to the west on a ridgeline over a thousand feet below us, but he was easily seen due to his mass and the open country. What a creature he was.

We packed up and climbed up and up some more. At the next impossibly beautiful stop, I watched my team employ their optics.

Then it happened, "I've got one," said Conan.

"Where?" Steve Replied.

They worked on it for a while, then Steve said with a certainty in his voice, "Yep that's a goat… Mike come see."

All I could say after looking through the spotting scope was, "my God that's exciting, " as I backed off.

The conversation continued between Steve and Conan. The goat was over 1,000 yards away. It was impossible to be certain of its actual size, but they were certain it was a billy. With smiles and exhales of excitement we packed up the spotting scope and climbed up and up. The journey continued throughout the day, much the same as it had been throughout the morning. We stopped at each venue and looked for goats.

It was just after midday when Conan said, "I've got one, no mate, I've got two."

"Where?" said Steve as he looked into the scope.

"Yes, you do and one is a stud. Mike come look we've found your goat."

I marveled at the huge white furry beast on the dark cliff of black granite, "Dear God, what a blessing. Let's go get him."

"Slow down man, we've got to come up with a plan, but we've got time."

The goat was indeed a stud of an old billy. He was accompanied by a nanny or a juvenile of either sex. Regardless, the smaller companion goat was not our target, but presented a second set of eyes to contend with. It was almost 2 p.m. and it was time to move out. We had about a half mile of alpine mountain to cover to get into range. The terrain was steep, rocky, and technical. We hiked, climbed, crawled, and scaled our way to within what Steve believed was rifle range without being seen by the goats, but it took too long. We stopped to catch our breath and Steve looked at me very seriously, then looked at his watch for the 27th time during the stalk.

Then he made a command decision, "We don't have time. We have to just go for it now. Cash all the stuff you don't need. Mike, just bring your rifle and keep up."

"You don't want the spotting scope or anything?", Conan questioned.

"We don't have time. We just have to go."

"Right Mate."

"Mike you ready?"

I simply nodded.

"Let's go."

Steve took off up an incline so steep that I had to follow by climbing on all fours like a primate, yet he was upright on his feet. Conan was trailing me, presumably to catch me if I took a wrong step. We crested every fissure and stopped. Steve looked down with his binoculars and I looked through my rifle scope. This went on for nearly an hour and it was apparent that we were running out of daylight. It was getting dark and I stopped thinking about the goat and started thinking about our safety. How would we survive out here after dark without our gear? Could we at least get back down to our packs? We certainly could not get back to the tent.

I was not paying attention, when Steve crested the next granite knife edge. His eyes grew wide with excitement and through a whispered scream he instructed, "Mike shoot him!"

So, I did.

The ancient old billy was asleep in a bed he scraped out of the mountainside. The first round was fatal, and he certainly died in his sleep, but gravity took over and he started to roll down the cliff. Steve barked orders… "Shoot him again."

I had planned to, and the gun barked before Steve finished his sentence. "Shit, he's still gonna roll off!"

Conan replied, "I've got him Mate."

What I witnessed next happened in slow motion. Conan leapt over the granite knife edge and scrambled down a sheer face to the goat. Nearing the small ledge, the goat was on, Conan slid as if to make it into second base. Then it was over. Conan had ahold of my goat and stood there smiling as if he had won the lottery. I forgot to breathe and once he was safe and holding my goat, the pressure of it all burst out of my chest like a whale breaching.

I exclaimed, "Holy shit Conan!"

"Don't ever do that again," chided Steve.

"No worries, I've got him Mate and he's a slammer," Conan responded in his easy confident way.

Steve and I climbed down to see the massive old billy. I could not believe it. Steve could not believe it. Conan acted like it was nothing special – his youth and confidence obviously getting the best of him. Steve and Conan began to talk about all the aspects of the stalk and what to do better next time. Their voices slowly faded away until I could not hear them. I was lost in the wonder of this animal. Mountain goats are engineered to live in places that are so dangerous and unforgiving, yet they call it home. You can call it God's plan or evolution, it matters not. The specific adaptations that allow them to not only live but thrive in the most unforgiving alpine terrain is more than impressive.

Steve woke me from my daydream, "Conan, let's just field dress him and get him pried open to cool. It will be dark soon. We won't make it back to basecamp. We're going to have to find a ledge to sleep on."

"Right, what's field dressing?" Conan replied.

Young Conan had only ever used the gutless method to bone out game. Steve and I had a hearty laugh at his expense, but it was getting dark and we had to climb down to our packs just to pitch a survival shelter. The wind was picking up and the temperature was dropping as Steve and Conan debated the issue.

I stepped in, "Let a Kentucky whitetail hunter show you how to field dress him young man." Conan and Steve laughed out loud as I opened my knife, but they could not deny the skill as I had the goat field dressed in mere minutes. Then with their help, we propped him open to cool overnight and climbed down to our packs.

In the fading grey light, Steve found a ledge big enough to stay the night. We all worked together to pitch a tarp using rocks as anchor points. Then we crawled under and laid out our bivy sacks and sleeping bags. As I crawled into my bag, I noticed Conan disappear in the darkness on the mountainside. Moments seemed like hours and I tried not to worry. "Where was Conan going?" I thought to myself. Then he reappeared with a bladder full of water and started the stove to heat it. In a few minutes we had boiling water. For the first time I realized what a luxury it was to be on a guided trip. Conan poured the boiling water into my foil pouch and the high winds and scary little ledge be damned, I had a hot meal. Chili Mac from Mountain House never tasted so good. As we finished our meals, the wind picked up and I was not sure the tarp would hold, but Steve did not look worried, so I just shook my head and smiled. I laid back and looked off the edge out the corner of the tarp. I could see over six thousand feet down to the Copper River. As the moonlight bounced off its surface, I fell into a deep happy sleep.

The wind beat the tarp like it owed it money. Twice it woke me up, but I did get some sleep. The next day really did not dawn, so much as the darkness faded. In stark contrast to the crystal blue previous morning, this morning was grey, cold, and punctuated with sleet. Undaunted, we had our coffee and cold breakfast. Then we broke camp and climbed up to the goat. Once again Steve pitched the tarp, this time over the goat and then they went to work.

I must say that I am not used to being guided on a hunting trip. I enjoyed watching them skin my goat and then debone all the meat, but I felt useless sitting on the edge of the tarp, which was the edge of a cliff, watching them work. When it was all done, there was not much left of the carcass. Conan took the majority of the meat in his pack. Steve took the balance of the meat. I took the hide and skull. By the time we dropped the tarp and began to head down the mountain it was snowing, and the visibility was less than fifty yards. I was apprehensive about the climb back down to base camp.

It would take us the rest of the day and going down was much harder than going up, especially with oversized very heavy loads to balance on our backs. I took my time and reminded myself, "Pay attention to your business. Do not even try to even keep up. Just be surefooted." At multiple points throughout the rest of the day as we climbed down to basecamp, Steve and Conan were out of my sight. The snow, the steep terrain, the weight of my pack and my unwillingness to move fast caused me to fall back. The hunt was over, and we had time to spare. I was in no hurry.

At each technical piece of terrain, I'd find Steve or Conan waiting in the distance until they saw I'd negotiated it. Hours went by and I noticed that the scree slopes were turning into the alpine tundra of grass and lichen again. Base camp was close. I rounded a knob to find Steve and Conan handing me a drink. We toasted our good fortune with something that tasted like grape Gatorade mixed with Scotch. I did not care. I was surprised that Conan had carried booze up the mountain. I suppose that's why they call him Conan, he's just that strong.

We climbed into the tent to avoid the sleet that was falling at this lower elevation and spent the evening hours of fading light reliving the hunt and telling sea stories. After a hot freeze-dried meal, I remember a wave of relief crashing over me before I fell into a deep sleep.

"What the hell is that?" I said to myself.

Then louder to my companions, "What the hell is that?"

There was confusion in the tent.

"Mike what's up. What are you talking about?" Steve said, trying to wake himself.

Something was in the vestibule on my end of the tent growling and pulling at my pack. It was trying to steal the mountain goat hide. For some reason I did not grab my rifle, but I grabbed my flashlight. I acted suddenly and rashly. I zipped open the tent and could see a set of eyes shining back at me, teeth locked on my goat hide, growling and thrashing. With my free hand I grabbed my boot. Initially there was no reaction from the animal, but as the boot crashed down on its head repeatedly it lost its resolve. I remember saying something out loud like, "I didn't come all this way for you to steal my goat you sunofabitch!" The boot beating it received was severe and it scrambled out of the vestibule.

"What the hell is it?", exclaimed Steve trying to unzip his bivy sack.

Conan was just waking, "Mate what the hell is going on?"

"Mike what was it?"

"I think it was a wolverine."

"Why didn't you just shoot it?"

"Wasn't thinking straight when it woke me up. My flashlight and boot were handy, so I just beat the shit out of it."

"Well it worked. It's gone. Let's try to get some sleep."

In some strange way, tempered by exhaustion and without pausing to think about the animal coming back. I followed Steve's order and fell back into a deep sleep.

The next morning as we ate breakfast, Conan caped out the goat skull. When he was done, we broke camp and packed. As we set off down the mountain all three packs were bursting at the seams. But we were all still strong and feeling triumphant, so the weight mattered not. Five hours later, the weight of the packs was certainly an issue.

The climb down seemed to never end. Once below tree line we contended with never ending willow and devil's club. Loose dirt and scree caused many an unplanned slide. The hours passed and it was just painful skull drudgery. Of course, Conan and Steve did a better job of maintaining their upright stature and dignity. I on the other hand had bonked. The days of waiting in my tent on the moose hunt, travel to get up the mountain on this hunt, and now the weight going down were overwhelming. I refused to let them help me, but I suffered more than a dozen slides on the way down.

The sand of the beach was firm, and the river smelled foreign. It didn't matter, we were down safe, and the boat was still there, unmolested by grizzlies. Dan saw us coming and began preparing the boat. For the first time of the hunt I let the pain in my back, knees and feet occupy my thoughts. By the time I got to the boat I was all in and all done. I climbed aboard and thanked God for the good weather.

The team got the boat in order and Steve headed back upriver. We made the gravel bar before dark and had the boat loaded shortly afterward. As we pulled away, Steve said, "Hey Conan, we were the last ones out and the first ones done!" In a sleepy voice from the backseat, "Your right Mate. I won't let the other guides live that down."

Then I realized it, I was four days late, but we got done two days early.

Recipe –

This is the final dish of the book. There are many more in my total history, but these were all picked as examples, some large and expensive and some small and easily attainable. That was done on purpose. The costs below are presented as if you did this hunt alone, not after another Alaska hunt like I did.

Ingredients:

_____ A willing soul, a stout heart, courage, never say die attitude, good legs, feet, and hips – priceless

_____ An excellent team of guide and packer – priceless

_____ Time Off – up to three weeks, start to finish, including travel, weather dependent

_____ Hunting License and Over-the-Counter mountain goat tag $865

_____ Hotels in Anchorage $400

_____ Round trip plane tickets Kentucky to Anchorage $600

_____ Outfitter Cost $10,000

_____ Rifle and ammunition; you should already have it; any of the .30 calibers with well-made accurate bullets will do just fine

_____ If you don't have proper gear already for a hunt like this buy the very best gear you can; Alaska will test it and you'll need it; plus, it will last a long time, some of it you might hand down to your kids or grandkids $unknown$

_____ Processing and transport of your hide and horns to the lower 48 $350

_____ Processing and transport of your meat to the lower 48 $200

Total Cost: $12,415

Directions:

Let me answer the question I get most often, "How big was the goat?" It made the Boone and Crockett All Time list, which means it was a rare big animal. Funny story is that my taxidermist is a trained measurer and when he got done and told me the score I said, "No way man." He said, "Nope that's it." My response, "Brother that's four inches bigger than the current world record." He measured again and it was not the new world record and we had a good laugh.

Okay, the recipe above is for a goat hunt that was NOT linked up with a moose hunt. I doubt anyone, especially after reading this article will try to do it the way I did.

I highly recommend you spend as much time researching your outfitter and guide as you do getting in shape for a hunt like this. They say you climb through sheep country to get to goat country. They are right. But whomever you choose, make sure you do your homework. Do not just call and speak with the outfitter, ask them for a list of references and call all of them. Great outfitters are not just skilled at what they do, they understand that it is a business and they will happily give you references to call. If the outfitter you are talking to takes offense when you ask for references – immediately move on.

Also, this is not a place to save money. The outfitter is responsible for everything, including getting you off the mountain alive, you want the best you can possibly afford. For any hunt, for any animal, anywhere in the world, you need to shoot the rifle you are most comfortable with, in an appropriate caliber for your game. Then pay close attention to the quality of your bullet because it is the bullet that does the killing.

If you choose to hunt mountain goats, I recommend a long action magnum rifle. Goats are tough critters and you want to anchor them and try to stop them before they roll off the mountain. I used a 180 grain Federal Trophy Bonded Bear Claw in .300 Winchester Magnum to be successful. Part of the success was shot placement and part was the ability of my guide to get me into position while the goat was asleep in his bed.

A pack with an external frame is really the best for these alpine hunts. I did not have one and I suffered. Conan and Steve were running frame packs and I watched how much easier they had it. I had one of the top-of-the line packs from a company famous for lightweight gear and it was terrible under the strain of an extreme load. The lightweight pack was strong enough and it never failed mechanically or ripped. But it swayed under the extreme load going down the mountain and no matter how tight I made it to my body it shifted with the Earth's gravity. Twice I had to force myself to fall on the uphill side, because the pack shifted and gravity threatened to pull me off the mountain. I will not go back up without a quality rigid external frame pack.

You must own a quality set of walking sticks if you plan to go alpine. They turn you into a four-legged creature, which is an absolute must.

Fitness is important, but your mental toughness and determination can get you, "there and back again." Of course, the stronger you are and the fitter you are, the more enjoyable the hunt will be. But even the fittest hunters will have to be determined and mentally tough. I was shocked at stories that Steve and Conan told me about multiple young fit clients that quit. It was mostly due to the steep terrain and weather, but my God I cannot imagine quitting.

One final lesson, be humble, listen and do your job. You are a member of a team on a hunt like this and without every member of the team doing their part, success is in jeopardy.

Epilogue

Some hunter, "Man I wish I could do a hunt like that."

Me, "You can."

Friends, this book is about inspiring you to think about your life in a different way. Is your son going to remember you drove the Audi or the Chevy?

If you drove the Chevy, then maybe you had the money to take him halibut fishing in Alaska when he graduated high school and then you had the money to take him on a plains game safari in Namibia when he graduated college.

I am not suggesting that everyone start hunting, fishing, hiking, and camping. I am suggesting you do something big, something that matters, something you will be proud of on your death bed.

Are you a NASCAR fan? Then go to a stock car driving school. Are you a good cook, who wishes you were a chef? Then go to Paris and take a cooking class, there's more than a dozen places open to the public in Paris for just that reason. Are you a horse lover? Ever consider going to Chincoteague Island, Maryland for the annual pony swim and auction? Do you love to paddle your canoe? Maybe you should get a team together and do the Texas Water Safari.

You do not have to do it my way.

Do it your way.

Yes, you might have to work on fundamentals and work up to being confident enough to do a wilderness adventure on your own. The first few chapters of this book will point you in the right direction and give you a start to being able to do a DIY wilderness adventure. But, if that is out of the question, then hire the appropriate guides and outfitters and go with their expertise as your safety net. There is an adventure that fits your dreams, trust me.

This book was meant to bring the idea of adventure to folks who think it is out of reach. The fundamentals listed in the beginning chapters are as necessary in daily life as they are if you are dropped off in the mountains of Alaska for two weeks.

Sadly, most people just do not know, nor understand what it takes. That is where this book comes in. Figure out what fundamentals are necessary for your adventures. Study the fundamentals. Practice the fundamentals. Take small trips first. Then when you are ready – go for it. Then after you come home in one piece with stories and pictures you will share for decades, do it again. But do it better the second time, because you learned from the first.

A sportsman once told me, "I'm too old and out of shape to hunt elk in the Rockies with you." I laughed out loud and responded, "That is all in your own head brother." If you are slower and weaker than you used to be, that is not a barrier to entry. It means that you have got to get in shape before you go. Maybe the best shape you can manage still falls short? Then you will need help. Maybe then you ask a favorite niece, who is a talented cross-country runner, to go with you. Help pay her way, swallow your pride, and ask her to be patient while you go slow.

Releasing yourself from the prison of disbelief is the first step. Then believing you can do it is the second step. The third step is doing it, whatever it is, your way, over and over until you have memories, not regrets.

Acknowledgements

Writing this book crosses off another goal on the "bucket list." I have not had much outside help, but I did get some good advice from my brother-in-law, David Dobson, and my friend Betty Ellison - thank you two.

The mistakes, be it grammar or sentence structure, are mine. Thank you to the reader for putting up with my mistakes throughout the book. I am a storyteller at heart, not an author. In fact, whenever I was deployed or in the field, I told stories to my Soldiers. They came to call them, "Abell's Fables." This book has really been a way for me to keep telling my stories to an imaginary group of Soldiers, now that they are gone from my life.

To be retired in my mid 40s with nothing to do but hunt, fish, camp, hike, write, shoot, and fight for our outdoor heritage is a blessing. It also means I have a whole lot of people to thank.

Aline, my love, my best friend… you are a smart, strong, skilled, and confident woman. Your trust in me to always return to you, your courage to hold down the fort while I am gone, and your willingness to go with me when you can mean the world to me. Also, your help in reading and sometimes reliving these adventures has been priceless - thank you.

There are entirely too many Soldiers to thank by name. My mentors were mostly Non-Commissioned Officers and that is probably why I did well. They realized I was malleable and so they took the time to temper me with the swing of their hammer, in the way only good Sergeants can. There were also a handful of Officers who mentored me and taught me the trade, thank you gentlemen.

In the end, the Army is about people. It is not an exaggeration to say that I have crossed paths with probably 10,000 different Soldiers in my decades of service. However, there are less than 50 that stand out, you know who you are – thank you.

There are times when you can go it alone and I did. But the big adventures require a team. It might just be a single teammate or it might be a fire team. Adventures are always best shared, and my best memories are those I got to share. To all my adventure teammates – thank you.

Finally, thank you to my friends in the wildlife conservation community. I have served on multiple boards, in multiple roles, and in multiple organizations, but always with good people. The common goal of leaving it better than we found it, courses through our veins, and the fight never ends – thank you.

About the Author

Colonel (Retired) Michael A. Abell

I grew up in metro Washington D.C. during the 1970s. It was a turbulent time. During the early years, I spent school days being bussed into neighborhoods where my skin tone helped with counties diversity statistics. On weekends, I rode with my family to western Maryland and learned about life on a dairy farm from my paternal grandfather. When school let out, I was lucky to learn how to fish with my maternal grandfather in Tennessee. Then I brought all those lessons back to the city when school started.

I started college thinking about becoming a game warden, but I ran out of money. The good Lord pointed me toward the ROTC Department and with the help of the cadre I won a scholarship. Two years after winning the scholarship I was the first Abell ever to earn a college degree. I was commissioned on December 7th, 1993. Assigned to be an infantry officer in Alpha Company, 3rd Battalion, 15th Infantry Regiment, 2nd Brigade, 24th Infantry Division.

In the spring of 1996, I met Miss Aline Mary Denoncourt and fell in love. We married the following year and I left the Regular Army, joined the Army National Guard, and started going back to school to become a teacher. The plan was to have summers off to travel, camp, and fish with my new wife. The good Lord had other plans for me. The mayor of the small town we lived in was a nefarious character and due to my public stance on his unethical dealings the local populace all wrote my name in during the next election. So, I became a small city mayor at 27 years old.

Time flew by and things were going well. Then 9-11-01 happened and everyone's lives changed.
I spent the next sixteen years back on active duty with the Army National Guard. It was a wonderful career and I was fortunate to come home from my deployments with my body and mind in one piece to the love of my life.

The thing that never wavered was our love for the outdoors, especially camping and fishing.
Whenever I had time off, Aline and I would be camping or fishing.

I had always hunted alone. Until I returned from my last deployment and tried to go turkey hunting. Aline would not let me out of her sight those first few weeks. So, she went turkey hunting with me. We did not even hear a gobble, but she got it. The alure was the woods, the wind, the birds, the smells, the flowers, and the feeling of belonging to it all sunk in. Later that summer she asked for a bow for her birthday. She practiced with it for weeks and took her first whitetail doe on the third day of the season.

We have hunted and fished all over the world and will continue to do so until the day the good Lord calls us home. Our passion for adventure is matched only by our passion for each other. Never forget, you will run out of time before you run out of money. Get after it, before it is too late.

If you enjoyed the book, please check out the website at www.theslowhunt.com. There are more stories, photos, packing lists, lessons learned, and much more available for you.